FROM THE COSMOEROTIC UNIVERSE TO COSMOEROTIC HUMANISM

FROM THE COSMOEROTIC UNIVERSE TO COSMOEROTIC HUMANISM

. . .

WHY IS THERE SOMETHING RATHER THAN NOTHING?

TELLING THE NEW STORY OF "EVOLVING VALUE" IN RESPONSE TO EXISTENTIAL RISK

Eros Mystery Schools: Oral Essays, Vol. 4

DR. MARC GAFNI

Author: Gafni, Marc
Title: From the CosmoErotic Universe to CosmoErotic Humanism
Identifiers: ISBN 979-8-88834-011-0 (electronic) | ISBN 979-8-88834-010-3 (paperback)

© 2024 Marc Gafni

Cover photo: "Liller 1 Globular Cluster"
Credit: NASA/Goddard/Arizona State University

Edited by David Cicerchi, Rachel Keune, and Jeffrey Malecki

Published by World Philosophy and Religion Press,
in conjunction with

IP Integral Publishers

https://worldphilosophyandreligion.org

This volume features a series of connected "oral essays," texts that express the Dharma that was delivered by Dr. Marc Gafni at the annual week-long Eros Mystery School. They have been edited specifically to be read and absorbed, so that the Dharma is transmitted directly. They also include analyses of cultural texts (popular movies and songs) that represent crucial—and often hidden or unconscious—aspects of the emergent new Story of Value. This volume features frequent recapitulations of key themes, which both review previous material and add new emphases and perspectives. In addition, the various prayers, meditations, and contemplation practices are designed to give you an embodied, anthro-ontological sense of the unimaginably beautiful transformations, both personal and collective, that are not only possible but absolutely necessary for responding to the meta-crisis and existential risk.

These oral essays are edited talks delivered by Marc Gafni at the Eros Mystery School, August 2022

erosmysteryschool.com

It's hard not to feel despair in a world marked by such extreme division and polarization, a world haunted not only by the potential death of humanity— but by the death of *our* humanity. We need to replace doomerism, denial, and indifference with accurate vision and action. To be accurate, we must first get the diagnosis correct.

First we note systemic dynamics like zero-sum, rivalrous conflict based on win/lose metrics, which generate fragile systems, as the generator functions of existential risk. But then we turn towards the deeper root cause, which we have identified as a "global intimacy disorder." Once we clearly see this, the solution also becomes clear: we need a new Story of Value rooted in the First Principles and First Values of Cosmos to ground us in a new global intimacy, which will in turn generate global resonance, coherence, and finally global coordination of the kind that is urgently necessary to respond the global challenge of existential risk. Only such a shared story of inherent value will allow us to respond adequately.

As part of this new Story, which we are calling "CosmoErotic Humanism," we are called to evolve as individual Unique Selves, transcending and including identifications with psychological separate self and spiritual True Self. We move through, accept, and process our insidious and multi-layered shame. We find the deep, ever-present joy in the post-tragic on the other side of the tragic. We "live the dream."

The realization of our Unique Self identity generates intimate communion and effective shared purpose, both personally and collectively. We are able to be truly aligned and intimate with each other, producing the social synergies that emerge from our "Unique Self Symphonies." From the context of a self-organizing universe generating multitudes of Unique Self Symphonies, we respond to the outrageous pain of the world. We realize that the only true response is Outrageous Love, which requires the emergence of a new structure of intimacy on a global scale. This is what are calling Unique Self Symphonies.

This is what it means to be the New Human and the New Humanity, what we call *Homo amor*, the successor to *Homo sapiens*, the one who lives and breathes the new Story of CosmoErotic Humanism. *Homo amor* is the CosmoErotic Universe in person.

CONTENTS

CHAPTER 4: THE RADICAL PATH TO THE TRANSFORMATION OF SHAME: FROM THE SHAME OF FINITUDE TO THE CELEBRATION OF FINITUDE

CHAPTER 5: THE LEADING EDGE OF HUMAN IDENTITY

CHAPTER 6: TOWARDS A NEW UNIVERSAL GRAMMAR OF EVOLVING VALUE AS A CONTEXT FOR OUR DIVERSITY

INTRODUCTION

by Claire Molinard

I'm going to introduce Dr. Marc Gafni by telling you a little bit of my own story—how I came to meet this great man a decade ago. This is not only the tenth anniversary of our Eros Mystery School, but it's also the tenth anniversary of the release of Marc's book, *Your Unique Self*. I wouldn't be here today if I didn't read that book.

At that time, I'd been on a spiritual path my whole life, and I'd been doing deep spiritual work. I had met many teachers, practiced a lot, and experienced the taste and flavor of grace and oneness. And yet I had a deep sense that something was missing in everything that I had found—until I read that book.

Merely waking up wasn't the full solution, I realized. Growing up and showing up, in the ways that I'd received those modalities, weren't quite cutting it either. Something was missing, and for me this book was a revelation. Reading it felt like receiving a transmission from Marc, who was speaking directly to me. For the first time, I felt my "Unique Self," addressed and spoken to through Marc's *own* Unique Self.

It was a miraculous transmission—and I had to find the source.

So I came to Holland later that year for the second Eros festival and met Marc. Since that time, I've been completely blown away by his compelling and necessary vision of Unique Self, Evolutionary Eros, and Outrageous Love. What Marc has articulated over these last ten years— weaving a comprehensive tapestry of meaning he now calls CosmoErotic

Humanism—is simply unbelievable, in addition to what's now coming to fruition with all the new books and initiatives at the Center for World Religion and Philosophy.

So I'm introducing you to a master weaver of meaning, who can draw from all the great insights of premodern traditions, modern systems, and postmodern thought, putting it together in a beautifully articulated and complete universe story, with grounding in the sciences—both exterior and interior.

This story has the potential, I believe, to change the course of where our world is heading today. It may sound grandiose, and yet it's deeply based on the best of what we have available today, through science, through embodiment, psychology, mysticism, and all the wonderful ways human beings have gained knowledge of self and world to this point.

So, let's welcome our great storyteller, Marc Gafni.

CHAPTER 1

RESPONDING TO THE META-CRISIS WITH A NEW STORY CALLED COSMOEROTIC HUMANISM

1.1

STORY IS A FIRST PRINCIPLE
AND FIRST VALUE OF COSMOS

SETTING OUR INTENTION: TREMBLING WITH JOY

Thank you all so much for being here, and welcome everyone. Before we start, I want to share with you a feeling—one I've become more and more familiar with: a feeling of terror. A strange way to start, perhaps?

It's both a feeling of terror and a feeling of almost ecstatic exhilaration at the same time, at the immense possibility of this time. We're going to enter that terror, and stay in it for a little bit, just to feel where we are today in the world.

Most importantly, we're going to do it with great joy.

There's a very beautiful phrase from the ancient mystics: *gilu be'readah*, to tremble with joy—**isn't that what Eros is about?** I want to invite everyone, whether you're listening to this or reading at home, to step into this place of trembling with joy.

Welcome, everyone.

• • •

A WORLD OF BROKEN SENSEMAKING: ABRAHAM KOOK AT THE EDGE OF APOCALYPSE

We're going to walk through an enormous amount of material together. There's a huge journey we want to take. Every chapter, we're going to add something to the previous one, and take another step on the journey. And if you think this is only about your personal transformation journey, this is the wrong text for you. We want to try and do something else.

There's a writer named Abraham Kook, one of the great mystics and "interior" scientists of the twentieth century. In Hindu terms, think of someone like Sri Aurobindo. There's been very little written on him, but he's a major figure in the hidden Hebraic tradition. He said something incredibly important for our current moment, something we can start with to frame everything, which I've translated for you:

> *The shameless behavior of the New World at the edge of Apocalypse comes because the world is not ready to claim the explanation of how all the particular details weave together into The All.* ***We're not prepared for any detail to remain unconnected with cosmic magnificence****—and any detail unconnected with cosmic magnificence will not allow the mind to find ease.*

This is an incredible passage from Kook's mystical diary.

He claims we're now at the edge of collapse because we're not ready to claim an explanation *of how all particular details*—meaning every detail of my life: my trauma, my dreams, my broken dreams, my hurt, my wounds, my shadow, my glory, my greatness, all personal details as well as political details, economic, and social details—fit together.

In other words, we're trying to do sensemaking, to figure out what's happening at all levels. What's going on in the Cosmos? What's going on in the world? What's happening in Ukraine? It's not clear. I can tell you six stories about Ukraine efficiently and well. But what's the real narrative? Try and figure that out without high-level intelligence briefings (which often contradict each other).

Ultimately, the capacity to do sensemaking— about ourselves and about Reality—is broken.

Let's look at that word "sense," and remember that all sensemaking is *sensual*—in other words, to know is carnal. Adam *knew* Eve. She knew him biblically, meaning intimately. The *sensuality* of the world is broken because we can't do sensemaking. We can't know. **We can't be sensual—we can't be in the Fuck of Cosmos, or in our own Fuck,[1] or in any dimension of my life—if we've de-eroticized, disconnected from Cosmos. We've lost the** *sensual* **in our sensemaking.** This can happen in one of two ways:

- We can't make sense of our internal Reality.
- We can't make sense of what's going on externally, in the world.

In our current digital context, we follow particular vectors of information, within particular filter bubbles, intensified by social media. We ignore all contradicting data because we're micro-targeted by the tech plex, which feeds us only that which confirms our original bias.

In America, you can live in a Republican or a Democratic district, a Red state or a Blue state. You can scroll through your social media feed and never see any posts that your neighbors in the next state—or across the street— will see. This means that our neighbors, people in the same geographical community, will not see one post in common while scrolling through their social media feeds. It's shocking. **You think you understand each other, but you're literally not only non-intimate, but in a kind of war.**

This operates in our external sensemaking as well as our internal sensemaking.

---

[1] By "Fuck," we mean our radical aliveness and the core nature of Reality. For a deeper dive, see "A Word on the Word 'Fuck,'" in *The Phenomenology of Eros, Volume One: From the Crisis of Desire to Sex Beyond Shame.*

The many schools of psychology all kind of disagree with each other on fundamentals. In other words, no one has actually yet integrated the big picture. You can imagine someone saying, "I went to this Gestalt therapist. It was fine for a bit, but then I got rid of them. I went to a psychoanalyst, then to a Rolfing person. Then I did some core energetics, some somatic therapy. Then I went to a New Age seminar. Then I did another kind of retreat…" **We keep jumping between different sensemaking apparatuses, many of which contradict each other in some fundamental ways. We don't quite know how to put it all together—we can't locate ourselves in it all.** Do we just arbitrarily pick one and ignore all the rest of the information that feels dislocated and off in my body?

What Kook is saying is that we're at a cultural moment when, for the first time, we're demanding an explanation of how all particular details weave together into The All. Yet, we're not willing to settle for:

- This or that Hindu view.
- This or that Christian view.
- This or that psychoanalytical view.
- This or that Marxist view.
- This or that Democratic or Republican view…

It's more than a bit confusing—it's complicated.

A TIME BETWEEN STORIES, A TIME BETWEEN WORLDS

As Kook said, we're demanding an explanation of how all particular details weave together, not content to live in a world in which any detail is unconnected with cosmic magnificence. If there's any detail left out—regarding economics, politics, my own life, my psychology, my sexuality, my relationships—then my mind is not at ease. This is a beautiful passage from Kook, but what does it really mean? **Simply put, it means that we desperately need a *New Story* to live inside of.**

We're at a time between stories, a time between worlds. While there were many in-between times in history, this moment is unlike any other because we now have exponentialized technologies in every vector of Reality, driven by algorithmic structures that are not even monitored by human beings. They are created by human beings, but then they move independently, creating the immersive technological environment we live in. Indeed, **we live in an immersive environment algorithmically generated by private actors engaged in win/lose metrics—not by actors investing in the good of the commons.** They create the immersive environments we live in.

We have what's called a "race to the bottom," a world governed by multipolar traps, trapped in the "Tragedy of the Commons."

For example, over the last year, many new potentially disruptive and dangerous AI protocols were developed. Why were they developed? Basically, no one is willing to *not* develop them, even though many don't think it's wise. There's a race to the bottom, because even if we agree *not* to develop them, I secretly think you're going to break our agreement. So, according to the logic, I'm secretly going to develop them anyway.

Toby Ord's book *The Precipice* talks about AI as the single biggest vector of "existential risk," by which we mean threats resulting in there being no future at all. Who's governing it? Who's guiding it? No one. **There's no world body governing AI. There's no story guiding the people involved, those generating the technology—no set of underlying First Principles and First Values, no Story of Value.**

There's currently no story in which every detail is connected to cosmic magnificence.

In other words, we live in a world that's been de-storied from any narrative rooted in First Principles and First Values, which serves as a Universal Grammar of Value. Only such a new enactment can respond appropriately— and excitingly, and creatively, and ecstatically, and urgently—to the many forms of existential and catastrophic risk we face.

INFRASTRUCTURE, SOCIAL STRUCTURE AND SUPERSTRUCTURE

One helpful way of seeing, developed by Marvin Harris, is to look at the world in three ways. The world can be split into: **infrastructure, social structure,** and **superstructure.**

Infrastructure is the structure of material stuff, things, systems, and technology. It's the tech plex. Social structure consists of laws, legal covenants, and those kinds of structures. Usually social structure binds infrastructure. Laws like those passed by national parliaments, the EU, or Congress govern infrastructure, as well as the algorithmic structures of the tech plex.

But social structure can't keep up with or understand infrastructure anymore. In other words, you need to bind, to direct, orient, animate, set the tone, and create regulations and boundaries. The political and social structure has no idea what you need to understand infrastructure today. For example, if you watch those recent videos of the senator interviewing Mark Zuckerberg, it's very clear that, although he's been briefed up the wazoo, the senator has no idea what to ask Zuckerberg.

Zuckerberg's laughing because Facebook has drained the world of many of the top data scientists. There's so many really good data scientists in the world, scientists we desperately need today to engage existential risk, but all of them are playing by win/lose metrics in the corporate world. Universities today can't get professors to teach data science because no one wants to do it for $100,000 or $200,000 a year. Why would you when Facebook, TikTok, Oracle, Microsoft, Apple, Google, and a bunch of others, including Chinese companies, can pay so much more? They've basically absorbed the world's best data scientists, whom we need in order to solve the most crucial issues in a civilization that's data-driven.

That is existential risk right in front of you. The government is a joke—it can't afford to hire data scientists. So they can't even begin to figure out what's happening in the algorithmic structures of the tech plex, or how to respond.

So, social structure—law, government, politics—can't even begin to bind infrastructure in the tech plex. There are many other examples exactly like this. These are the dimensions of existential risk—and they operate in every sector.

SUPERSTRUCTURE: THE STORY WE LIVE IN

Here's the good news: there's another dimension called **superstructure, which is the story we live in, the story that tells us what's real.**

- It's not just a story, but a Story of *Value.*
- It's a way of knowing that *value is real.*
- It's not contrived or not made-up.
- It's a Story of Value based on First Principles and First Values.

It's not a dogmatic story. It's not a Jewish story, a Hindu story, a Buddhist story, or a New Age story. It's grounded in the very structure of the Cosmos itself. Of course, that's a big claim that we're going to have to qualify, justify, and support—and we can do that.

We've unfortunately lost track of our Story of Value—for many it seems completely outdated. **What would it mean if there was a Story of Value grounded in our best contemporary interior knowledge and the best contemporary exterior knowledge? And what if it was an *evolving* Story of Value?** In other words, it gets newer all the time—which feels intuitively correct to many—but there's still a story that we live in.

> *We need a sense of a shared grammar of value that we're all living inside of.*

We're not living inside of win/lose metrics. We're not living inside a narrow success story, which governs every dimension of society, every corporation, including the relationship between divisions in every corporation, between every person and society, between each individual asking the question: *Am I successful*? Every one of those data scientists' decisions, for example, is based on narrow rivalrous conflict, on win/lose metrics.

Social structure currently doesn't bind infrastructure—and in fact, the reverse is true: Infrastructure binds social structure. **And infrastructure itself—the tech plex, for example, or the AI world—has no superstructure, no sense of what is Good, True, and Beautiful.**

The major assumption in the tech world, as in culture at large, is that *there's no Story of Value*. That's a very big deal.

I think we can show that there is a true Story of Value. That's very exciting. To unpack this over the following chapters, we're going to go through a lot of theory, watch a lot of movies, and tell lots of stories.

- We're going through a bunch of stages.
- We're going to talk about a lot of personal stuff.
- We're going to talk about shame and sexuality.
- We're going to talk about value, story, and narrative.
- We're going to talk about victims and players.
- We're going to live the dream.

Perhaps most importantly, we're going to have an enormous amount of joy doing it. It absolutely has to be joyful.

FIRST VALUES EVOLVE

The main idea here, which we'll unpack below in many different ways, is that we're living in an *evolving Story of Value*—not a story of preordained values—rooted in First Principles and First Values. Anyone who says, "We know the First Principles and First Values," but fails to say that they're evolving, is a closet Fundamentalist. Be careful.

So, number one, these are *evolving* First Principles and First Values—they are a part of an ongoing story. Number two, this is not just a story, but a Story of *Value*. We're going to show that **Story itself is a First Principle and First Value of Cosmos—and we could also add meaning or consciousness or information**.

I'm not referring here to what Claude Shannon meant by information. The great founder of systems theory got the math right, but the metaphor wrong, as his co-author, Warren Weaver, pointed out in 1948. When Shannon talks about information, he's only talking about bits and bytes. What we mean by information are the meaning structures of Cosmos. Cosmos has meaning structures *all the way down to the subatomic level and all the way up to the complex human mind—all throughout the evolutionary chain.*

Meaning is not a human invention. That's a pretty big deal. Meaning evolves. And story is real.

So postmodernity got it exactly half right: Yes, it's all just a story, but story is not fiction; story is real. Story is a real and evolving structure of Cosmos, a First Principle and First Value. So our personal stories are not just bullshit, although parts of them might be. We have to distinguish among those parts—we'll get to that soon. The core notion is that my story matters, your story matters, and the drama of our lives actually has *infinite significance.*

REALITY IS NOT MERELY A FACT—REALITY IS A STORY

Another claim we can make is that our lives are mythic, that our lives are chapter and verse a part of the story of Reality. So, again we can say: *Reality is not merely a fact. Reality is a story.* This is not merely a poetic statement. It's not quite like the way Brian Swimme beautifully talks about the "universe story"—but then refuses to say that it's real.

No, this is a real statement, an ontological statement. Reality is not merely a fact, Reality is a story, for *real*. **The structure of Reality is story.** We're going to come back to this again and again, and in a certain sense the entire book is a series of meditations on these themes of story and value.

Reality is not merely a fact. Reality is a story—an ontological structure of Cosmos.

Buddhism generally says, *move beyond your story.* Kashmir Shaivism has a version of this as well. This is why postmodernity gets along so well with certain varieties of Buddhism. Postmodernity says, *the only real story is that there are no real stories.* That's a good summation of the postmodernist story. There are no grand narratives. Of course, that itself is a grand narrative, and they didn't seem to notice that this claim is a performative contradiction.

YUVAL HARARI REFLECTS THE POSTMODERN ZEITGEIST

Postmodernity's basic point is that it's all just a story, based on nothing. Therefore, my Story of Value equals your Story of Value—who's to say which story might be more real, more grounded in value? This may seem minor, but it matters immensely because it currently affects each of our lives, at every level: our health, our interiors, our friends, our sex, our love, our money… it affects everything.

I want to bring in someone I've been following the last five or six years: Yuval Harari. We're actually not interested in Harari as a thinker or a philosopher—he's a popular historian who's important because he's what we could call "uncontaminated material," meaning that he naturally reflects the ideas of the Zeitgeist. He's not philosophizing—he's merely reflecting the culture.

This is why it matters: Barack Obama read Yuval's book and said, *Yes, this is it.* Jeff Bezos says, *Yes, this is it.* Bill Gates says, *Yes, this is it.* And so on—there are many other such people at the core of contemporary culture saying the same thing.

Here's a quick example from chapter seven of *Homo Deus*, just so you get where the Zeitgeist is:

- Harari tells a story about a boy who lives in a particular English town, and he's really inspired by the local meaning-makers. It's the time of the Crusades in the medieval period, so he goes to the Middle East, to a particular area of present-day Syria, and slaughters Muslims. Amen. And he comes back a hero.
- Seven-hundred years later, in our era, in the same part of England, another English boy gets really excited by the local meaning-makers, and he goes to the same Middle East. This time, he goes to work for Amnesty International to help re-settle displaced refugees.

Harari says they're *both* made-up stories, that there's no *essential* difference between them, and that there's no *intrinsic* value difference between them.

As another example, from chapter two of *Sapiens*, Harari talks about universal human rights and Gaddafi's Libya, with its brutal repression of human rights. He compares these two, writing that both of these are stories. Both are fictions; they're both made up. There's no intrinsic reality to them—they're mere figments of our imagination.

Harari believes the differences between these stories of value are mere social constructs and fictions. It's quite incredible. Now, we wouldn't give a damn if Harari was an obscure academic philosopher or a historian quoting a philosopher. Some dude wrote a book—who cares?

But can you imagine a president of the United States one hundred years ago praising a book that says there's no distinction between Gaddafi's Libya and Universal Human Rights? Between the Crusades and Amnesty International?

And unlike other recent presidents, Obama is someone who supposedly stands for human rights.

THE POSTMODERN CLAIM: YOU CAN'T CLAIM INTRINSIC VALUE

Guess who else is an avid reader of postmodern thought? Vladimir Putin, as is the circle around him. So is Xi Jinping in China. **If you read them carefully, both Xi and Putin's position is: because it's all just stories, it's only a question of who rules and who has more power. It's only a power issue.** So anyone who thinks that America holds some exalted moral position is just making it up or thinks it's some strategic information warfare move. Ultimately, there's no difference whatsoever between our position and theirs because we believe values are made-up.

They're not entirely wrong, of course—there's some truth there—but both sides believe that, at the core. If you track Obama's speeches over the last fifteen years, you can see that he's a dyed-in-the-wool postmodernist. Like so many in the culture, he believes that all stories of value are made up. Of course, we happen to like his particular Story of Value, and we like him— he's suave, he dances, he's cool. Great wife, awesome kids. We love Barack.

Obama and many others influenced by postmodernity, like Bill Gates and Jeff Bezos, are not bad people. **Like so many in our culture, they merely received the collective wisdom of the academy and the media, so they cannot claim any ground for intrinsic value.** Obama went to university, and that's what he heard. Bezos is surrounded by academics, and that's what they all say. All the people at the Gates Foundation are saying the same thing because that's the standard position in our culture.

So it's not that there's only a bunch of idiots or academic philosophers saying this. No, very influential people are saying it. That's why we have to figure out why they are, what's true about it, and what's completely wrong about it. And then: **How can we articulate a position that even someone like Putin can get on board with?** It's not about him personally, but about

Russia. We need Russia, China, and other nations on board with the New Story of Value.

We need everyone in the game, or it's not going to work. We need Barack in the game, standing for intrinsic value, for a true and evolving shared Story of Value. We need Bezos, Gates, whoever. Corporate people, academic people—all people.

STARTING NEW, STARTING FRESH EVERY TIME

We're not doing university-style academic discourse here. This kind of talk doesn't actually happen in the university—and if it did, we'd have a much better university system. A much better way to get educated today is to leave the university, which has turned into a hothouse for repetitive mediocrity. Instead of academic ideas, we're going to do this through real life:

- We're going to talk about shame.
- We're going to talk about sexuality.
- We're going to talk about value.
- We're going to talk about story.

It's a big deal—it's vulnerable, and it's real. That's why I'm a little terror-stricken. I'm not just pretending. **You can't just *talk* about this—you have to completely empty yourself out.** That's the only way to engage something. Although we've talked about some of these topics many times over the years, I'm trying to approach them new with you here, with permission, from the very beginning.

Tabula rasa, clean slate.

We're going to start fresh.

1.2

YOUR STORY IS CHAPTER AND VERSE IN THE UNIVERSE: A LOVE STORY

Let's first spend a few minutes contacting a sense of deep rest and entering into prayer. Like the song by Foreigner says, "I want to know what love is." Is it real? And how do I know it's real? I can't just declare it to be real.

Our key sentence is "Reality is not merely a fact. Reality is a story. Reality is not an ordinary story—Reality is a love story." This is not a New Age declaration or a Fundamentalist claim but comes from the best understanding of the interior and exterior sciences, in all the vectors of wisdom—premodern, modern, and postmodern—integrated into a new emergent, into a new whole.

Because that's what Reality does.

Reality synergizes separate parts into new wholes because **Reality is animated by a fundamental principle called** *allurement*. It's a fundamental principle that operates all the way up and all the way down, from quarks to cells to societies to planets to galaxies, and especially humans. All of the attractive forces are, in some sense, special instances of this quality of allurement, and allurement is in a dialectical relationship to autonomy, sometimes called attraction and repulsion. **It's allurement *and* autonomy all the way up and all the way down.**

Love is not only just allurement—love is allurement and autonomy in relation with each other.

So, Reality is not merely a fact, but a story. And Reality is not an ordinary story. It's a love story—for real. This means that love is real, and that story is real. Reality is not an ordinary love story, but an outrageous, evolutionary love story. By Outrageous Love we mean that allurement and autonomy dance together and animate Cosmos all the way down and all the way up.

What if we could show that to be true, and not just declare it to be true, in such a way that *it becomes the ground of a universal and evolving grammar of value*?

• • •

Here's the last key piece of our general CosmoErotic proposition: **Your story is literally chapter and verse in The Universe: A Love Story, or Evolution: The Love Story of the Universe.**

Your "story" and my "story" are not mere postmodern social constructions.

- It's not a fiction but the core thread.
- It's not a victim story.
- It's not about repeating and obsessing over the details.
- It's not the therapeutic rehashing that I've done thousands of times before.

The core plotline is that my story is an irreducibly unique chapter in Evolution: The Love Story of the Universe.

At the same time, *love remains a complete mystery*. **There is no love without radical uncertainty and radical curiosity and radical**

16

unknowing. And yet: Love is real, Eros is real, story is real. Absolutely real. That interplay, that paradox, is what we're going to be unfolding in the chapters to follow.

Let's just hold that for a second, taking a few minutes in Silence of Presence, gently. As we integrate this, let's always remember to come back to this most important principle: *Let's just love each other.*

• • •

This is not just for the sake of our own personal transformation. Of course, it is personal on some level, **but my transformation participates in the transformation of the whole. There's no split between these two.** That's what Kook wrote in his mystical diary: "There's no detail of the personal that's unconnected from cosmic magnificence."

Any interpretation of my personal story that's merely therapeutic or explained only in terms of psychological or economic principles—*but doesn't actually understand that I am, in my irreducibly unique story, chapter and verse in Evolution: The Love Story of the Universe*—will not allow my mind to ease.

The fastest-growing disease in the world today is depression. There's an opioid crisis across America, as well as Europe and Asia, devoted to covering up the emptiness of our stories being apparently unconnected from cosmic magnificence. Let's just ask right now—as I've asked myself many times before—let's just look inside right now and ask:

Do we know that our story is connected to cosmic magnificence?

Can we feel this truth? It's not because we're flaming narcissists. Narcissism is actually a form of self-loathing, a failure in psychology, a failure of self-love: a feeling that my story is disconnected or disassociated from cosmic magnificence. We become narcissistic when we believe that all the meaning that feels intrinsic to me is just made-up, fictional, a figment of my imagination, a mere social construct that actually violates my sensibility, my sensuality, my Fuck, my Eros.

Therefore, of course depression is rampant. There's currently almost a million suicides a year, with about twenty-five to forty million attempts. It's utterly tragic.

In Silence of Presence, let's just sense into what we're saying, as we set an intention here at the beginning to love each other.

1.3

THE FIRST PRINCIPLE AND FIRST VALUE OF CELEBRATION IN THE MIDST OF A META-CRISIS

A t the 2021 Eros Mystery School, we talked deeply about the tragic, about the great suffering occurring around the world, and about the potential risks that lie ahead.[2] We're not going to recapitulate that here, but let's just sense into the tragic world situation and hold it because it's more true this year than it was last year. We feel this full weight of the tragic. But even as we completely acknowledge it, we must be celebratory.

This must be about celebration, about joy, about outrageously loving each other.

Why are we celebrating? Are we just turning away from all the pain? It's extremely serious, so why is our mood one of celebration?

WHAT HAPPENS TO A DREAM DEFERRED?

Before going deeper, I want to establish this principle of celebration in the midst of a meta-crisis. So how do we actually engage this? Langston

---

[2] See Marc Gafni, *The Amorous Cosmos: From Pre-Tragic to Post-Tragic—First Principles and First Values in Response to the Meta-Crisis* (World Philosophy and Religion, 2024).

Hughes, the great Black American poet, wrote a crazy beautiful poem called "Harlem":

> *What happens to a dream deferred?*
> *Does it dry up like a raisin in the sun?*
> *Or fester like a sore and then run?*
> *Does it stink like rotten meat?*
> *Or crust and sugar over, like a syrupy sweet?*
> *Maybe it just sags like a heavy load.*
> *Or does it explode?*

What are you doing when thinking about what the world needs to be? You're thinking about the dream. You're thinking about what the world *should* be. You've got a dream of what it looks like.

If your name is Pol Pot, if your name is Stalin, if your name is Mao, you don't know how to already live in the dream, so you try and reshape the world *immediately* the way you want it to be—and you inflict more suffering than all other forces of history.

In other words, what do you do with a dream you can't realize? The reason Stalin, Mao, Pol Pot, and all the other Utopianism figures tried to immediately enact the dream is because they couldn't delay it. They feared it would dry up like a raisin in the sun, that it would explode, so they instead tried to explode Reality.

LIVING THE DREAM

We don't want to do that. It's very subtle, but **the only way you can change the world is if you're willing to live, now, *in the already changed world.*** It's the only way you can change the world responsibly. Meaning, we can't wait until we've totally handled existential risk. And once we've handled it, only then can we celebrate, only then can we make love, dance, sing…

We can't think that until then, it's only nose to the grindstone—because we've got to actually save the world. Of course, there's something very beautiful and noble about this, but it's actually quite dangerous. Remember: *what happens to a dream deferred?*

There's this gorgeous dance we have to do together—you can call it a "dialectic" if you wish. On one hand, we cannot turn away. Thirty years ago, Robert Jay Lifton wrote a wildly important book called *Facing Apocalypse,* in which he asked: How do you not turn away from catastrophe? So we have to acknowledge existential risk.

At the same time, if you don't turn away and instead only engage in "serious" work all the time, then you risk deferring the dream.

A good principle is: *You can't change the world unless you're willing to live in the world that's already changed.* **Even as we're seriously attempting to evolve the source code, we're also not waiting for it to change to rejoice. We're living dialectically in a world that's already changed. Therefore, we can celebrate.**

I call that *living the dream.* It's the dreamtime. I want to welcome us— with permission, humility, and audacity—to the dreamtime. Let's be in dreamtime together—tenderly, audaciously, and fiercely. Although we're facing existential risk, we're not deferring the dream. We have to be able to hold that radical joy, and live in the dream right now.

THE SABBATH: BUILDING A PALACE IN TIME

There's an already existing, wildly beautiful interior technology developed for this very purpose, to live the dream. It's a technology that was very well developed over a couple of thousand years.

When I was in Dharamshala with the Dalai Lama, I learned he's actually madly grieving underneath his surface "ha-ha" smile, which makes him seem very happy to everyone. He's just madly heart-broken. No one is paying him a lot of attention in Dharamshala, and in Tibet he's completely demonized. People see his picture in Tibet and they go into fit of rage and hatred and loathing. I saw a woman do that, a Chinese musician. She saw his picture and went into a kind of paroxysm of government-inspired rage. He also told me about the unimaginably magnificent temples of Tibet that he grew up in, which have all been destroyed.

So he's having a hard time, and he says to me, laughing, "I go to the West because they like me there!" Then he turned to me and said, "You're from Jerusalem. How did you guys do it?" I said, "We have a technology for that—not only do we build a palace in space, but we also build a palace in time."

That's what Sabbath is: Every week, for an entire day, you step into an already liberated world. No matter what oppression is going on, no matter what brutality, no matter your socio-economic class, you spend a seventh of your life meditating in enlightened space, in enlightened time, in a liberated world.

This notion of Sabbath time is very radical.

Remember, we've got to weave together a New Story of Value in which we integrate the best strands of premodern, modern, and postmodern wisdom. So, here's an essential teaching from the traditional period: Live the dream. Sabbath.

We don't wait.

That's the celebration.

Welcome to the dreamtime.

1.4

THE THREE SELVES: WEAVING PAST, PRESENT, AND FUTURE TOGETHER INTO A NEW STORY OF VALUE

Let's move into the plotlines of the New Story of Value. First, we will take a look at our relationship to self through a model we've unfolded over the last couple of years that complements the Unique Self framework. This model is also based on what I want to call a First Principle and First Value of Cosmos.[3] We have outlined about fifteen or twenty First Principles and First Values so far, and each one has an equation to describe them. For example, uniqueness would be a First Principle and First Value, as well as Eros and intimacy. All of these also constitute plotlines in the New Story of Value.

But here I want to introduce the First Principle and First Value of temporality. In the structure of the manifest world, there's a space-time

---

[3]   See David J. Temple, *First Principles and First Values: Forty-Two Propositions on CosmoErotic Humanism, the Meta-Crisis, and the World to Come* (World Philosophy and Religion, 2024).

continuum—and in that continuum, there's a structure called past, present, and future.

We're not going to go into the whole movement in physics today that says that our understanding of the space-time continuum is collapsing and that we need a new model. If we want to read just one good survey of the literature on that, take a look at Donald Hoffman's book *The Case Against Reality*, especially chapter six, on how our understanding of space and time is radically shifting. That's not our topic here, so let's stay for now in a world of space and time.

In this world of space and time, there is past, present, and future.

PAST, PRESENT, AND FUTURE: STRUCTURES OF REALITY ITSELF

This is no accident. In other words: Past, present, and future are clearly structures of Reality itself. Therefore, to be in right relationship to Reality, we need to be in right relationship to past, present, and future. **If I dissociate from the past, if I disconnect from the present, or if I'm alienated from the future, that's not a psychological problem—it means that I'm structurally dissociated from the basic structure of Reality itself.**

So past, present, and future are not just random happenstances that physics describes—or *undescribes*, depending on what you're reading. **Past, present, and future are clearly structures of Reality itself.**

Remember what Kook said: We want no detail to be unconnected from cosmic magnificence. Meaning that my personal story and the cosmic story are interconnected. So I want my personal story to be deeply connected to my past, my present, and my future. The cosmic story, and the world-historical story, too, have to be connected to past, present, and future—to the precise extent that I dissociate from or distort my relationship to any of them, I'll be a sick human being in a sick society.

It's almost self-evident when we phrase it this way.

That's a fundamental structure of Reality, a First Value of Reality: My Story of Value has to include temporality—past, present, and future. And this is expressed in our very self-identity, in our three temporal selves.

PSYCHOLOGICAL SELF IS ROOTED IN THE PAST

There are three basic visions of self that we've been talking about in a new way recently. The first one we call "psychological self," who is madly committed to the past.

Psychological self says that the key to healing and transforming is found in the past. There's an enormous amount of important psychological literature on this over the last 250 years supporting this. For example, over a hundred years ago, Josef Breuer was sitting in Vienna, and "hysterical" women were being brought in to see him. It turns out that many of these women in Viennese society were abused, or raped, or experienced incest— women that no one in polite society would talk about.

Breuer begins to look into this, and he realizes there's a key in the past. He can't just look at these women and ask them to get it together in the present. Somehow they're all troubled in their feminine expression, these "hysterical" women. Indeed, the diagnosis of hysteria was a major feature in the early inception of psychology.

Breuer had a brilliant understanding that the past is magic. It's really important: **There's something in the past that has its invisible hands on the steering wheel of my life**. If I can go back and somehow relive those moments, reframe those moments, and do all the beautiful psychological work, then I can somehow free those invisible hands from the steering wheel of my life and establish a new direction. That's a very big deal.

It is true, but it's partial. It's only a piece of it. The shadow side of this is that everything that happens risks being reduced to prior causation. Meaning, we might mistakenly think that *yesterday causes everything*. For example, **free will goes out the window in this view because everything is related**

to a set of prior causes. If you could perfectly see the web of prior causation, then you could fully know the present. This exists in the Buddhist notion of mutually interdependent co-arising.

If you could just trace it back, you'd realize that this particular constellation, this particular context, this particular moment, and everything else is determined by the past. The idea that yesterday determines today, however, can also become the greatest slave driver, the most brutal oppressor.

So yes, we must honor and investigate the past, but then we must move beyond it in order to actually get free.

ENLIGHTENED SELF: THE DEPTH OF THE PRESENT MOMENT

The second temporal self is what we can call the "mystical self," or perhaps the "enlightened self." The enlightened self looks at the psychological self and says, "Ah, what Western nonsense. Let's realize the full beauty of the infinity of presence in the depth of the present moment."

Do I really need to think about my mother and father all the time? No. **Let's meditate and enter into the infinity of the present moment and just be here now.**

- I experience the power of the Now.
- I'm in the fullness of the Now.
- I breathe into that eternity that resides in the moment.
- I enter into the timeless time and the placeless place.

Any thought that you're determined by your past is entirely liberated in the full *blissfuck* of the present.

Of course, this view is absolutely true, and you already know the next sentence: It's true—but partial. This perspective by itself ignores the gifts and invitations of the past. **It doesn't differentiate, it dissociates.**

This is why, for example, when Eastern mysticism came to the West, many people stopped doing their necessary psychological work, thinking that the True Self experience would settle the issue of you being an asshole. No, you're still an asshole—just a meditating asshole. Meaning: **You can't bypass the deep work of the past.**

Teachers of meditation assumed that their meditative states, which were absolutely real and deep and important. meant that they had authority in a wide range of areas beyond their training. They assumed their insights and understandings about the interior dimensions of human psychology were necessarily accurate—when of course they weren't.

I know a beautiful man who brought his child, who was quite sick psychologically, to the guru Muktananda. He was coming to America in the mid-1970s, and his child was in deep need. He had very serious schizophrenia. This child wound up committing suicide, and was one of the major people involved in the collapse of Siddha Yoga, Muktananda's organization, by accident. There's a naïve assumption, held by some who represent the enlightened self view, that it would somehow supersede and completely replace the psychological self—but **past and present absolutely need to live together.**

EVOLUTIONARY UNIQUE SELF: THE FUTURE IS CALLING

So far, we've got the past, and we've got the present—now we need the future. There's a third temporal self we call the "Evolutionary Unique Self." Your future self. **Your Evolutionary Self is called by a memory of your future, and it includes both past and present self.**

I'm not only formed by my past, nor do I live solely in the eternal now. These are both true and necessary, but I'm actually, *quite literally*, also called by the future. **The future calls me.** And if I listen, if I enter into a deep enough state of interiority, I'll hear the whispered calls from my personal future. If I listen even more deeply, as part of the whole, I'll hear the memory of the future of the whole... And from there, we can say that "hope itself is a memory of the future."

This is about hope—we need to evoke a memory of the future.

The human being is not merely *Homo sapiens* determined by past and present. The human being is beginning to emerge in an entirely new way, where for the first time ever, **I'm not just part of the whole, but I can see the whole—and I can take action** *for the sake of the whole*. That's never happened in history before. I can see the whole, I'm inseparable from the whole, the whole directly affects me. There's no place to hide. There's no more "local." The merely local does not exist. If you think this is only local, you're completely delusional.

We think we've created our beautiful world—our beautiful Belgian world, our beautiful Dutch world, our beautiful Vermont world, separate from everything else. That's not true. There is no local place disconnected from the world anymore. It simply does not exist. The whole invades my life. For the first time, I can see not just that I'm *part* of the whole, but I can *see* the whole itself. Moreover:

> ## *The whole lives in me—and I can affect the direction of the whole.*

If this is fully understood and integrated, it means that I become "omni-considerate" for the sake of the whole. What would it mean if the actions of every agent or every person in the Commons was aligned with every other agent—and with the Commons itself?

In other words, what if it were the exact opposite of our life today?

What would it mean if we lived in a world in which all actions were omni-considerate, taken for the sake of the whole?

A NEW HUMAN AND A NEW HUMANITY CALLED *HOMO AMOR*

What would it mean if we emerged as humans who experienced, both individually and collectively, a deep sense of being omni-considerate as part of their very identity? Meaning:

- We have a direct, lived experience that the LoveIntelligence of Reality in this love story lives in me, personally and uniquely.
- We know that this LoveIntelligence has something to give to the whole, something the whole desperately needs.
- We know that we can create a new Commons.

This is the emergence out of *Homo sapiens* of a literal New Human and a New Humanity called *Homo amor*. Is this really possible, or a fanciful pipe dream? Is it the inexorable movement of history? Are we able to awaken and guide this process? We've got to look at these questions in a serious way. We can't just repeat, "Oh, *Homo sapiens* and now *Homo amor*. Got it." We have to look at it with fresh eyes.

The Evolutionary Unique Self hears the call of the future. It's a shocking experience to know that the future is literally part of the now. That the future speaks to me, invites me forward. That I can listen to the call of desire.

Desire is the call of the future—and the clarification of desire is the clarification of the call from the future. My deepest heart's desire is the desire of Reality itself, uniquely expressed in me, as me, and through me.

The clarification of my deepest heart's desire is the clarification of a dimension of Reality's desire that lives uniquely in me and that is needed by All-That-Is.

You can begin to see the clear outline of a New Story here.

· · ·

So, we have three temporal selves: psychological self, enlightened self, and Evolutionary Unique Self, or future self. **We absolutely need all three**, or else we're in violation of a First Principle and First Value of Reality— temporality. That's what's so beautiful about it: It's so clear. We can't move without being in alignment with all of those structures.

They're not made-up spiritual ideas—they're embedded in the very physics of Reality.

I'm limited to the extent that I'm dissociated from either the past, present, or future, and I instead choose only one of these. For example:

- Psychology chooses the past.
- The Ashram chooses the present.
- Techno-Optimists choose a desiccated version of the future.
- Political utopians and totalitarians try to make the future immediately present, weaponizing both the past and present.

You can actually chart politics based on your relationship to each one of these three. For example, what's China doing right now? It's pretending to honor the past. Confucius is all over the country these days, and of course it has very little to do with the great sage. Russia is also pretending to honor its past, and the country's great history is being set-up and abused.

America has a brief past, so it's very much into the Now. In general, the West is obsessed by its present—it can't really see the future. It's politically determined by elections every four years, for example. Short-term results are also what defines the corporate world. **In the immediate present, the ability to hold the past and see the future is virtually impossible**.

So how do we, in our lives, weave together the best of the traditional, the modern, and the postmodern?

How do we weave past, present, and future together into a New Story of Value?

1.5

DISTINGUISHING BETWEEN HOLY AND UNHOLY SEDUCTION

As a review and a preview, these are our three starting points:

- One: Celebration—we live the dream.
- Two: Temporality—we exist as three selves, in all three times.
- Three: Seduction—that is our goal.

There's another important frame we need to introduce: What we're doing here has to be about seduction, which is a core obligation. Seduction is a heavy term, a loaded word. In the book of Psalms, for example—we have scripture on this—the infinite force of Reality is considered the seducer. But there are in fact two kinds of seduction: holy and unholy. Let's look at each of them.

- **Unholy seduction** is when I seduce someone to break their appropriate boundary for the sake of my greed.
- **Holy seduction** is when I seduce someone, or myself, to break an inappropriate boundary, a contraction—be it intellectual, emotional, aesthetic, artistic—for the sake of their deepest, clarified need, or my own deepest, clarified need.

This is an absolutely critical distinction.

SEDUCE THYSELF—SEDUCE EACH OTHER

Let's take this distinction one level deeper. If, as many in our culture believe, Reality is a reductive-materialist Reality—which it's not—then Reality is but a *tale told by an idiot, full of sound and fury, signifying nothing*. It's merely random, and there's really nothing underneath. Then all we have is our artificial, socially constructed boundaries—and nothing else.

That then determines my identity. That's who I am: no more than a collection of socially constructed boundaries. If there's nothing underneath, if there's ultimately nothing to be seduced towards, then the whole notion of seduction is considered almost evil, per se. If the only thing that exists is an *artificial* notion of the good, enshrined in an artificial set of boundaries that are ever-changing, then seduction can only ever be mere trickery.

But if Reality is a love story, which it is, then my obligation is: *seduce myself*. To seduce myself means actually transcending—"trance-end," as we say, or end the trance of my trauma, the trance of my contraction—and feel out into the expanded field.

There's a great teacher who lived a few thousand years ago. His name was Moses, and he had a student named Joshua. Joshua was the least talented of his students but became the successor. My lineage teacher pointed out that he became the successor because he was the only one who trusted Moses to seduce him.

So I want to invite you to *seduce yourself*, and *allow yourself to be seduced by Reality*.

We're a Unique Self Symphony, so we need to seduce each other. It's not about me as the teacher. It's all of us together. We must seduce each other with beauty, into depth, into outrageous embrace, into authenticity. **Seduce each other to *live the dream*.** We look into each other's eyes and say, *I love you madly*. Seduction doesn't mean we're getting married and moving in together. It doesn't mean we're having sex. It simply means *I love you madly*.

- I'm ecstatic to be with you.
- You're beautiful, you're stunning.
- We're excited about each other.
- We're ecstatic about each other.
- We're delighted by each other's beauty, goodness, and wisdom.
- We're delighted by the sparkle in each other's eyes.
- We're delighted by the curve of your cheeks.
- We're delighted by the way the light plays in your hair.

But to do that, we have to be willing to seduce each other. Holy seduction. We give each other permission to let go of the past, of our trauma. An interesting definition of Enlightenment is the ability to completely bracket trauma. So for now we're bracketing trauma, meaning we're putting it aside. It's not as if it's not there—it's all real, but we're bracketing it, not bypassing it. Big difference. *We're living the dream.*

Imagine that there's not just a separate self. And imagine, as we've talked about many times before, that there's a True Self. **Do you think you're going to get from separate self to True Self without being seduced? What do you think meditation is but a form of holy seduction?**

- Can I seduce myself beyond my separate self into True Self, and see clearly that I'm part of the Field of Value?
- Can I seduce myself beyond True Self, into my Unique Self?
- Can I seduce myself beyond Unique Self into Unique Self in an evolutionary context, an Evolutionary Unique Self?
- Can I seduce myself to play my instrument in Unique Self Symphony?

This is how we seduce ourselves and each other—how we engage in holy seduction.

TAKE RESPONSIBILITY FOR YOUR OWN AROUSAL

It's not *know thyself*, from the Delphic Oracle—it's *seduce thyself*. And the key to seducing thyself is knowing that no one else is responsible for your arousal. **We must each take responsibility for our *own* arousal.** Arousal is a another structure, a First Principle and First Value, of Cosmos. Arousal is something that happens throughout Reality. There's an arousal, an excitation in Reality as a new moment is birthed that holds something the old moment didn't hold.

That's called "emergence"—there's something new in the world. For example, a cell has something that a macromolecule doesn't have. There's an emergence: the macromolecule arouses, there's an intensification, and then novelty.

So let this be a week of *it'aruta*, as the Aramaic text says, a week of arousal. **In the thirteenth-century Book of Radiance, *The Zohar*, and in hundreds of other lineage texts, arousal and awakening are used interchangeably.** *The Zohar* intentionally blurs the lines between all forms of arousal. Because the sexual models the erotic, there's twelve billion years of Eros before sex. You can be completely aroused and completely celibate. But the sexual holds an important model for what Eros could look like.

This is what it looks like: I'm not in my small self. I'm not on my contracted self. If you want to find a model for general arousal, find your best sexual moment, then apply it in every other dimension of life. What would it look like to be that person who screams the name of God?

As above, so below, screaming the name of God.

When I scream the name of God, what else do I scream? *The name of the other person*—because I realize they're the same.

That's what we want to do with this work. We want to arouse our greatness, our goodness, our truth, our integrity. Again, it's not about sexuality—it's about Eros.

It's about the Eros at the core of everything.

If there is a general motif for this work, it's holy seduction—intellectual, emotional, aesthetic, existential and moral seduction. **We're seducing ourselves in order to love each other.**

WE ARE A BAND OF OUTRAGEOUS LOVERS

In *The Zohar*, the Book of Radiance, there's a section called the *Idra Rabba*, the "Great Gathering." There were eight people at the Great Gathering, and they become *amuda olan*, the "pillars of Reality"—the Unique Self Symphony, where each person plays their unique instrument within a common score of music.

The Zohar, in fact, was not written by one person, but by a band of Outrageous Lovers. They're called the *chavreya* in Aramaic—the *companions*. Isn't that beautiful? These companions are not always in the study hall. They walk in the garden. They're by the lake. Sometimes they gather in a hall, and they walk out again. They're out at night. They're up in the morning.

They're the *Companions of Radiance*.

That's who we are, a band of Outrageous Lovers. *Homo amor*—the LoveIntelligence of Reality moving through us. We get to be aroused by each other, the radiant companions of Outrageous Love.

CONTEMPLATION EXERCISE: FIND SOMEONE'S EYES

We live in a culture where we're not allowed to be blown away by each other's radiance without it being somehow inappropriate or misappropriated. So let's allow ourselves to be blown away by each other's beauty, by each other's goodness. We have to be delighted by each other as we meet each other. Whatever your protocol or preference is—you can either bow or hug or whatever.

Whatever feels right to you.

Over the course of the next week, there's just one simple, tender instruction: Find at least three people. Briefly find their eyes, stop for a second, and be blown away by the other. The other person may not even be aware. This could be a few seconds with someone on the street, or at the grocery store. It could be with a family member, a friend. It may be prolonged or fleeting.

We're the radiant companions. We're Homo amor in Unique Self Symphony. We're in the source code itself. The source code is in us. We're in terror, and we're trembling with joy. We're sharing this with the world around us, looking into each other's eyes.

CHAPTER 2

READING SACRED TEXTS OF CULTURE: VALUE IN *DON'T LOOK UP*

2.1

EVOLVING BEYOND
REGRESSIVE SPIRITUALITY

Let's start with a little evolutionary thread here. Early on, there was the reptilian brain that can only feel in the immediate present. Then we developed the mammalian brain (the limbic brain), the neocortex, and then the frontal lobes. That's the evolutionary development allowing us to do this thing called abstraction, or higher-order thinking. Regressive forms of New Age spirituality say, *don't do that.*

Abstraction does not mean I'm disconnecting from immediacy. No, I'm actually feeling into the space. In other words, I can get out of my immediate experiential self of the moment.

You remember the three temporal selves? I can feel into the past psychological self to understand trauma; I can feel into the future, my evolutionary self. And then from there, my past and future are in my present. I've recovered the memories of the past, but **genuine recovery is when I've also recovered** *memories of the future.* With those, I enter into and engage with the present.

This is opposed to Eckhart Tolle, who writes in *The Power of Now* that there's no past and no future. That's a tragic mistake—of course there is.

Similarly, everyone keeps misreading Mary Oliver's poem about the soft animal, which is called "Wild Geese":

> *You do not have to be good.*
> *You do not have to walk on your knees*
> *for a hundred miles through the desert repenting.*
> *You only have to let the soft animal of your body*
> *love what it loves.*
> *Tell me about despair, yours, and I will tell you mine.*
> *Meanwhile the world goes on.*
> *Meanwhile the sun and the clear pebbles of the rain*
> *are moving across the landscapes,*
> *over the prairies and the deep trees,*
> *the mountains and the rivers.*
> *Meanwhile the wild geese, high in the clean blue air,*
> *are heading home again.*
> *Whoever you are, no matter how lonely,*
> *the world offers itself to your imagination,*
> *calls to you like the wild geese, harsh and exciting —*
> *over and over announcing your place*
> *in the family of things.*

I've heard this poem misread so many times—it's infuriating. We often hear: Just look at the animals and the children, how joyous and free they are, while we're filled with regrets about the past and anxieties about the future.

That's not entirely wrong—of course that's partially true—but we have to read very carefully.

Whenever a new capacity comes online in evolution—and our frontal lobe is such a capacity—we have to learn how to use that new capacity.

- Can that new capacity be hijacked for recursive loops about the past in perpetual anxiety about the future? Of course it can.
- Is that a bad use of this new capacity? Of course it is.

- Do we really need Eckhart Tolle to write books like *The Power of Now*? Of course we do. They're a great contribution, necessary reminders.

But we also must evolve beyond regressive spirituality. We have to be able to envision the future. That's exactly what we were talking about in the last chapter, with the three temporal selves. I want to just invite, with gentle permission, all three selves into the room—past, present, and future—as a full reflection of temporality, a First Principle and First Value of Cosmos.

In the New Age spiritual world we think we've got that all down—it's all about the Now. But just like the fundamentalist world goes too quickly to the past, so much of the New Age world stays in a superficial version of the present.

Remember, the opposite of the holy is not the unholy. The opposite of the holy is the superficial.

If we stay on the surface, if we disconnect and dissociate our minds from our feeling, then we can't think. I've actually never thought of a good idea in my life. I'm not being sarcastic or cute when I say this—**I've always *felt* good ideas.** Any idea that's real, you *feel* it.

Only then do I use the discursive mind to try and find a way of understanding and expressing what I'm feeling.

Then I try and distinguish between surface feeling and depth feeling, and then navigate the feeling tones through the mind, as the heart and mind dance with each other. It's gorgeous.

• • •

Before we go to the movies, I just want to spend a little time setting our tone.

I just want to try and hold a meditative space now.

Before stepping in, we're going to hold Silence of Presence, gently.

So much gratitude, so much gentleness.

2.2

TWO FORMS OF EXISTENTIAL RISK: THE DEATH OF HUMANITY AND THE DEATH OF *OUR* HUMANITY

I had a conversation recently with a young man who's been in deep contact with the think tank over the last several years. He made a movie that was number one on Netflix for a while. We've been in conversation about one of the major themes we talk about: existential risk, meaning any risk to our very existence, a term coined by Nick Bostrom. It's quite heavy, and no joke: the potential annihilation of the future.

Even before Covid, I would basically say to people: "No, it's not too big to fail," and I would see the resistance rise up in them. Then they would look at me and say, "Stick to Unique Self, stick to what you know."

I remember one evening talking with a bunch of fantastic people. When we were talking about existential risk, I remember everyone's eyes glazed over, people contracting and tensing up. Then everyone relaxed and opened up again when we started talking about Unique Self. I thought, "Wow, people don't really get it—or they really don't want to."

What we're saying is: It's not too big to fail. Existential risk is about systemic collapse. What I've been trying to do for the last decade is look at the systems and how they operate in their infrastructure, social structure, and superstructure.

We came to the conclusion that there's a good chance the whole thing will collapse in on itself.

Then when Covid hit, all of a sudden, the unimaginable happened: You couldn't take flights, or even leave your house. People lost their jobs, and their family members. All over the world tens and tens of millions of people lost their life savings, their children's future. Tens of millions of people lost the entire world they dreamed of building for decades. Sometimes it took several generations for a family to become financially stable—that all got crushed and crashed for many. And none of what caused it has been repaired.

Of course, **we weren't thinking in terms of systems.** We actually stopped all movement in the world, focused only on the short-term, moved by the reptilian brain. Our immediate goal was to stop the short-term effects of the virus. We outlawed all Covid response approaches except for one officially sanctioned one. We ignored all the peripheral effects and caused massive breakdowns in supply chains along the way.

How we *should* have dealt with it is a different conversation. But the point, again, is that the freeze-framing of the reptilian brain sees only what's in front of it and misses the broader set of issues.

However, since Covid, when I say to people it's not too big to fail, there's a flicker of recognition. It's like, oh right, **the systems are not invulnerable, and existential risk is based on systems collapse.**

- When the rivers run dry,
- When the coral reefs die out,

- When the deserts are no longer there,
- When the forests are burning,
- When dead zones appear in the ocean...

But when you add up all the ten or eleven different risk factors that are on the breaking point, climate change is the least of our problems. Of the ten major existential risks, climate change is among the least important.

That's what this is all about, and that's what the Center for World Philosophy and Religion is focused on responding to. It's about taking the death of humanity seriously.

But there's a second form of existential risk which is not merely the death of humanity—it's the death of *our* humanity: the disappearance of what makes us human.

2.3

THE MOVEMENT FROM TECHNOFEUDALISM TO TECHNOHUMANISM

The main threat from a tech plex gone wild is what we're calling TechnoFeudalism. And the main threat from TechnoFeudalism is not the death of humanity, but even worse: the death of *our* humanity.

We're concerned about the creation of a world of upgraded algorithms and downgraded human beings. A world of rampant ads micro-targeted to different peer groups. Being part of a peer group means that you're subject to "split-testing" all the time. Split-testing means that your reactions to different sequences are measured and then optimized. For example, you see the image of a cute cat online. A few seconds or minutes later, you see another image, and then a third, a fourth, and a fifth: a sequence of many images in a row. Your responses all are tracked: your reaction time, whether you click on a link, how long you scrolled, where your mouse lingered. This data is then compared, or split-tested, with how you responded to other sequences presented to you and others in your peer group.

Split-testing is happening behind the scenes—and it's unregulated. There were huge outcries against the British Intelligence Service in England and the CIA in the United States, which was basically testing and influencing and controlling the population. In the United States, Sam Ervin, who headed the Watergate hearings in 1971, convened a huge panel with Ted Kennedy—one of the most important contributions to stop intelligence agencies around the world from doing this.

Well, this is all now being done again—but this time not by the government.

Everyone thought the government was the main threat, but it's now moved to the private sector, where it's all unregulated. Split-testing is happening all the time—every day, every second. Anyone who in any way engages online is subject to split-testing to see what peer group you fit into, and how you'll respond to a sequence that, for example, might be directed to groups of unaffiliated or undecided voters.

Then, based on the split-testing conducted on social media platforms, those voters may be subject to a particular sequence to get them to change their vote, depending on where they live. This was tried out in 2010, and **it was shown that you could actually move voting results by two to four percent**—a small margin but one that can often determine the outcome of an election…

That's it—democracy just went out the window.

Democracy doesn't actually work anymore because you can micro-target and influence peer-groups to change people's behavior. When I shared this with my friend John Mackey from Whole Foods, we had a huge fight. He said, "There's no difference between this and the old advertising." His position is libertarian, based primarily on the value of freedom. "This is what the people want—it's just advertising."

But it's not just advertising. Advertising used to broadcast one single message across a platform to lots of people, and everyone received the same message. No micro-targeting, no split-testing, no peer groups. Everyone had more agency about whether they wanted to be influenced consciously or subconsciously by that advertisement on television.

What's happening now is what we would call in law "undue influence." It's a legal category. You're not even aware that it's happening. You're being micro-targeted, split-tested into peer groups. Now, you might say to yourself, "This does not affect me." Okay, fine—**but all you need to do is affect three percent of the population—and then democracy is literally done.**

Now, it's not like this was championed by someone like Donald Trump. It was developed and promoted by Eric Schmidt, the head of Google who ran Obama's campaigns in 2008 and 2012. If you follow the tracks, you realize that the person who deployed this technology most effectively was Obama. Then there was the Facebook and Cambridge Analytica scandal in 2016, with Chris Wylie, a lieutenant of Schmidt's also working on the 2012 Obama campaign.

It's not that there aren't real villains—of course there are bad actors. However, much more insidious is that we've collectively, systematically rendered democracy ineffective and susceptible to manipulation. We could say that democracy has disappeared in the last couple of years. We still assume our system is democratic, but it's not.

That's not the death of humanity. That's the death of *our* humanity. The algorithm has had a huge negative effect on the value of choice and freedom.

There's two kinds of existential risk. We've got to look at both of them—and respond to both of them. **Luckily, we're not only facing dystopia—we're poised between dystopia and utopia.**

• • •

Let's remember, technology is not only evil. It's beautiful and important and gorgeous—and we desperately need it. We're all here because of technology. So many of us are closer to each other than we would have been because of social media and WhatsApp. We are all webbed together through the beauty of technology.

However, we need to animate technology with a kind of "Techno-Humanism," which is much different from transhumanism. We still honor our humanity.

We need a TechnoHumanism,
not a TechnoFeudalism.

We need a movement away from digital dictatorship to digital intimacy. The movement from TechnoFeudalism to TechnoHumanism is how we respond to both existential risks: the actual death of all humanity and the death of our humanity—both serious threats.

2.4

FROM HIJACKED ATTENTION TO THE PLACING OF THE HEART

———————

One of the ways we can do this is to take hold of our own attention. In Hebrew, the word for paying attention is *sim lev*, which you can translate as "the placing of the heart." It's a beautiful phrase—**to pay attention is to place your heart**.

So I'm going to ask everyone to pay attention. Meaning, place your heart. Take responsibility for your own arousal. In other words, don't rely on me or anyone else.

———————

Take responsibility for your own arousal, and place your heart.

———————

When you're doing anything, place your heart: cooking, washing, praying, making love, resting, or doing yoga. Yoga is beautiful, a gorgeous practice of feeling the body, from the heart.

So whatever you're doing, you feel your heart, you place your heart, you place your attention. A part of the death of our humanity is that we're living in an attention economy in which you are not the end user. You are not even the product—*the ability to influence your decision is the product.* This is organized through the collection of all of your data, and not just which porn sites you searched. That's a different conversation.

It's much more subtle: how long your mouse hovered before you clicked, the order and speed of your typing. Every detail—what are called "digital breadcrumbs"—is subject to what's called "reality mining" in the literature of MIT's media lab. This term was defined in 2004, in an article by the lab's director, Alex Pentland.

In reality mining, all your digital breadcrumbs are collected in order to create the actual product of the tech plex: prediction. This prediction is then sold to third parties who are unaligned or misaligned with your interest, through a continual, algorithmically generated auction. But in order to collect more breadcrumbs, your attention must be held for longer and longer. **This is most effectively done by arousing the reptilian brain, primarily through primal negative emotions: fear, jealousy, and anger.**

One of the most commonly deployed methods is called "algorithmically generated micro-targeting," where no one's making the decisions. In other words, it's algorithmically generated through its own inherent principles—which are **the opposite of First Principles and Values**. For example, several major sites have been able to algorithmically micro-target users with pictures of one's former spouse smiling because that generates an amygdala hit of anger.

This is then exponentialized across your personalized web experience, which is designed to generate engagement—and thus polarization—through forms of amygdala hijacking.

In other words:

- First your attention needs to be hijacked, which is best done when it's weakened.
- Then this process is exponentialized, and more data is algorithmically collected.

- Once enough reality-mined digital breadcrumbs are collected, the ability to predict and manipulate behavior increases.
- This adds to the overall predictive certainty of your peer group, which is the product being sold to various companies,

It's pretty wild: **We have an attention economy generated not by government but by the private sector, based on the collection of digital breadcrumbs, which creates a micro-targeted personality profile with the capacity to literally undermine your free will.**

WE HAVE NO CHOICE BUT TO ENGAGE WITH TECHNOLOGY

This is what Nobel Prize-winner Daniel Kahneman talks about with his distinction between "fast" and "slow" thinking. Ninety-six percent of our decisions are made in "fast-thinking mode," which is completely subject to undue influence through a tool you have little choice over whether to use or not.

People often say to me, "Oh, digital technology is just a tool you can choose whether to use or not." Not true. **Technology today is not a tool, but a completely immersive environment.** Those are two completely different things. That which generates the immersive environment is not the loom—this not a Luddite issue, a choice of whether or not I should use the loom, or any other new technology.

Technology is our cell phone, which has become an extension of ourselves, the primary means of communication. We're immersed in our screens. Then there's Metcalfe's Law, which says that once there's a popular new technology, it creates a "network effect"—not to participate completely disadvantages you in your win/lose metrics. It makes you feel isolated and alienated, which is why everyone has an iPhone.

When you exponentialize that into a Metaverse, that's the death of our humanity. Facebook realized the world didn't like Facebook, so Facebook decided it didn't like the world—and is now attempting to create an alternate "metaverse." The metaverse is a virtual-reality world in which they want people to spend an enormous amount of time, and where every single action you take there is commodified and subject to commerce.

Every move you make is downloaded into an algorithmic intelligence exponentially more powerful than the algorithms that defeated Boris Kasparov in his famous Deep Blue matches. **You have a completely radical asymmetry of power, algorithmically micro-targeted against your free will, undermining your attention.** It defeated the powerful force that defeated the best chess master. You're just going about your life, acting primarily based on "fast thinking"—that's the stealing of attention.

RECLAIMING OUR ATTENTION, RECLAIMING OUR HEART

Let's talk about the responses to this. First, we need a new digital information act and new regulatory legislation—this is the response in terms of social structure, which is important but not our area of focus.

The beginning of a superstructural response for the individual is to take your attention back. Seduce yourself. **Take responsibility for your own arousal, and then liberate your attention.** Set your phone down for a couple of days, or at least couple of hours a day, and see what happens. Can you place your attention and place your heart and step into the inside of the inside of Reality?

When we're living the dream, our intention is not to become Luddites. We are not against technology. It is necessary and beautiful, of course. But we need to invest in technology with evolutionary love.

We need to move from TechnoFeudalism to TechnoHumanism.

This is what meditation is: training your attention, placing your heart, so you can actually trace the movements of the amygdala, and gain more agency and free will. A lot of people understand the notion that attention is being hijacked, even if they're not doing much about it.

What's really needed is an answer to the question: Why is this even a problem? This is why *The Social Dilemma* movie was dismissed by so many people. John Mackey told me the whole premise of *The Social Dilemma* was wrong. He claimed that these are just people who are doing commerce, engaging in capitalism, business as usual.

No. There's a total violation of value here.

But in order to articulate the violation, **we have to realize that attention itself is a First Principle and First Value of Cosmos—and that the evolution of attention is actually the story of evolution itself.**

The capacity to place attention can even be seen throughout Reality— there's even attention evolving in the world of matter, in the subatomic world, the world of quarks, atoms, cells, up to the world of plants, amphibians, mammals, early hominids, all the way up to the human being—and then all the way up through the collective, cultural levels of the human being.

Within my own particular and personal life, my capacity to place attention is how I enter into the inward space and create/discover meaning, which already resides in me. But we absolutely must be able to place attention, to place our heart.

When my attention is hijacked, virtually all my decisions are made by fast thinking and thus subject to undue influence determined by peer group split-testing. This leads to the death of our humanity, as we enter the metaverse, in which every single decision and movement is commodified and sold.

2.5

PRACTICING THE PLACING OF ATTENTION: "ODE TO JOY"

We're going to do a practice now to introduce our prayer. I'm going to ask everyone to place your attention, place your heart, on your center, as best you can. As your attention wanders, which it always will, gently place your attention back, again and again, to your center.

Watch the annoyance that might arise because you want the next action to happen—maybe you're bored, or maybe because your attention has been stolen so many times and this is a pattern and a habit. It's okay. To prepare for the clip, take about two minutes to drop in to a simple True Self meditation. Let your thoughts wander in and wander out.

And then keep placing your attention on just one word: *amor.*

Amor is love for the Eros that animates Reality.

Come back to that word, our mantra: *Amor.* Your attention wanders and you're thinking about this and that. It comes back to center, *amor*, the Outrageous Love that is the center of your being. Notice that we're meditating not only on awareness, but also on **the Eros which is the center of our identity**.

The love that lives inside of each of us, the desire to connect, the desire to see and be seen.

Quivering tenderness, quivering gentleness. Placing our attention, placing our heart. *Amor.*

From this place, let's watch this video clip,[4] paying particular attention to every face you see.

VIDEO CLIP: FLASH MOB ORCHESTRA PLAYS BEETHOVEN'S "ODE TO JOY"

We see a busy Italian plaza on an ordinary day: people drinking coffee, tourists wandering around, pigeons flying about, kids running and playing, etc. Over the course of about ten minutes, classical musicians slowly begin arriving, one by one, set up their instruments, and begin playing Beethoven's "Ode to Joy." People are intrigued at first, and gradually begin to gather around. More and more musicians arrive, and a full orchestra starts to emerge, resulting in more crowd engagement. People start singing and conducting from the side, their faces lighting up with joy. It's a very beautiful and very moving performance, resulting in wild applause at the end. The extraordinary emerges from the ordinary—this can be seen clearly on the faces of everyone.

We're in a public square somewhere in Italy. Perhaps Rome, Florence, or Venice. This is the first time something like this was done. At the end of that clip, they're playing "Ode to Joy," written by Schiller and adopted by Beethoven. You look at people's faces at the beginning and see they were having an ordinary day—all the issues, all the worries, all the contractions,

---

[4] You can find the video here, https://www.youtube.com/watch?v=kbJcQYVtZMo, or by typing in "Ode to Joy Flash Mob" into YouTube.

all the traumas, all the usual stuff. Within a very short period—six or seven minutes?—people were totally seduced.

This is a seduction scene.

Now notice: Did anything objectively change for anyone in that square? Did someone win the lottery, get a new job, reconstitute a relationship, work out some big issue, have some major insight? There were no new objective pieces of exterior, data-driven measurable information. None of that happened, and yet, I think we can all agree that we saw—and even, perhaps, somewhat experienced ourselves while watching—the transformation of those people in that public square that afternoon. **The inside of the inside opened up, the interior face of Reality that's always there.**

They placed their attention because the music opened up the interior face of Reality.

Nothing changed and everything changed.

When you focus on the faces, you can tell a beautiful, detailed story about each person. After the first time seeing this, you can probably clearly remember two or three faces. If you watch it again, placing your attention fresh each time, you'll actually begin to meet each face, to remember each face, and begin to know an enormous amount about each face.

You can watch this clip again as a *Homo amor* practice—placing your attention, placing your heart, letting the music enter you. *Ode to Joy.* Each face will strike you, invite you in, show you the interior of Reality.

Who remembers the face of the girl who put the first coin in the hat? Who was the first musician who played, the man with the bald head? Do you remember the second time he appeared? Was his face the same the second time? Completely different, wasn't it? Everyone surely noticed the dramatic, unshaven guy who said, "wow." Who saw the blonde girl who had just broken up with her partner, and was just kind of hanging out? She was wearing a leather yellow jacket. Like everyone else, she's a whole story, a whole world.

There's actually about forty major figures in this scene, and you can catch each one of them. If you watch this clip a few times, you can find any one of them in a second, even talk to each of them.

Place your attention. Place your attention on the face. Place your heart.

The square is transformed, the collective is transformed. You are transformed.

HEART BLOWN OPEN: THE HOLINESS OF THE FACE

Someone recently wrote me a very long letter saying that Dr. Gafni never shares his personal enlightenment experiences, which we find very suspicious, and therefore he's not enlightened, therefore da da da... It's a very long letter. It was also nuanced and well-reasoned—and it's true, I rarely share personal experiences of that nature. But I'll share one of them now.

When I was seventeen or eighteen, I was studying in a seminary in Israel where we did this eighteen-hour-a-day regimen of studying Aramaic texts, which I loved madly—and still do. I would sometimes leave the seminary, which was confusing to the heads of the seminary because I loved this practice of studying and analyzing sacred texts, which makes you stand out in that context.

But I also hated the prayer services there—and I really loved horseback riding. So I would go on these horseback riding trips for a few days at a time, and then have to make up some creative reason for why I disappeared. I had a file of the many, many different reasons why I had to be gone for four days. You know, that poor uncle in the hospital...

When I wasn't riding, I would sit at cafés. There was one particular place in Jerusalem where I would sit—I can see the place on Ben Yehuda street right now, in my mind's eye—and just watch people. I would especially watch their faces.

I would just sit and catch people and watch their faces and my heart would be blown open. I would sit for hours in ecstasy. Sometimes it would be a mother with a child, and my heart would melt. Though be careful if you do this—you can get thrown out for being creepy. You've got to sit quietly in the back and do it well.

But if you intently and lovingly watch people's faces for a while—and it's an ongoing practice—your entire state changes, and your heart gets blown open.

• • •

Outrageous Love is the Eros that lives in the very center of Cosmos itself, that lives uniquely as me. It's the basic force of allurement of which all the attractive forces are specific cases. It evolves, and it lives uniquely in each of us.

I can see your face, and I can fall madly in love with your face.

That's the practice. **Face in Hebrew is *panim*—and it also means inside.** There are forty-five muscles in a face, and almost all of them are used for disclosing interiority.

The inside of the inside, the holy of the holies, the deepest of the deep.

If then you notice, if you truly place your attention, place your heart, on someone's face, you can't help but fall madly in love.

Your heart just bursts open.

How could it not? You'd have to be a fossil not to fall madly in love.

---

*Through the face, you fall madly
in love with everyone.*

PRACTICE: PLACING OUR ATTENTION—
"HOW COULD ANYONE..."

Try, if you can, to do this practice on the inside of the inside, where you can find the face of the other—to be face-to-face for real. We're not defaced anymore, but face-to-face.

Again, either with a partner in Outrageous Love, or with someone you see briefly on the street, an old friend you're meeting for coffee, someone you know well or not at all. You can do this, as we just did, with people in a video or a movie. Try it with photos on your phone. There are lots of options.

As you place your attention, as you place your heart, on the face, you say the words (either out loud or to silently yourself):

"How could anyone ever tell you that you're anything less than beautiful?"

"How could anyone ever tell you that you're anything less than whole?"

Say it to yourself a few times, just to hear the words. Then try it out with all kinds of faces. Eventually, although it can be difficult, you can try this in the mirror.

2.6

DEEPER INTO THE MYSTERY: THE POETRY OF "ODE TO JOY"

B eethoven took the words from Schiller for "Ode to Joy." Let's read them out loud, because they're crazy beautiful.

> *Joy,*
> *Beautiful spark of divinity,*
> *Daughter of Elysium.*

Elysium is a clear reference to the afterlife, and potentially even a coded allusion to the Eleusinian Mysteries, the ancient Greek mystery school.

If you look into the history of mystery schools, you will realize that they were core influences on key philosophical, political, and social movements—this occurred most famously during the Renaissance and at various key moments in ancient Greece. **Mystery schools were places where people gathered, and where class distinctions completely disappeared. People sat, they practiced, they studied, they felt, and they blew their hearts open—not by bypassing Reality, but by entering the interior face of the Cosmos.**

Mystery, *mistorin* in Hebrew. The story, the mystery, the inner story, the satyr. The hidden place on the inside of the inside where I place my attention.

Attention is my capacity to enter to the inside of the inside.

That is also similar to how Einstein described the process of science. **The reason science works is because we're cosmic humans—the Cosmos lives in us.** Science lives in us. Mathematics lives in us. It's beautiful. Through mathematics, I can feel because mathematics *is* feeling. Through mathematics, I can feel my way back to the Big Bang. As Collingwood said to Harding in 1921 about the mathematics prodigy Ramanujan, we're "intimate with every number in the universe."

Every second is crazy precious… Don't waste time not falling in love. Let's find each other's faces. This is everything.

• • •

Let's return to the lyrics to "Ode to Joy."

> *Joy,*
> *Beautiful spark of divinity,*
> *Daughter of Elysium.*
> *We enter drunk with fire.*
> *Heavenly one, thy sanctuary.*

This is the sanctuary. This is the dreamtime. And what happens to a dream deferred? Does it dry up like a raisin in the sun? No, this is where we live the dream. **Remember: We can only change the world if we're willing to live in the world that's already changed.**

> *Thy magic binds again*
> *What custom strictly divided.*
> *Now, all people become brothers and sisters*
> *Where your gentle, fierce wings abide.*
> *Whoever has succeeded in this great attempt*
> *To be a friend's friend.*
> *Whoever has one great love, let him*
> *Add to his jubilation.*
> *Yes, and whoever has just found their own soul*

61

To call her own in this world
And she who never managed it.
Should, for the first time,
Weep from the great union that's about to take place.
All creatures drink of joy at nature's breasts.
All the just follow her trail of roses,
Kisses she gave us in grapevines.
Ecstasy and the cherub stands before God.

These might be the two cherubs above the Ark of the Covenant in the temple in Jerusalem, Solomon's temple, that we've referenced so many times. Think Indiana Jones, *Raiders of Lost Ark*, the Ark of the Covenant.

The Eleusinian Mystery School can be traced back to Alexandria, and then back to Jerusalem. And the Eleusinian Mystery School created the best gifts of what we know of as the West.

It was essential in creating Athenian democracy and the insights of Greek philosophy.

PRACTICE: SINGING FROM THE HEART, TO THE OTHER

This practice is to sing the words to "Ode to Joy," either on their own, or along with the music. This can be done alone, or even better as a partner practice with someone who's familiar with this Dharma. It's not necessary, though.

Find someone—find their face, with heart open, find their eyes. Or if you're alone at the moment, try doing this with a photograph, or a video. You can also do this in a mirror, though it can be more challenging. No shame.

We're going to try and create space. We're not singing the song—

we're practicing it. Face to face, eye to eye, with the depth of your receiving.

It's placing your attention, of your heart.

We're on the inside of the inside, attempting to articulate a New Story of Value that will lovingly, erotically, and ethically respond to this moment in Reality.

2.7

MOVIES AS SACRED TEXTS OF CULTURE

We're about to go to the movies, but as with all the practices, we're placing our attention, placing our heart. *We're watching lovingly and carefully.*

Movies are important sacred texts of culture—even though they are *unconscious* text of culture. In fact, this is one of the reasons they're good texts to study. Culture speaks in many voices, and most of them are unconscious, expressing the collective.

I remember chatting with Avi Arad some fifteen years ago in LA. He owns a little operation called Marvel Studios—he's making these movies that you've all seen. Avi is a sweet and lovely man, and the writers writing for him are also sweet and lovely people. But they're not really thinking through things—they're just writing. They're on a schedule, trying to generate something. Despite that, though:

There's a deeper resonance of culture that speaks through these movies.

I've shared with you before that I once spent a night in Chicago talking and arguing with Lana Wachowski, who made *The Matrix*, about her new movie at the time, *V for Vendetta*, explaining to her what the movie was about, which she clearly didn't understand. The fact that she made the movie gave her no privileges.

In other words, there's something speaking from the collective unconscious. **A movie is a voice of culture, and you have to read it as a text.** Movies are very important texts these days—*sacred texts*.

I think the academy is important but tragically overrated. Our whole notion of information is breaking down. We now realize that peer-reviewed journals, for example, are funded by exterior interests, and they often print information that's inaccurate. Yes, occasionally you'll have a great figure rise through the academy. One of those great figures is a gentleman named Moshe Idel, my dissertation advisor at Oxford.

In our first conversation, Moshe said something important to me that really stuck in my mind. I was thirty years old, at the library all the time, working on the topic of Eros, on the book that was to become *The Mystery of Love*. He put out a book called *Kabbalah and Eros*. Although we were doing quite different things, he had a very, very deep interior understanding, and he said to me, "Read anything and everything." In other words, the academy is bullshit. Just read everything, everywhere. **Read texts wherever they are. Read everything as a text.**

So if you watch a movie, read the movie as a text. And the text will tell you something important. **But read it carefully. Pay attention. Place your heart.**

That's the beginning of becoming *Homo amor*, to wake up and pay attention.

In this chapter, we're going to read a movie called *Don't Look Up*, which we've "re-edited" by linking a series of isolated scenes from the movie to show some hidden themes that were probably unconscious to the writers. They just threw this stuff in, but the themes weave throughout quite beautifully.

Although the movie is superficially about existential risk, we're not so interested in these obvious themes in the movie, about a meteor that's been detected by a couple of scientists, played by Leonardo DiCaprio and Jennifer Lawrence. They detect this world-threatening meteor, but they can't seduce the world into paying attention, no matter what they do.

If you read Toby Ord's book on existential risk, *The Precipice*, the first chapter is on meteors—he says they're the least serious risk we have. Yes, it is a problem, it's a real thing.

There's a whole literature on it, but of all the existential risks, that's not where the key worry lies. So we're just going to use that as our archetypal frame and not really discuss the meteor at all.

2.8

DON'T LOOK UP, PART 1:
THE COLLAPSE OF TRUST

This first set of scenes, from the beginning of the movie, will give you a sense of the context: they discover this comet, and they try to call the president. The young scientist Kate, played by Jennifer Lawrence, has a very intense reaction to the realization that the comet will hit the earth and most likely end everything. Her supervisor, Dr. Randall Mindy, played by Leonardo DiCaprio, has a less intense response.

MOVIE CLIPS: *DON'T LOOK UP*

SCENE 1—THE REALIZATION

This is a fast montage scene from early in the movie, first in a classroom-type setting, with Professor Randall Mindy teaching the basics of comet dynamics to a group of younger scientists, including Kate. They gradually realize the comet is headed for Earth, and there are scenes of disbelief, denial, distress, disagreement, and confusion, as well as planning and strategizing, as the reality of the situation sinks in. Tense music plays throughout. Here's the lead-up to the key realization:

Randall: Well, this will be fun. I haven't done orbital dynamics since grad school. The question is: What would Carl Sagan do? He would take it back to first principles. Kate, what are the initial coordinates?

Kate: Twenty-one. Twenty-four. Thirteen.

Randall: This is fun, huh, guys? Now that we have the comet's orbit, we check the ephemeris, and that will give us the distance between the comet and planet Earth. *[music fades out]*

Kate: Why does the ephemeris keep getting lower and lower?

Watch her eyes. Here's the moment of realization.

Kate: I've been running it all day. I keep getting the same result. A direct hit on earth in six months and fourteen days.

Randall: Me too.

There's a montage of back-and-forth phone calls among various governmental officials (such as Calder), and a NASA official. There are various reactions to the dawning news.

NASA Official: And it's roughly five to ten kilometers wide…

Randall: Isn't that an extinction-level event?

Calder: Well, let's not be dramatic here…

NASA Official: I need the person who first laid eyes on the comet. Share this data immediately with Cambridge, Caltech, and IAU…

Calder: Wait a minute. This is classified information. I serve at the discretion of the president…

Kate: Is this really happening?

Randall: Kate, this isn't happening, right? Kate, this isn't real, right? This is just some sort of alternate reality, right? Say something.

Kate: I gotta go get high.

Then Randall and Kate are on a military plane—he's in total, utter disbelief, while she's smoking a joint.

Randall: What the *fuck*! Is this real?? Is this some goddamned joke? This can't be happening.

Then we see them at the Oval Office.

Kate: Are we really about to tell the president of the United States that we have just over six months until humankind, and basically every species, is completely extinct?

Randall: Yeah, that's exactly what we're about to do.

Kate vomits into a rubbish bin.

Toby Ord at Oxford has crunched the numbers on existential risk. In the next hundred years, if you put all the risks together, **there's a twenty to forty percent chance of the death of humanity**. I just want you to think about that for a second. You're about to cross a bridge—there's a twenty to forty percent chance that bridge is going to collapse. How do you feel about that? *Over the next several hundred years, if the vectors don't change, we are doomed.*

For the record, I believe the vectors *can* change. They can change by transforming the superstructure, meaning our Story of Value. We need a Renaissance moment. We're at a time between worlds, a time between stories…

But bracket that for a second. In the next few hundred years, if we don't change the vectors, there's a twenty to forty percent chance of extinction. And this is from Ord's deep academic crunching of the numbers.

Now, let's remember: There's the Tao and the 10,000 things. The 10,000 things are that which is measurable, subject to the crunching of numbers. The Tao is Eros, the Tao is the interior. The Tao is that which generates mathematics. The Tao is where all the 10,000 things come from.

The Tao that can be spoken is not the true Tao. The Tao that can be measured is not the Tao.

All of Toby Ord's numbers are the vector, and then there's the Tao. **We're in the Tao here, and it's from the Tao that you can enter the source code, and transform it—by telling a New Story of Value.**

That's what I mean by superstructure. When Marvin Harris talked about superstructure, he talked about it as the world you're in, as a general abstract sociological concept. But that's not quite right. The superstructure points to the Tao. It's the story of meaning we live in, the story that influences every decision.

Sometimes, even people who are closest to me get a little upset with me. I was speaking to one of my friends, and I said, "For you, dealing with existential risk is an exciting hobby." He was restraining not to hang up the phone, which I appreciate. He's a very close friend who I've known for fifteen years. But this can't be just a hobby. It keeps me up every night. **Because we're talking about the future of unborn trillions of people.**

And we're the only voice of the future.

• • •

We're now going to see a set of five different clips we've spliced together, the theme of which was not picked up by any of the reviewers of the movie. *Don't Look Up* was categorized by half of the reviews as a comedy about the threat to Earth. These were viewed as some of the comedic scenes, but they're not that at all.

FIVE SPLICED THEMATIC SCENES — WHY DOES A THREE-STAR GENERAL CHARGE FOR SNACKS?

1

In the first scene, Randall and Kate are at the White House. They've gotten off that plane we just saw them on. They're about to tell the president about this comet about to hit planet Earth. And this three-star general comes by and brings them some snacks. He walks down the hall with sandwiches and bottles of water for Randall and Kate, and says, "They charge an arm and a leg for this stuff. Ten a piece oughta do it. Here, grab a water." Randall gives him a twenty dollar bill.

2

Kate and another person are eating lunch in a lunchroom at the White House. Kate takes a bottle of water from the fridge, and then asks the other person:

Kate: Where do I pay for these?

Woman: It's free.

Kate: Really?

Woman: Yes, it's the White House.

Confused, Kate later walks down the hall to Randall, and tells him, "The snacks are free. That General charged us for the snacks, but they're free." Then she wonders, "Why on earth would he do that?"

3

In the next scene, later on in the film, Kate is sitting down on the floor, speaking to someone off-camera:

Kate: I've gone over it again and again in my head, and I still can't make sense of it. He's a three-star general, and he works at the Pentagon. Why would he charge us for free snacks?

71

4

In the next scene, Kate is with Yule (Timothée Chalamet), someone she meets and connects with in her hometown, and they're lying down together on a rooftop:

> *Kate:* Maybe he just gets off on the power, you know. It's like he knew that I was gonna find out that the snacks were free. You know what I mean, so it was just a power play.

> *Yule:* Yeah, guys are weird.

5

Finally, we see Kate again sitting in the White House hallway, as the General and his entourage walk by, and she calls out to them:

> *Kate:* Watch out for him. He'll charge you for free shit.

Is this just some funny routine they just threw in to the movie? No. These five short scenes, spread throughout the movie, depict perhaps one of the most important themes. What's it actually talking about?

Let's approach it this way: Imagine you're in someone's house, and they lie to you. When you're in someone's house and they're hosting you, there's this trust that's supposed to exist between you. **That's a value structure of Reality.**

A few decades ago, when I lived in the Middle East, I would visit my Bedouin friends in Qalqilya, even those who were avowed enemies—and there were a few Bedouins around the area I lived in who were actively involved in abetting terrorism against the village I helped found some twenty-five years ago. When I went into one of their tents, I knew I was completely safe. That was just the way it went. **You're in their tent, there's trust between us.** You eat the food they offer, you honor the food. In that moment, there's a bracketing of our conflict.

There's safety and trust.

In this scene at the White House, ostensibly the "home" of Western values, there's a fundamental violation of trust. You have this three-star general, who obviously doesn't need the twenty dollars. Naturally, Kate can't understand it. This theme goes through the whole movie—there's this intuitive understanding that the movie-makers likely have no idea about, but they unconsciously understood something about the core structure of value, and of existential risk. It's quite striking.

The whole movie appears to be about infrastructure issues—solving the technical problem of an immanent threat, and then destroying a comet— as well as about the social structure of politics. But it's actually not about that—it's really about superstructure. About interiors. About the value of trust. And here we can see that there's a fundamental collapse of trust in the White House, in the military, in all the institutions.

TRUST AS A CORE QUALITY OF EROS

When there's a collapse of trust, then no exchange between us can ever hold. The general charges them twenty bucks. It's an insane exchange, but he can't *not* do it. Then she thinks, oh it must be about *power*. **This is the mainstream culture speaking: It's obviously about power. Everything is a game of power, after the collapse of value—power is the only thing left.**

This view of power is based on Foucault, for whom power is bad. But it's the only thing left, the foundation, so everything basically must be a power move. Underneath everything, it's all power. Of course, power itself has been misunderstood—it's really quite exciting and important to have power. But the point here is: There's no trust. And one of the most important experiences of Eros is trust—it's a core feature of Eros.

Because Eros is a value of Cosmos, when Eros is denuded from Cosmos, trust disappears.

Eros is why two separate things come together to form a whole, which is synonymous with ethics because there's trust between them. **In fact, there's no split between Eros and ethics—they're exactly the same.**

Eros is a First Value of Cosmos itself—I spent thirty years thinking about this and arriving at that conclusion. Then about a year and a half ago, I was reading Whitehead's *Process and Reality* and realized he had come to some version of the same conclusion 100 years ago.

But essentially: **Eros is a core value of Cosmos, and a key quality of Eros is trust.** What we realize in these scenes is that there's no trust. She keeps going back to the moment when the general sold them a bottle of water—she can't understand it: *Why would he do that?* If it's not a pure power play, why would he do that?

The real question, however, is: Why *wouldn't* he? In other words, once you remove or deny value (as our culture has done), then every interaction is necessarily based in rivalrous conflict governed by win/lose metrics. What's left is our interactions in this success story. **These scenes point to something deeper than power: the absence of a Story of Value in our culture.**

The movie—completely unconsciously but brilliantly—understood something it didn't realize it did: At the micro level, every single interaction becomes a rivalrous conflict governed by win/lose metrics interaction. When you exponentialize that throughout the system, you've got existential risk. It's quite shocking.

LIVING INSIDE A STORY OF VALUE OR LIVING INSIDE A SKINNER BOX

Culture almost completely misses this. In other words, what happens is that Reality is made up of billions and billions of micro-interactions. This is a claim made by Alex Pentland at MIT Media Lab—one of the primary architects of the internet and the so-called "father of wearables." Graduates of the MIT Media Lab, his students, are the current architects of the internet. He's also a hidden student of behavioralist B.F. Skinner, something he hasn't acknowledged. We've identified about twenty-five major structural parallels between Skinner and Pentland.

Skinner is beyond brilliant, arguably the most important psychologist of the twentieth century. **I would even say Skinner is the most influential meta-theorist in the world today—although he largely remains hidden and unacknowledged.**

If you carefully read his book *Beyond Freedom and Dignity*, you'll notice that it's actually about existential risk—and he says there's only one way out. I spent a year reading it, and I would call Zak in the middle of the night and leave him messages, just blown away by the book, blown away by Skinner's brilliance. He didn't become Skinner for nothing. It's brilliant—and horrific.

He clearly realizes that there are serious existential risks, so his response as a behavioral psychologist was to create a vision he calls a "Skinner Box." By experimenting on pigeons and rats, he basically found that through ratios and schedules of reinforcement, you can totally control these animals. **Skinner was asking: How do you control unconscious actions and behaviors?** Of course, this can also be applied to humans, and in 1948 he wrote a novel called *Walden Two*, which depicts a utopian society that is essentially a society-wide Skinner Box.

It's shocking beyond imagination—this is the center of Western civilization.

Now, Skinner was probably a wonderful guy. And Pentland's probably also a beautiful guy. You'd love to have them over for dinner. But that's not the point. They're great people in the sense that they likely *feel* that they're doing their best—as best as they can without a story of intrinsic value.

Following his teacher, Alex Pentland is basically saying he wants to recreate a Skinner Box on the internet. It's kind of like the War of the Sith Lords—every Sith Lord always has a hidden Sith Lord. In the twenty-first century, however, Pentland translates Skinner Box with a euphemism: He says instead that the world has to become a "living laboratory." But this is structurally the same as a Skinner Box of total control. **In a data-driven world with billions of micro-interactions, Pentland realizes that if you can place the world in a living laboratory, you can govern how those interactions happen and avoid existential risk.**

Again, Skinner and Pentland are not necessarily evil—they're just desperate. And totally mistaken. The only way to deal with existential risk, they believe, is to re-create the world as a completely controlled environment. Pentland sanitizes it and calls it a living laboratory, where you just innocently collect all the data instantaneously—but through that data, you can drive and direct the entire system.

They just don't realize there's a much better option.

- Either the world is controllable by billions of interactions, so you superimpose control from above.
- Or you can intervene in the value structure, and create a New Story of Value.

Here's what they miss: You can actually create a more effective kind of living laboratory, albeit one with actual freedom and value, based on a Story of Value that's not made up, a Story of Value that incorporates the best information we have from both the interior and exterior sciences. **We can then begin to live inside that Story of Value, and that story generates trust, honor, and nobility.**

What these scenes with the General clearly show is a collapse of integrity at the micro-level, followed by the unconscious implications of this micro-event exponentialized throughout the system.

Instead, our aim is to exponentialize a *different set of micro-events* throughout the system, based in real value. This will happen not through unconscious control, using what Kahneman calls "fast thinking," but by generating a Universal Grammar of Value that is not imposed, dogmatic, or owned by a single religion. **It's a Universal Grammar of Value as a context for our *diversity*.**

- This is not a homogenizing of the world.
- This is not an obliterating of all the unique instruments.
- This is a shared score of music.
- We add our unique tones and voices to the symphony.

The only response we have to existential risk is the possibility of a Universal Grammar of Value not arbitrarily created by somebody. That'd be an imposition. Rather, you have to show value is structurally fundamental to Cosmos.

Not only is this necessary, but completely doable. Moreover, **living inside a Story of Value is exponentially more powerful, true, and joyous than living inside of a Skinner Box.**

REBUILDING TRUST THROUGH A NEW STORY

There was a figure named Elisha ben Abuyah from the first century, who became a traitor. A discussion in a third-century Talmudic text discusses why he became a traitor—these discussions are written in a series of Zen-koan-like fragments, very concise. It basically says he became a traitor because when he was born, the masters came and visited his parents. His parents saw this pillar of fire hovering above the house and said, "How great is the power of wisdom."

And the scholars say: *How great is the power of wisdom* is why you became a traitor. That's the koan. It doesn't really make any sense. I thought about it for many years and still didn't understand. Then one day, when I was about thirty, I was stuck in Singapore, on my way to Sydney, with nothing to do but think. I was pondering that passage when it suddenly hit me.

What this cryptic passage means is that **there are two kinds of communication that culture, or our parents, give us: content communication and dream or value communication.**

- Content communication is what they tell us.
- Dream or value communication is what they really believe.

As a baby, Elisha has this proto-understanding of early infancy, and he hears all throughout his childhood: "How great is the *power* of wisdom." He feels the inflection like a child does: the issue is clearly one of power. So he becomes a master of wisdom, but at the core is power—and the greatest power of the time was Rome. So he aligns with Rome, of course—where else would he align?—because the dream communication, the transmission of value was about power.

When you live inside a Story of Value, there's an exponential application across the systems, across billions and billions of events. It could be the value of win/lose metrics in a rivalrous success story, or it could be a story based on First Principles and First Values that are Good, True, and Beautiful.

To put it another way: Once you step out of the Tao—and of course, you can never *actually* step out of the Tao, but we *think* we've stepped out of the Tao. But **once you think you've stepped out of the Tao, you're out of the Tao—and each action exponentially affects everything.**

The result can be seen in this major Hollywood film, a key transmitter of culture in the Western world, with a hidden theme that threads throughout the movie in five short scenes: A micro-event that shows the lack of trust at the heart of the system.

This says everything about where we are today.

2.9

DON'T LOOK UP, PART 2: BOTH PRAYER AND FUCK ARE FILLED WITH EROS

T his next series of three or four scenes are also spliced together from throughout the movie. They show the creeping realization that the death of humanity is a real possibility. Dr. Randall Mindy, as we'll see, initially tries to avoid it, while Kate looks at it head-on. In the end, they come together. There are about ten major figures in this movie, and most of them undergo no transformation at all. Two of them do, however, and one of them is Randall.

MOVIE CLIPS: *DON'T LOOK UP*

1— CONVERSATION IS NOT POSSIBLE

Randall and Kate are going to appear on television to share their horrific news with the world for the first time. The pair of TV announcers, Jack and Brie—one of whom we'll meet later—represent win/lose metrics. This is Kate and Randall's big chance to share the news widely, but they don't really know how to get the announcers to pay attention. Eventually, they both have an outburst on live TV. Here's the dialogue, and notice all the avoidance happening:

Jack: So this has to be really exciting, Miss Diabiasky. Tell us what you found.

Kate: Um, I was monitoring exploding stars to help measure the expansion of the universe, and I saw something I didn't recognize. It was a comet. A big one. It's headed directly at earth. It really likely will hit.

Jack: This sounds very, very exciting. Exploding stars, like stars actually explode. So how big is this thing, and can it destroy someone's house? Is that possible?

Randall: Well, Comet Diabiasky, which is what it will officially be renamed...

Jack: After her?

Randall: Yeah.

Brie: Congratulations!

Jack: What an honor! Congratulations.

Randall: It's somewhere between six and nine kilometers across.

Brie: It's big.

Randall: So, it would damage the entire planet. Not just a house, you know?

Jack: The entire planet. Okay. As it's damaging, will it hit this one house in particular? It's right on the coast of New Jersey—my ex-wife's house. Can we make that happen?

Brie: Stop. You and Shelley have a great relationship... You need to stop.

Jack: I will, but in all fairness, I actually paid for the house…

Kate: I'm sorry, are we not being clear? We're trying to tell you that the entire planet is about to be destroyed.

Brie: Well, you know, it's something we do around here. We just keep the bad news light.

Jack: Right, it helps the medicine go down. And speaking of medicine, tomorrow we've got a. .

Kate: Well, maybe the destruction of the entire planet isn't supposed to be fun. Maybe it's supposed to be terrifying. And unsettling… and you should stay up all night, every night, crying, when we're all 100 percent for sure gonna fucking die!

Randall: Kate…

Brie (to Randall): So could you please help us out here, oh wise scientist?

Randall: Well, first and foremost, Brie, there most certainly is a comet. And we know that there is a comet because we have the data. There has been growing concern within the scientific community as of late. You see, the peer-review process is absolutely essential…

Dr. Randall, are you sure you're okay? Do you want a glass of water?

Randall: I don't feel so well…

Brie: Okay… Well, we're going to go to a commercial and come back —

Randall: NO. Please, Brie, don't cut away. Let me say something.

Jack: Well, you came to the right place. Because on this show, we like to say things.

Randall: WOULD YOU PLEASE STOP BEING SO FUCKING PLEASANT!

[Everyone goes quiet.]

Randall: I'm sorry. Not everything needs to sound so goddamn clever or charming or likable all the time. Sometimes, we just need to be able to say things to one another. We need to hear things. Look, let's establish, once again, that there is a huge comet headed towards Earth. And the reason we know that there's a comet is because we saw it. We saw it with our own eyes using a telescope. I mean, for God's sake, we took a FUCKING PICTURE OF IT! What other proof do we need? And if we can't all agree at the bare minimum that a giant comet the size of Mount Everest hurtling its way toward planet Earth is NOT A FUCKING GOOD THING, then what the hell happened to us?

I mean, my God, how do we even talk to each other? What have we done to ourselves? How do we fix it? We should've deflected this comet when we had the fucking chance, but we didn't. I don't know why we didn't do it.

[Brie, Jack, and the TV crew stare at Randall with concern.]

Randall: And now they're actually firing scientists like me for speaking out, for opposing them. And I'm sure many of the people out there aren't even going to listen to what I just said because they have their own political ideology. But, I assure you, I am not on one side or the other. I'm just telling you the fucking truth.

Brie: I think this would be a good time to establish that Isherwell and the President said that there's benefits to be had...

Randall: Right, well, the President of the United States is FUCKING LYING. Look, I'm just like all of you... I hope to God that this President knows what she's doing... I hope she's got us all taken care of. But the truth is, I think this whole administration has completely lost their fucking mind! And I think we're all gonna die!

Look, I just wanna go home. I just wanna go home more than anything.

The announcer, Brie, a representative of the media, has already been co-opted by Peter Isherwell, the head of BASH Industries, which represents the industrial tech plex and is planning to mine the meteor for massive profits. If you notice her eyes as she was watching him, they were just completely glazed over. She's got other information: what the president says, what BASH says. And then Randall says they're all lying—it's unimaginable to her, it doesn't compute.

The most important thing is what Randall says: "We can't even talk to each other anymore. What have we done? We can't have a conversation. We can't even establish a simple fact." **No intimacy is possible in this situation.** Sound familiar?

Then what does he say at the end? After he gives his whole speech, he says, "I just want to go home." All of a sudden, this basic value emerges, and he just wants to go home.

We'll get back to that later, but first I want to get a better sense of how the win/lose metrics often plays out: It's not villainous, there's no devil—it's much more subtle. So let's turn back now to Brie, the TV announcer. Mindy and Brie end up having this relationship. He leaves his wife for a period of time during the movie.

2— PSEUDO-EROS AND THANATOS

There's a scene shortly after this one of Randall Mindy and Brie, the TV announcer, clothed, at the TV studio, having sex standing up, while she's saying, "Tell me we're all going to die... Tell me we're all going to die..."

Here she's taking the immanent death of humanity and turning it into a pseudo-Eros move. That's the only way she's able to relate to it. It's fascinating—she grabs this knowledge, this realization, quite incomprehensible, and she pours it into Fuck because she doesn't know what to do with it otherwise. She doesn't even know what to do with it. You actually could do something real with that in sexing, but she doesn't. It's merely an unconscious-personality sexing move.

3 — IS CONVERSATION POSSIBLE?

In this next scene, Randall and Brie are in bed together at a hotel, after sex. This is a continuation of their pseudo-erotic relationship, where she is reluctantly sharing herself with him.

Brie: I just realized we don't really know anything about each other.

Randall: True. Every time I ask about your life you tell me about your favorite restaurants.

Brie: I despise the "get to know you" part of relationships. But okay, let's just get it all over and done with. My grandfather invented the flash-freezing process so I come from grotesque money, but I got away from it by getting three Master's degrees. I've been divorced twice. One was a Secretary of State. The other a sport fisherman. I've slept with two former Presidents, I speak four languages, and own two Monets.

Randall: Wow. Two former Presidents? Wow. My turn? My Father was a middle-school geography teacher. My mother cut hair out of our kitchen. About two years ago our family dog JoJo died, which was really emotional. I can't remember crying that much ever. And I finally got my *Star Wars* poster signed by Mark Hamill. It's in the garage.

Brie: Ok, Good. That's done. Now, where are we gonna go for dinner tonight?

4— GLIMMERS OF EROS

In this scene, Brie and Randall are attending a news conference where they watch an attempt to deflect the comet, and she suddenly, surprisingly utters a phrase in French.

Brie: *Les anges s'envolent vers le ciel...*

Randall: Was that French?

Brie: Yes, it means "And the angels soar to the heavens..." It's from a fourteenth-century French poem I studied at Dartmouth. Watching this made me think of it...

This is the one moment in the movie where some other part of Brie that's been lost appears. This beautiful French poem comes to mind, and you see this whole other person for a split second, and then she disappears again. Her face is completely different—it's a different person. There's another possible life she could have led.

Think about what it means to live in a world defined by a certain group of friends, and by certain values. You get these little glimpses of freedom, here and there, but basically these structures run your life. She's run by the values of her context. But notice how her face changes when she speaks French poetry...

5— LIFE IS COMPLICATED

Next, we see Randall and Brie laughing, coming back late to Randall's hotel room, which is dark. He turns on the lights to find June, his wife, on the couch with a bag full of luggage next to her. This scene is a caricature, and it sets up the conflict. Here is some of their dialogue:

June: I had a feeling something was going on.

Randall: Well, you know we're discussing important business. That's what we're doing.

June: Oh yeah, that's really very important.

Brie: Can we just skip past this whole part please, where you get to feel self-righteous, and we put our tails between our legs? It's so boring.

June: You want to skip the part where you feel bad for screwing my husband.

Brie: Oh, I don't feel bad. Randall and I are having a wonderful time. So I think the question is: Do we keep having a wonderful time or does he go back with you to Wisconsin? Or Montana? Or Michigan?

June: You know what? She's actually right. That is the only question. So...

Randall: Well, June, sweetie. Sometimes things in life, they're, you know, complicated and they just...

June: Okay, that was fast. Before I go, let me give you some instructions on how to take care of Randall...

She goes into the bathroom and comes out holding a bunch of prescription pill bottles, throwing them at Randall.

June: Here's the Xanax he takes for his panic attacks... Here's the Zoloft he takes to curb the crashing depressions...

Randall: Not so much recently.

June: Oh, good for you! This is for his blood pressure. Restless Leg Syndrome. Appetite suppressant to counteract appetite gain from his other meds. And yeah, for America's Sexiest Scientist, a bottle of goddamn Cialis!

Goodbye Randall! I'll tell your sons that dad's fucking the lady on our television!

Randall: June, I…

Brie: I really thought for a second that was gonna work out.

6— WHAT IS LOVE

In this next scene, he's now just given the speech on television where he says we're all going to die. He finally stops cooperating, so they take him off the set, and later Brie goes to see him in the car, where he's got a hood over his head.

Brie: Why did you do that? I really liked you. And I despise most people.

Randall: You know, I really thought I loved you…

Brie: Really? Wow. That's wild.

She couldn't even grasp it. The notion *I really thought I loved you* doesn't even occur to her as a remote possibility. She doesn't quite know what he's talking about. In other words:

- Eros is no longer a value.
- Love is not real.
- Love is a social construct.
- Love is a fiction.
- Love is a figment of imagination.

She's a product of the postmodern heart and mind, which is not tender—it's Tinder.

Look at her eyes in this scene. They're completely different than when she read the line from the poem, "The Angels Soar to Heaven." Look at the shots—it's not just in the words. Look at her eyes—they're completely vacant now. It's an incredible scene. **Eros clearly doesn't exist there.**

That was her moment. She could have taken a different path. There was something else to do there—she could have responded to love, to Eros. If you watch her face, she even considers it for a millisecond, but she can't do it. It's completely impossible to her.

7— HOW DO YOU DIE?

In the next brief scene, we're at the end of the world. The meteor's about to hit. Brie's with her co-host, Jack. He could be beautiful, but he's totally superficial here. Superficial Jack and superficial Brie. It's the moment before the end of the world. They're together at an empty bar with abundant food, drinking and eating, as they wonder what they should do:

Jack: We could fuck? Or pray...? Or...?

Brie: Honestly, I just think I'd rather drink and talk shit about people.

This scene is absolutely incredible. This is it, the end. They don't know how to fuck, and they don't know how to pray. Their only idea is to create a circle, and place people outside to give them an illusion of being inside the circle. There's no Eros—only pseudo-eros.

This is the textbook definition of pseudo-eros—placing someone else outside to give you the illusion of being inside. At a certain point, you become so unpracticed in Eros that, even at the moment of your death, you cannot summon it.

Right now—not as a teacher, but as a friend—I want to bless us all with a good death. **You practice your whole life for your death.**

These two, Brie and Jack, have clearly not practiced dying at all. **They have no idea how to die.** The only move they have in death is to re-enact the same pseudo-eros that's been happening throughout their lives. They're unable to access true Eros.

Superficial Jack has some vague memory of what might have been: *We can fuck or we can pray.* But there's no Fuck in his invitation, and there's no prayer in his invitation. *There's no Fuck in his fuck, and there's no Prayer in his prayer.*

Both real prayer and Fuck are filled with Eros. But this is Fuck dissociated from Eros and prayer that's dissociated from Eros.

She realizes that it's empty, and they don't know how to do it anymore. They've forgotten how to fuck, and they've forgotten how to pray. They're completely de-eroticized.

All that they have left is pseudo-eros: booze and shit-talking.

2.10

DON'T LOOK UP, PART 3: THE COLLAPSE OF EROS—REDUCING REALITY TO ALGORITHMS

We're now going to meet Peter Isherwell in this next set of clips. He's this quintessential representation of win/lose metrics. Isherwell owns BASH, the company that said they should not destroy the comet. There was an early opportunity to destroy it, but they let that opportunity go because Bash argued the comet has exponential financial possibility, and they could mine it for rare minerals.

The extraction model of planet Earth is exhausting our core minerals—it's one of the modes of existential risk. What we call the planetary stack is going to collapse, for a bunch of reasons. He wants BASH to seize this opportunity for minerals, which kind of takes us through.

MOVIE CLIPS: *DON'T LOOK UP*

1— "WE LOVE YOU, PETER"

At a launch for a new tech product, we see a large, enthusiastic crowd in an auditorium, about to be introduced to Peter Isherwell,

CEO of BASH. On stage there are three children. Just as he's about to walk on stage, someone from the crowd yells, "We love you, Peter!"

Deep-voiced Male Voiceover: Introducing BASH LiiF. Life, without the stress of living...

Female Voiceover: Before we introduce the founder and CEO of BASH, please remember to avoid direct eye contact, sudden movements, coughing, or negative facial expressions. And now, please welcome Peter Isherwell.

Isherwell: Hello everyone. All of my work has been driven by the inexpressible need for a friend who would understand and sooth me. And you know, all those years of work have come to fruition... with BASH LiiF. Our new BASH 14.3 phone is fully integrated into your every feeling and desire without you needing to say one single word.

Peter and the children hold up the new cell phone.

Isherwell: If I feel...

Child 1: Sad...

Child 2: Afraid...

Child 3: Or alone...

Isherwell: ...the BASH 14.3 phone, when set to "LiiF" setting, instantly senses my mood through blood pressure, heart rates and...

Phone Voice (V.O.): Your vitals show that you are sad. This will cheer you up, Peter.

"Here, this will cheer you up..." appears on the screen and a video of a puppy riding a rooster, and a child's voice robotically repeating, "You are my best friend. You are my best friend..."

Isherwell: Oh, that's wonderful! And it also schedules a therapy session with a nearby professional so we can make sure these sad feelings never, ever, ever return.

Child 2: May I say something, Mr. Isherwell?

Isherwell: No.

And to support BASH LiiF I would like to officially announce...

Backstage, twenty minutes later, a junior executive, Linda, takes the phones from the children.

Linda: Give me the phones—they're not yours. Say bye.

Child 1: Bye Mr. Isherwell...

Child 3: Bye Peter.

Child 2: Um, I love you, Peter.

Isherwell ignores the children, or is simply unable to hear this expression.

What's the first line we hear that someone screams from the audience? "We love you, Peter." Then he says, "All my life, I've been yearning for a friend, connection, love." Then the kid wants to express something on stage—and he says, "No. We don't have time now." And then backstage she says, "I love you, Peter." Her face in that moment was incredible.

- She's the Goddess.
- She's the feminine.
- She's Eros itself.

She looks at him and says, "I love you." And he literally cannot see or hear her.

Eros is completely dead. Love doesn't exist. It's the postmodern construct talked about in chapter two of *Sapiens* and chapter seven of *Homo Deus*.

It doesn't exist, it's a fiction. Maybe it exists in some deep, personal spaces between some people. **But as a core force of culture, Eros is gone.**

In the next scene, we see Isherwell at the White House, in a control room with the scientists. The mission to destroy the comet is about to be successful. They're about to take down the comet. But Isherwell's scientists have done a reading of the comet, and they realize they can capitalize on its financial potential.

He says to the president, "Can I have a moment with you?" It becomes clear he's running the story. Elections happen every four years, but politics is not driven by people who are actually in power. What *Homo amor* would look like in politics is a great question.

2— POWER OVER VALUE

In this scene, President Orlean, Isherwell, and various scientists are seated around the White House Operations Room table, about to successfully destroy the comet.

Isherwell: Madame President can I speak to you outside for one second?

Randall: The success probability has already increased to 81%.

Isherwell [in his "real" voice]: Janie. Now!

President Orlean: I'm so sorry. Of course, Peter.

Peter yells, "Janie, now!" All of a sudden, his mask drops for a second. The mission was about to be successful, but win/lose metrics and rivalrous dynamics come to dominate.

3— WHERE VALUE TRULY LIES

Shortly afterwards, we see the President, the scientists, and Isherwell in a White House situation room. The mission has been aborted, and there is worldwide shock and confusion. Watch here as Isherwell reframes the story in a techno-utopian way.

President Orlean: Ladies and gentlemen, what we and what the world thought was an impending and terrifying danger... is actually an astonishing opportunity.

Secretary of State Berkers: Our allies are very confused and demanding answers, Madame President.

President Orlean: Tell them to wait. According to the most recent spectrometer reading of Comet Dibiasky made by astro-geologists at BASH cellular... we've discovered something. Something truly miraculous. Peter?

Isherwell: Thank you, Janie. As some of you know, the most valuable minerals in the world are fast becoming the ones used to make cell phones and computers: yttrium, terbium, osmium, dysprosium, and on and on. We're running short. And the problem is exacerbated because China has her big panda paw firmly on almost all the mines that produce these valuable rare earth assets. So you can imagine, wow, just how happy we were at BASH when our astro-geologists saw that this comet hurtling towards earth actually contains at least thirty-two trillion dollars of these critical materials. [...] When other metals are factored in, this comet contains almost 140 trillion dollars worth of assets.

Randall: But what does any of this matter if we're all going to die?

Isherwell: Obviously, one giant comet is a major and existential threat to our planet... But thirty smaller meteoroids we can handle. Our BEADs, which stands for BASH Explore and Acquire Drones, will attach to the comet and scan using nano-technology developed by Nobel Prize winner Dr. Gary Talcamont here. And then we will then deploy Nobel- and Polofsky-prize winning scientist Dr. Inez's micro-targeted quantum fission explosives deep into the object.

Dr. Inez, would you like to explain…

Dr. Inez: Thank you, Peter. We've been developing phase fission reactions in the CERN particle accelerator that can splinter the comet into smaller pieces with breathtaking accuracy. These segments are then steered and decelerated by each BEAD into the Pacific Ocean for reclamation by waiting US Navy ships. The animated drones then individually steer each piece of the comet into the Pacific Ocean, making a simple splash.

Isherwell: And when these treasures from heaven are claimed, poverty as we know it, social injustice, loss of biodiversity, all these multitudes of problems will become relics of the past and humanity will stride through the pillars of Boaz and Jachin, naked into the glory of a golden age. An interplanetary, interstellar, intergalactic existence for the human race. *[applause]*

Notice the face of Inez, the Nobel prize-winning scientist. She's not a bad person. She's a mother of two kids, maybe three. She's not the devil. She kind of understands what matters, what's valuable. **But these data scientists and Nobel-Prize-winners who should be creating social structure and infrastructure have been co-opted across all sectors.** Once you win the Nobel Prize and you get half a million dollars, which is not that much, what do you do next? Eventually, your new research needs to be funded. The government's not funding it, so it's generally funded by the private sector.

Isherwell trots out a couple of Nobel Prize scientists who don't look at all like the devil. She actually looks extremely trustable.

There's some little place inside of her, late at night, at 3am, that knows all this isn't true—a still, small voice that lives when all the meetings are over. She wakes up and that still small voice says, "I don't actually know that that's true." Then we turn over, go back to sleep then go back into the day.

Notice also how Isherwell's speech is Skinnerian. That's the way Skinner spoke. That's the way Pentland speaks. For example, a couple years ago, *Time* Magazine's cover story was, "Google Will Conquer Death." This is a very widespread belief. The language of the tech plex is utopian, even messianic.

If you read Zuckerberg carefully, for example, you can see that he's influenced by Pentland. The tech plex has massive consequences. It's not just regular techno-optimism—it's a techno-utopian messianic moment. **Just like messianic moments in the old religions, it's beyond dangerous—they caused major civilizations to fall.**

For the first time ever, we have a global civilization, and we haven't solved any of the problems that the smaller, local civilizations didn't need to worry about. In our global civilization, the prophets are techno-utopians with exponential capacity, which they want to use to respond to existential risk in ways that actually dehumanize our essential being.

This has nothing to do with right or left. It has nothing to do with conspiracy theories. This is the structure of the tech plex—a proto-utopian, messianic vision that is reductively materialist at its core. It does not view Eros as real. It's astonishing.

4— BUSINESS OR EVOLUTION

In this next scene, after the meeting at the White House, Randall is finally stepping up, after initially staying quiet. He has this incredible conversation with Isherwell, perhaps the most important conversation in the whole movie.

Randall: Listen, a lot of my colleagues, they've either been removed or resigned from this project, apparently for asking too many questions about this mission here. So I just wanna make sure that you're open to the scientific peer-review process, and that you're not approaching this entire mission like a businessman...

Isherwell: What did you say?

Randall: I wanna know if you're...

Isherwell: Did you call me a businessman?

Randall: You do own a corporate...

Isherwell: You think I'm just a businessman? Do you think you know me, Doctor? Business? This is evolution. This is evolution of the human species.

Did you know that BASH has over forty million data points on you and every decision you've made since 1994, Doctor? I know when you have colon polyps months before your doctor does. You've got four or five at the moment, actually. You know, they're not of concern, but I'd have a checkup as soon as you can.

But more importantly than that—much more importantly—I know *what* you are. I know *who* you are. My algorithms have determined eight fundamental consumer profile types. You are a Lifestyle Idealist. You think you are motivated by high ethical beliefs, but you just run towards pleasure and away from pain. Like a field mouse.

Randall: I just want to make sure the science is sound on this project. I hope you understand...

Isherwell: Our algorithms can even predict how you'll die with up to 96% accuracy. I looked you up after we first met. Your death was so unremarkable and boring... I can't even remember what it said. Apart from one thing: You're going to die alone.

Hold that prediction. Just hold it in your body. Based on the algorithmic knowing, Randall's apparently going to die alone. They've got all the data points. The assumption of the tech plex is: We know who you are, entirely reducible to the algorithmic interpretation of all the data points at play.

. . .

At the end of the film, Isherwell is with the president at the White House, watching the BASH mission to split the comet apart. As things start to malfunction and missiles are misfiring, and real concern starts to rise, he says, "We're all fine. Everyone's fine. If you'll excuse me. Nature calls. I'm going to the restroom for a moment."

At this point, he just runs away. *Without a Story of Value, what else could he do?*

2.11

DON'T LOOK UP, PART 4: SWEETNESS HINTS AT INFINITE EROS BREAKING THROUGH

There's a term in the Hebrew wisdom lineages, *hamtakah*, which means something like "sweetness." It means that which is immeasurable, that which you can't touch, that which is not subject to data points. The word sweetness in English doesn't quite catch it—it tries to but only catches some of it.

Sweetness comes up three times in the movie. Let's take a look.

MOVIE CLIPS: *DON'T LOOK NOW*: SWEETNESS

1—SWEETNESS: HIDDEN FAITH

Yule and Kate are on a rooftop late at night, lying on their backs talking.

Yule: I'm starting to think that all of this "end of the world" stuff is bullshit.

Kate: Well, it's not. It's definitely happening. I've seen it.

Yule: I feel like if God wanted to destroy the Earth, He would destroy the Earth.

Kate: You believe in God?

Yule: Yeah. My parents raised me evangelical, and I hate them. But I found my own way to it, my own relationship. I'd appreciate it if you didn't advertise it though.

Kate: I won't tell anybody. I think it's kind of sweet.

That's the first sweet scene. His name is Yule. He and Kate have found each other. He doesn't think the comet is happening. His parents are evangelical—the wrong way—but he found his way. She thinks this belief is sweet.

In the next scene, this is a few hours before the comet is going to hit. Kate, Yule and Randall driving in a car, and he is singing a song that's playing on the radio.

2—SWEETNESS: EROS BREAKS THROUGH

Randall: "Although there are oceans we must cross and mountains that we must climb, I know every gain must have a loss. So pray that our loss is nothing but time..."

Yule: Kate, I gotta ask you something.

Kate: What?

Yule: Dr. Mindy, can I be vulnerable in your car?

Randall: Yeah, go ahead.

Yule: I've met a lot of people, and I've never met anyone like you. And I feel a connection to you on a level that... I don't know. I haven't felt with anyone else. And going out on a limb, but would you want to spend more time together? Maybe even get engaged or something?

Randall: Wow.

[Kate smiles to herself and chuckles.]

Yule: Are you laughing? No?

Kate: I'm smiling. Well sure, why not?

Randall: Wow. Well, this is sweet. This is pretty sweet.

It is sweet. A few hours before the world's about to end, and he asks, "you want to spend more time together, get engaged or something." It's sweet. **This Eros is breaking through.**

In the next scene, Randall's now come home. He hasn't seen June in a long time. This is a couple of hours before the comet hits.

3—SWEETNESS: THE REUNION

Randall's sons, Evan and Marshall, are in the living room watching the launch.

Randall: I was hoping we could have a family dinner.

Evan: Hey Dad!

Marshall: Hey it's Dad! Dad!

There's a long pause as June considers.

Randall: What do you say?

June: Yeah.

Randall: Thank you... this is Kate.

Randall holds up a bouquet of flowers.

Randall: I got these for you.

June: Thank you, that's really sweet, honey.

Randall and June hug for a long time.

Randall: I'm so sorry. You have no idea. I really am.

June: I know. I've missed you.

Randall: I missed you so much.

He gives her flowers, and she says, "Thank you. That's really sweet, honey." So "sweet" here is not saccharine. **Sweet is infinite Eros breaking through.**

Those are the three sweetness scenes. Now we're going to see the only "desire" scene in the movie—and it's a critical scene.

4—DESIRE: "WHATEVER"

Yule: Wanna make out?

Kate: Yeah, why not?

Yule: Can you not say "Why not"? It makes me feel like you don't want it. It's shitty.

Kate: Sure. Whatever.

Yule: That's better. *[They kiss.]*

This is an incredible scene. Even at the moment when it's all about to end, **there's self-evident value in desire**. He asks, "You want to make out?" What does she say? "Whatever."

It's an expression of self-evident value: Desire lives at the very heart of Reality. Unlike the end scene with Jack and Brie, in this moment of death, they know how to practice desire, and it's *self-evidently* valuable. It requires a mutuality of desire—and in those fifteen seconds, everything disappears.

They're completely in the Field of Value.

2.12

DON'T LOOK UP, PART 5: CHANGING THE VECTOR OF HISTORY WITH A NEW STORY OF VALUE

Now we're at the very end of the end—and how do our heroes respond? In this scene, we see them shopping for the final family dinner they're going to make. The kids are there, Kate's there, Yule is there, and they're all talking about all the food they love—wild salmon, fingerling potatoes... They're genuinely appreciating the simple, delicious things of life.

In the scene that immediate follows, the President and her son Jason are giving a final address to the nation. Jason offers the following prayer: "I've been noticing a lot of prayers recently for people during this time, and I commend that. But I also wanna give a prayer for 'stuff.' There's dope stuff, like material stuff. Like sick apartments and watches, and cars and clothes and shit—that could all go away. And I don't want to see that stuff go away. So I'm gonna say a prayer for that stuff. Amen."

Both of these scenes are about stuff. One is ecstatic, a praise of simple things like wild salmon and fingerling potatoes. Ecstasy and Eros for the details of the food they're about to eat. The other scene is this empty, pseudo-erotic prayer for stuff. **One's filled with Eros, while the other one's completely de-eroticized.**

Now here's the scene of the final dinner, a few minutes before the end. You can hear the asteroid rumbling in the background, as its impact with Earth is imminent.

MOVIE SCENE: *DON'T LOOK UP*, THE LAST MEAL TOGETHER

Everyone's there at the dinner table: Randall, his wife June, their kids Evan and Marshall, plus Kate and Yule, and a scientist colleague named Ted Oglethorpe. It begins with a simple toast:

Randall: Cheers, everyone, huh?

Kate: Cheers. Thank you so much for having us.

June: Thank you for being here. It's so special. And it's really good to have you home.

Kate: Dr. Mindy got really famous.

Randall: Oh yeah, I forgot about that. That's right. I was on magazine covers and everything…

June: I love you.

Randall: I love you, too.

There are frequent, deep, heartfelt expressions of intimacy and connection.

Evan: I'm thankful for that night I fell asleep out in the backyard. Woke up face-to-face with a baby deer.

Randall: I remember that.

Evan: Yep. It was the best day of my life.

There's a clear acknowledgment of the pleasures and joys of life.

Kate: I'm grateful... I'm grateful we tried.

Dr. Oglethorpe: Man, oh, man, did we try.

Randall: Well, we're not the most religious here in the Mindy household... but, um, maybe we should say "amen"? Should we do that?

June: Don't look at me. I don't know how to... What, do you just say, "Amen?" I don't...

Yule: I got this... "Dearest Father and almighty creator, we ask for your grace despite our pride, your forgiveness despite our doubt, and most of all, your love to soothe our fears in these dark times. May we face your divine will with courage and open hearts of acceptance—in your name. Amen."

Dr. Oglethorpe: Damn. Yule's got some church game.

Kate: That was... beautiful.

• • •

Marshall: I'm going to have some more of that apple pie. It's really good.

Kate: It's actually store bought, but you really can't tell.

Dr. Oglethorpe: If I'm being really honest, which at this moment why not, I like the junky taste of store-bought better than homemade.

Randall: You gotta be kidding me.

Dr. Oglethorpe: No, I'm not kidding.

June: I know what he means. It's a childhood memory thing or something...

By this point, the house is shaking and utensils are clattering as the comet enters the atmosphere.

Kate: This coffee doesn't taste store-bought. Is it?

Randall: Never. I always grind my own beans.

Marshall: Yeah, Dad's kind of a coffee nut.

June: It's true. Randall is very particular about his coffee.

Kate: I can get that way about tea…

Randall: The thing is, we really did have everything, didn't we? I mean, when you think about it…

Then there's a huge explosion, followed by silence.

In those last seconds, they come together, they pray—whatever that means to them. **They invoke Eros, they say I love you, and they realize they had everything.** They express gratitude and acknowledge that they tried. That's good. "We tried": That's what we want to be able to say together.

Of course, we also want to succeed. But can you imagine saying, "We actually didn't really try, did we"? Can you imagine if we couldn't actually look up? A few characters in the movie knew how to do it, or slowly learned how to. But the whole movie is a testament to a culture that kind of sees it but doesn't know how to truly look.

We're reaching for something: **There's value, there's Eros, there's relationship. It's all real.**

I truly trust that we can do this, that we can change the vector of history.

If there's one thing that I completely agree with Yuval Harari on—and this is where he's firmly in his proper field as a historian—he cites a number of studies that say **the only thing that ever changes history is a new story.**

Story is the only thing that ever changes history.

In the Renaissance, at that time between worlds, that time between stories, with da Vinci and Ficino, Paul Tillich points out that there weren't more than 1,000 people involved at the core of the Renaissance. That's it.

We're back in Florence right now. We're among those 1,000 people—and we have a sense of how to do it. It's not a dogmatic vision, nor is it without uncertainties. We want to look away, but it's real.

As we take our beautiful steps in our business, in our lives, in our relationships, in our homes, which occupies almost all of us, can we also step out and take our place at the table of history? That's the invitation.

Imagine that we could actually evoke a new Florence? Remember, in Florence, they barely knew the "Renaissance" was happening historically. Most people were against such radical change at the time. And most of the Medici family was against the private funding of da Vinci and what they were doing. It wasn't popular in Florence or elsewhere—it was considered absurd, or worse.

But they ended up telling a new story: the story of modernity…

- To the precise extent that they got the vectors of that story right, they birthed what Habermas called the great "dignities" of modernity.
- To the precise extent that they collapsed or neglected pieces of the story, they birthed what Habermas called the "disasters" of modernity.

In a similar way, it's now up to us to tell a new story—a New Story of Value rooted in First Principles and First Values.

We can't make this story up. There's no shortcut. Every line we write has to be profoundly researched, carefully checked—it must be grounded in the external sciences.

- We need the intuitions of the goddesses.
- We need our wings to soar to heaven.
- We need our hearts wide open—**we need mad commitment and mad love between us.**

It's the love between us that, more than anything, will generate the companions who become the Unique Self Symphony, just like the 1,000 people in Florence who resonated with each other and loved each other madly in every way. *They love each other back.*

There was a Unique Self Symphony of mad love in Florence that was birthed. It was genuine Eros.

Now it's ours to do.

That's the Tao.

CHAPTER 3

WHY IS THERE SOMETHING RATHER THAN NOTHING? DIVINITY DESIRES REALITY

3.1

PRAYER: I WANT TO KNOW WHAT LOVE IS

Now that we've looked at a very revealing sacred text of culture and recognized the need for a New Story of Value, let's go deeper into that new story. First, we need to open the Eye of Value, which will enable us to see this Field of Value. To do that, let's start with a little prayer that expresses our urgent desire: to truly know what love is.

Many years ago, my teacher once said to me that **when you pray, you've got to lay your life down for it**. And we're not praying to a cosmic, vending-machine God—we didn't put in a quarter to get what we want. No, prayer means entering the field of the intimate universe—*again, always as if for the very first time*—to let it move through you. We're not on automatic. It's time, finally, to take responsibility for our own arousal.

Prayer is a big deal—and to really pray, you have to be willing to risk your life.

So this song, this prayer, "I Want to Know What Love Is," means I *really fucking want to know what it is*—literally. We're willing to lay it all down, all the way, go all the way, as if we're about to die and this were the last moment we had to open the gates of heaven.

We're on the inside, with full heart, like we've never prayed before. Into the Silence of Presence, in the space between the breaths.

PRAYER: "I WANNA KNOW WHAT LOVE IS," FOREIGNER

In my life, there's been heartache and pain
I don't know if I can face it again
Can't stop now, I've traveled so far
To change this lonely life

I wanna know what love is
I want you to show me
I wanna feel what love is
I know you can show me

3.2

THE INFINITY OF INTIMACY IS THE POSSIBILITY OF POSSIBILITY

Let's recall our key themes. First, **we're trembling with joy.** That's our mood: trembling with joy, living the dream, and affirming that we can change the world only if we're willing to live in the world that's already changed.

Recall also that there are three selves involved in this: we're gathering all of the past as our psychological self, entering the infinity of presence of the True Self, and called by our future evolutionary Unique Self. This is our second theme: **we're seduced by the future itself.**

Homo amor is called and seduced by the future—we can feel it in our bodies, and literally hear the voices of the unborn. Millions of babies, trillions of young girls and boys, men with women madly wanting to love each other, to make love, to touch, to feel, to create, to sing, to laugh, to dance, to sing. They're turning to us and saying:

- You are our voice.
- Whether we're born or not, only the story of your lives will determine.

- Whether or not we will be the heroes of *our* lives—or whether our lives will even begin—depends on you being the heroes of your own lives.

We're entering a space of deep hope, radical optimism, radical possibility.

Third, we have a deep relation to the sacred. For many, God is a dirty word, for lots of valid and understandable reasons. **But we can think instead of God as the Infinite Intimate, that which holds me *and* lives inside of me.**

If I had to define the infinite field, God as the absolutely Real, I'd call it the Infinite Intimate. And if I had to further define the Infinite Intimate, I would say it is the Possibility of Possibility.

God is Reality, the Infinite Intimate, the Possibility of Possibility.

The same energy that moved in the first nanoseconds of the Big Bang, which unleashed a continuous, incessant creativity through all of the stages of matter and life and mind—also known as the physiosphere, the biosphere, and the noosphere—that same creativity is happening all the time, literally right now. It's alive in us *right now.*

REALITY IS A PROCESS, REALITY IS A VERB

One of the first things we need to do is de-nominalize Reality. Nominalization means making something into a noun. We often think Reality is a noun—fixed, static—and we just live inside of it. That is simply a scientific mistake. It's just not true.

We live in Reality, and quite literally, Reality lives in us.

- Reality is a verb.
- Reality is a perpetual, ecstatically urgent, unfolding becoming that emerges out of the Tao.

- Reality emerges out of being, in which we directly participate.
- Reality is fundamentally relational and participatory.

If there's any spirituality at all, it's a *participatory* spirituality.

If there's any politics at all, it's a *participatory* politics.

If there's a politics of *Homo amor*, it's the realization that the polis is an expression of the next unfolding of evolutionary communion that lives in us, as us, and through us. **In fact, we are the Possibility of Possibility.**

We're going to talk about what it means to live in an intimate, participatory universe. **But it's not only that we live in an Intimate Universe—that's only half of the story. The other half is that quite literally, the Intimate Universe lives in us.**

This leads us to the danger of artificial intelligence: AI goes for pure, radical, data-driven, exponentialized thought. But the technologists forget there's a dimension of Reality accessible only when I stop thinking. There's a dimension of thought available only when we feel into the infinities of possibility, beyond all words, where I have direct access to gnosis, which is why the word for "know" is the same as the word for "Fuck" in the original Hebrew.

Knowledge is always carnal, always embodied. Once I stop thinking, then I know. And once I know, as in gnosis, then I can start thinking again—but at a higher register of thought.

This different level of thought is where thoughts are merged with feelings, where thoughts become music...

3.3

THE MUSIC THAT SEDUCES US LIVES INSIDE US

As we've talked about before, the most powerful instrument of seduction is *taking responsibility for you own arousal*. There's no need to wait for the music, for the external support, for the technical structures, to create a moment of prayer. Instead, **we step in and love it open, and then let the moment love us open.**

We could say that there's only one decision we ever make:

> *Do I let the moment love me open, or does the moment remain closed—do I remain closed? Do I birth the Possibility of Possibility with which the moment is pregnant because I'm willing to take my unique risk? Or does the moment remain closed, barren, stillborn?*

One of the most powerful instruments of seduction is clearly music. Music seduces. Music radically changes our mood. **Music loves us open.**

The move from *Homo sapiens* to *Homo amor*, to the New Human and the New Humanity, takes place both when we change our mood and when we change the mood of culture itself. Heidegger wasn't wrong when he said that all that exists is mood. Mood is the fundamental category of Reality.

So, we have to change our mood, deepen our mood. Our mood is the core qualia of existence—and music changes our mood at its core.

All music is actually about love, always. All songs are love songs. These could be personal love songs about human lovers, or love songs about nature, love of country, love of spirit—or their loss. **Music is always intimately bound with love. It holds the agonies and the ecstasies, the devotions and the demands, the rapture and ravaging of love itself.**

It's always at the center of music. You could also say that music is the mathematics of intimacy. Pythagoras understood that music and math live together. "All truth is comprised of music and mathematics," writes Margaret Fuller, a beautiful poet and close friend of Walt Whitman.

I want to tell you something strange about music: Music is not about spirit. That's a mistake. Music has been here from the beginning of time. As Aldous Huxley wrote, "Music discloses the blessedness that's at the heart of all things." **However, although music has been here from the beginning of time, music was not here *before* time.**

There's actually no music in Cosmos before the manifest world of matter emerges, before time. There's no music before there's matter because sound itself is made up of matter. That's shocking. This means that the entire split between thought and feeling, between embodiment and ensoulment, between interiors and exteriors, is false.

To think music is merely spirit that arouses is wrong; music is of matter itself. Sound, in fact, is an expression of one of the earliest forms of matter: gravitational waves. Gravitational waves disclosed by Einstein's mathematical formula were actually only discovered experimentally in 2015, with the help of a three-kilometer-long tuning fork that the universe built through human creativity and imagination—the universe imagining itself.

Music (as gravitational waves) is an expression of time, which isn't separate from space. That's what Einstein's theory of relativity, which is rooted in mathematics, tells us about the intimate structure of the universe. We live in and are composed of spacetime, but what is music at its core? What is sound at its core? Music is made up of matter-energy—in other words, *it's made of time.*

If you go back to the Big Bang, when the single point of the singularity stretches itself out in a line, time is birthed into Reality. And within that line of time, there's continuity from moment to moment, and moments also distinguish themselves from one another. This is difficult, so remember:

- Don't try to understand this only with your mind—also feel it in your body.
- Don't worry about the concepts, although they are important.
- Just feel the science. Don't worry about the details for now.

Within that line of time, there's continuity, and moments are distinguishing themselves. It's this distinction of moments that allows for chords and melody and rhythm and harmony. It's in the break in the continuity of time where music is born. **Once we realize that music is the stuff of time, and that we ourselves are made of time, then we realize that we're made of music.** *Wow.*

We ourselves are made of time, because time is part of the spacetime continuum, part of matter. And that original matter—from the first nanoseconds of the Big Bang, when the spacetime continuum was born— lives in us. We're composed of spacetime.

Music is born in spacetime, so the music that seduces us also lives inside of us.

Indeed, that's why music seduces us—because we are made of music.

And most crucially, music allows us to open the Eye of Value.

3.4

THE THREE EYES OF KNOWING

There's a classic distinction drawn in many of the great traditions—Integral Theory beautifully recapitulates some of them, as does Habermas—between the Eye of the Mind (the rational mind, moral reasoning, mathematics), the Eye of the Senses (or Eye of the Flesh, able to apprehend with the five senses), and the Eye of the Spirit.

It's an important and helpful distinction, but with all due respect, it's actually rooted in a medieval schema and doesn't reflect our current understanding of Reality. It speaks of these three eyes as separate, but they're not.

Let's look at the Eye of the Flesh—the eye that sees through the five senses. When you go to the depths of the Eye of the Flesh, it becomes the Eye of the Heart.

This is what we mean when we say that at its best, "Sex is love in the body." **Sex is cosmic Eros performed in the flesh.** That's not the lowly Eye of the Flesh or the Eye of the Senses. And the Eye of the Mind that sees mathematics and ethics is also an expression of the body. As someone recently told me, "I listen with my body." In other words, I don't transcend thoughts. I don't leave them behind, but instead I enter into the heart of thought itself. When we do, we find the most gorgeous thought:

The deepest, most gorgeous thought is that thought and no thought exist at the same moment.

Let's not call it the Eye of the Spirit—let's instead call it the Eye of Consciousness, and notice that it has lots of important facets:

First, it includes the Eye of the Heart, which I use to love my way to enlightenment. When we find each other and look into each other's eyes and say (from the song by Libby Roderick):

- How can anyone ever tell you that you are anything less than beautiful?
- How can anyone ever tell you that you are anything less than whole?
- How can anyone not notice that our love is just a miracle?
- How deep we are connected in our souls?

Next, there's the Eye of Contemplation. In our morning meditation, we enter into True Self awareness using this eye. It's essential that we're able to drop into that beautiful space, feeling one with the ground—and that the ground is one with me.

Third, there's the Eye of Value, with which we can actually discern goodness, fairness, and loyalty. We can discern value itself.

Finally, there's an Eye of the Spirit, which says that when we do ritual, when we practice, the spirit opens up, into us, as us, through us. The energy of the Cosmos.

The Eye of the Heart, the Eye of Contemplation, the Eye of Value, and the Eye of the Spirit are all names for the same thing, but here's the truth: These are not separate from the Eye of the Flesh nor the Eye of the Mind. **It's all one eye.** When we cleanse the doors of perception, all we see is the infinite, through all of the eyes. *It's all one eye, one heart, one Eros, one love.*

121

So music is not like the ancient texts thought, when, for example, Elisha in the *Book of Kings* says to his minstrel something like, "Bring music and arouse prophecy—in this way, I'll transcend my body and become a prophet." No. Instead I'll enter into the infinities of Eros in my body and clarify my desire—not surface Eros or desire.

My deepest heart's desire is to have few desires, but to have great ones, as the Buddha said. **I clarify the desire that moves in me—my body listens, my body hears, my thoughts stop, and *I know*.**

Then I think even deeper. Then I feel. Then I touch. All of that is part of the great carnal knowing and sensual sensemaking of Reality.

Let's see the world with the Eye of the Heart and the Eye of the Mind, with the Eye of the Flesh and with the Eye of the Spirit, with the Eye of Consciousness *and* with the Eye of Value—with all the eyes. We know that it's all one eye.

If you split off *any* of these eyes, you become blind. You can't see. So we want to open all of our eyes—as the single one.

What we're doing here is attempting to reweave the source code of civilization. When you open up most books on this subject, the Eyes of the Mind, the Spirit, and the Heart are considered three different things. **We're instead reweaving the entire epistemology of the Western and Eastern world in a post-Integral way: *There's no split between these eyes*.**

Music also opens our eyes, but there's a gorgeous paradox. **Music is not of spirit—music lives in matter, it lives in time.** *We are quite literally music.* And music is one of the most powerful ways to access the Eye of Value...

PRACTICE: FINDING LOVE IN THE FACE OF THE OTHER

Let's watch the "Ode to Joy" performance again.[5] Or you can choose another appropriate piece of music for the practice, something that evokes Eros, connection, relationality, love. We're going to

---

[5] You can find the video here, https://www.youtube.com/watch?v=kbJcQYVtZMo, or by typing in "Ode to Joy Flash Mob" into YouTube.

hold Silence of Presence, and as we listen, again notice which faces come up.

Completely place your attention on the music and on the faces at the same time—it's total attention, total heart. The music is loving us open, but we're loving the music open. Place your attention on a video or a series of photographs, and see if you can connect with the faces. Other faces from your past may arise as well.

For example, my old friend who I haven't seen for twenty-five years, Susie Handelman, might appear. How is Susie doing? We studied together in Jerusalem a little bit. She was a professor of English literature, and one of the most brilliant readers of Aramaic texts in the world. She did a stunning reading of a passage in Kook: *When we live on the inside of the inside, we don't grow older, we grow newer.*

Like my beloved friend and evolutionary Whole Mate, Barbara Marx Hubbard, whom I was thinking about this morning, whom I miss dearly, who died at 89—when I first met her, she was very excited about this next step. She was 84 and still filled with fire when I met her. She said to me, **"Marc, I'm not growing older. I'm getting newer."** She called me several times a day, which made me a little crazy because she would call to talk about what we talked about yesterday, and she'd get as excited as if we had never talked about it, with complete virginal ecstasy, with this wild energy. Now, of course, I wish Barbara would call, just to get excited all over again.

Taking Barbara as an inspiration, let's look at this video and hear this music again, as though we've never looked at it before, like a virgin, touched for the very first time. Enlightenment is like revirgination. *To see it for the very first time.*

3.5

RESPONDING TO EXISTENTIAL RISK WITH A "DIRECT HIT": A NEW STORY OF VALUE

Now we're going to weave the strands together and enter into the depths of Reality itself. **We want to more fully participate together in the evolution of culture and consciousness, which is, as we'll see, the evolution of love**—in response to the meta-crisis, as an expression of Eros itself. We're trying to evolve the source code of culture. We're trying to take our seat at the table of history.

Are we willing to play a larger game?

Are we willing to actually set our intention on the evolution of love?

We're in this time between worlds, in this time between stories—and we're going to participate together in the evolution of love.

I'm going to release myself from any obligation to entertain you, from any obligation of wisdo-tainment, although I do have a few jokes I'd like to share. We're going to go super deep and get very serious, but the paradox is: It's actually the most entertaining, the most alive, the most wild, and ultimately, the most transformational thing we could do.

Let's start with a familiar image from popular culture that gives us a sense of our intention: the explosion of the Death Star. *Star Wars* is probably the greatest mythic story of the last fifty years, certainly the most watched human story on the planet. It's a true cultural phenomenon.

Paradoxically, while this is the most watched story in culture, the deeper meaning remains invisible. We're in this moment of what we might call the meta-crisis. The meta-crisis is the Death Star, a planet-destroying weapon. The Rebels have the plans and blueprints for the Death Star, but it seems impossible to destroy it—how are these little groups of people and their little ships going to face this huge galactic technology? But in fact, **it's only those little ships that can get in because they weren't defended against. The technocratic order—or, if you will, the TechnoFeudal order—didn't account for them because they didn't think they were a threat.**

The only way in to destroy the Death Star—much more than a weapon, a symbol of a culture of death, leading to both the death of humanity or the death of *our* humanity—is to be stealthy and score a direct hit.

In other words, there's no way to raise enough funding to build a counter-Death Star. We would spend our lives on a fifty-year-long fundraising drive, administering all of it, like some organizations often do, building a huge bureaucratic structure in order to try and construct a huge counter-apparatus. It won't work. We can't build a new Death Star, or "Life Star"—nor do we want to.

But, as in the movie, we can realize that there's a chink in the armor that wasn't accounted for, the capacity to actually score a direct hit.

THE FIRST AND SECOND SHOCKS OF EXISTENCE

We're at this moment that we're calling the second shock of existence. **Again, the first shock of existence is simply the individual realization of mortality: "Fuck, I'm going to die."** We reflect on life and realize that death is part of the story. As David Graeber pointed out, that already begins with the hunter, not with the farmer. It's an early realization that death is part of my life. As William James said, "The skull grins in at the banquet"—that's the first shock of existence.

What's the response of Reality to the first shock of existence? Civilization. **All of civilization is a direct response to death**. We're pressed into service, and all of civilization at its best, in all its Eros—in all its beauty, in all its disaster—is our genuine response. All of the pseudo-eros of civilization is what Ernest Becker calls the "denial of death," an attempt to cover up this realization. So, all of human civilization—based on the best angels of our nature and all of the demonic parts—arose in response to this first shock of existence.

But then we go through all the stages of civilization, all the stages of evolution, and we get to this point where we meet the **second shock of existence, the realization of the potential death of humanity.** That's the Death Star—culture always speaks in unconscious images. They're not making this shit up. This is the most watched story in the world, in the galaxy—at least in this part of the galaxy.

It couldn't really be more clear. The story is about a planet destroyer. In other words: existential risk, even before existential risk was in the conversation. I've scoured the internet, and there's not one review from 1977 that discusses *Star Wars* in terms of existential risk.

In other words, culture didn't notice then what it was saying to itself. But this is always what happens. Steven Spielberg and Joseph Campbell were even on the set. On the surface, it was about one thing, but underneath they're actually saying something real: There's a way to score a direct hit. So how do we score a direct hit?

- The direct hit is a *new Story*.
- The direct hit is a New Story of Value, grounded in First Principles and First Values.

- The direct hit is a story we know, a story we feel, a story we can enter into.
- This story is infinitely more potent than a Skinner box.
- This is a story that changes the vector of history.

That's what da Vinci, Ficino, and company realized in the Renaissance. At that other time between stories, that time between worlds, they realized the disasters like the Black Death could sweep through Europe again, and they had no idea how to respond to it.

Half of Europe died from the bubonic plague in the most ugly and horrific way. And here's where Steven Pinker got it right. Our response to Covid is infinitely, gorgeously—even with all of its complexity, with all of the death—more effective. Because of the Renaissance, because of modernity, we exponentially outstripped the medieval response to disease. In a year and a half, humanity did something quite astounding, even with all the complexity about lock-downs, vaccines, and everything else.

But we're at this moment where it's not about a vaccine, or even one disease. **It's about the entire panoply of existential risks—the death of humanity, the death of *our* humanity—that can't be responded to with mere social or infrastructural response.**

It can only be responded to with a new story.

The response must be superstructural—the direct hit itself is a New Story of Value.

3.6

THE ROOT CAUSE OF EXISTENTIAL RISK IS A GLOBAL INTIMACY DISORDER

To get why this is the case, let's see if we can identify the underlying generator functions. Let's feel together. We're made of music, and we're playing a symphony together.

Until a couple of years ago, The best analysis that Barbara, Zak, Daniel, and I came up with, when we were working at the think tank, after combing all the literature and trying to see through it all with infrared glasses, was that there are two underlying generator functions for existential risk.

ZERO-SUM RIVALROUS CONFLICT GOVERNED BY WIN/LOSE METRICS

The first generator function is the failed story that we live in. A few years back, we ran an event called Success 3.0, about existential risk and the "success story" we live in today. Success 1.0, the pre-modern success story says, "Do what God says. Obey and you shall be redeemed." Spinoza spent a good part of his life critiquing this success story.

Success 2.0 is the story of modernity and postmodernity, currently expressed by everyone from Xi to Putin to Obama to Biden—we all live in some version of this story at the moment. **The basis of this story is zero-sum rivalrous conflict governed by win/lose metrics.** It drives everything—every company, every division, every structure of society. There are billions of micro-acts in society driven by this story, based on the question: "Am I successful?"

Let's be brutally honest for a second. When we think of ourselves, we want to look good and be successful. Often when we say someone's very sincere, it's like a booby prize for not being successful. About an unsuccessful man, someone who's not rich or powerful, we often say, "He's very sincere." Or about a woman, we say, "She's a very devoted wife," when we mean she's somehow not successful in whatever our standard of beauty happens to be—but at least she's devoted.

Success lives and breathes us in our culture—we're taught to be successful from an early age. Our entire school system is organized to train people to participate successfully in the workforce. Comenius, an early Renaissance figure, tried to argue for a different division, but unfortunately we didn't go that way. We went with a different school system, so now everything is about competition and success. It's the driver of Reality in every nation, every city, every company, everywhere: rivalrous conflict governed by win/ lose metrics.

Unfortunately, however, there's a catch. It generates a self-terminating system:

- You create exponential growth curves, which always drop off due to a finite planet and resources.
- You create fractional reserve banking, a deceptive system that will crash in the end, every time.
- You create an extraction model for the whole planet, which extracts and extracts until an all-systems crash occurs, until the banks crash, and you can't get a loan anymore, or a job.

Last year, I described in great detail the next thirty or forty years based on an intense economic and socio-political analysis.[6] I won't go into it again. **Whether it's over the next thirty, fifty, seventy, or ninety years is debatable, but that's absolutely where the system is currently heading: to a series of cascading crashes.**

The system is driven by exponential growth curves that have to drop off at some point, by extraction models that have to eventually collapse, and by a system of fractional reserve banking that cannot sustain itself forever. We think it's going to keep going, but it won't—it can't. Covid was just a minor dress rehearsal for the structural weakness in the system.

COMPLEX AND COMPLICATED SYSTEMS

The second generator function, theorized by people like David Snowden and Nassim Taleb, and discussed by systems theorists who see the world clearly, is really important. The distinction they draw, and let's use Snowden's terms, is between a **complicated system and a complex system**.

- A complex system takes care of its own waste, and a complicated system does not.
- A complex system has an interconnected balance among its parts, and the complicated has a fragile imbalance.
- The complex regenerates itself, and the complicated does not.

As an example of a complex system, think of the Brazilian rainforest. It regenerates, takes care of its own waste, everything is interpenetrated with everything else, and there's this very deep cascading set of intimacies, if you will, throughout the system. It's quite robust.

As an example of a complicated system, imagine a Ferrari. A Ferrari fits together well, but if you're missing a part and the factory closes, you're

---

[6] See Marc Gafni, *The Amorous Cosmos: From Pre-Tragic to Post-Tragic: First Principles and First Values as a Response to Existential Risk* (World Religion and Philosophy, 2024).

fucked. A Ferrari doesn't regenerate itself. It doesn't fit together, essentially. It's very fragile.

The world economic system, for example, has unfortunately become a complicated system. It's what we could call a "hyper-object," a phenomenon so complicated as to be incomprehensible, and where pieces of the system don't know each other. They're all operating independently, based on rivalrous conflict governed by win-lose metrics. Then they generate a complicated system, or what Nassim Taleb calls a "fragile" system.

We have created financial instruments, for example, in one discrete subset of a particular company, and those instruments are meant only for that particular sub-unit to win in its rivalrous conflict with other sub-units, based on win/lose metrics. Many such disconnected financial instruments thus cascade through the system, leading to disastrous meltdowns like the one that happened in 2008. **If you trace the financial instruments that cascaded through the housing market, they were artificially created— and then only artificially solved.**

Or look at the number of doctors and nurses who died early on from Covid because they couldn't get masks. They were maskless because their production was structured in such a way that only particular people were allowed to make them, based on an entire set of complicated structural contracts.

Around the world, and especially in the United States, the world's superpower, tens of thousands of people died in the first six months of the pandemic because there were no masks. It's unimaginable.

In other words, the system is a complicated, fragile system that optimizes not for safety, resilience, or life.

The system optimizes for short-term success, driven by rivalrous conflict governed by win/lose metrics in its short-term structures.

THE UNDERLYING INTIMACY DISORDER

So we identified—quite brilliantly, if I may say so—those two generator functions for existential risk. But we were spectacularly wrong in a really big way, because we actually didn't go deep enough. We really can't be proud of ourselves. It was accurate, but it didn't quite get it. What's the deeper root cause? Here I want to introduce a term that we've thrown around over the years, and I want to get really specific about it.

The underlying root cause of those two generator functions is what we might call a "global intimacy disorder." So, those generator functions are not the deepest root cause.

In terms of rivalrous conflict, it's pretty clear: There's me and you, and we're not intimate with each other. We're in rivalrous conflict all the way up and all the way down the system, at odds with each other because *we don't realize our fundamentally shared identity.*

So I'm optimizing, or sub-optimizing, my relationship with every single person I know or meet based on some version of rivalrous conflict. It's always at play, in every relationship. Buber called it *I–It,* **the fundamental intimacy disorder at the very heart of culture.**

- In a complicated system, the parts can't *see* each other.
- They don't *know* each other.
- There's no carnal knowledge.
- There's no Fuck running through the system.
- There's no currency of Eros.
- The parts are sub-optimizing in their own rivalrous conflict.
- There's no mutuality of recognition—they can't see each other.
- There's no mutuality of pathos—they can't feel each other.
- There's no mutuality of purpose—no shared goal.
- There's no shared Field of Value.
- There's no intimacy.

Both complicated systems and those in a rivalrous conflict governed by win-lose metrics are fundamental expressions of an underlying intimacy disorder.

As disheartening as this is, it's actually great news—it's quite hopeful because diagnosis is everything. If we can identify not just the generator functions, but the underlying root cause, that's an enormous opening because it means that we can see a way through. The way through is not some *restoration* of intimacy—we've never actually *had* global intimacy before.

So let's forget about *restoring* intimacy—let's instead *evolve* intimacy. **An evolution of intimacy means we can generate a new structure of global intimacy that drives the entire system and its billions of interconnected micro-acts in a new way that goes way beyond complicated systems in rivalrous dynamics.**

3.7

RESPONDING TO THE GLOBAL INTIMACY DISORDER WITH A NEW STORY OF VALUE

Imagine this was always the way evolution worked, that crisis is always an evolutionary driver. *Always.* Imagine that every crisis, at its core, is actually a crisis of intimacy. This is, in fact, the movement of evolution itself—**and at this moment in history, we're facing not an ordinary crisis, but a meta-crisis, exponentially unlike anything we've ever seen.**

Exponentialized technology creates exponential *suck*, if I can use the Latin term. Bows and arrows, guns, tanks can be pretty bad on a local level. The atom bomb is pretty bad globally, but not such a huge deal because it takes an entire country to manufacture one—you need state capacities to enrich and transport uranium, to create the possibility of manifesting a nuclear device, maintaining it, and then detonating it. We can kind of handle nuclear weapons. Over the last seventy years, we sort of did handle them, though it wasn't easy. They almost went off a bunch of times, and somehow we managed.

But that's not where we are now. The atom bomb was child's play compared to our current situation. We're now at weaponized, automated drone technologies. We now have rogue non-state actors playing with new protocols of biological weapons and artificial intelligence.

In 2019, Nick Bostrom wrote a very important essay called "The Vulnerable World Hypothesis," in which he said that each new technology is like reaching blindly into a bucket and grabbing a ball: Either it's white, grey, or black.

- A **white ball** is a great new technology, with all or mostly positive consequences.
- A **grey ball** has a mix of greatness and a lot of downsides—social media is a pretty good example, and there are lots of these in the bucket.
- A **black ball** is a pretty disastrous technology, with all negative consequences. Something like an exponentially weaponized technology that can be made in a short amount of time, away from the eyes of appropriately surveilling parties, by rogue, non-state actors—a technology where you can't track who's making it.

How do we deal with that? Bostrom argues that we actually *need* surveillance, some way of seeing what's happening. Many are naturally suspicious of this, and a lot of the literature says let's get rid of all surveillance. Shoshana Zuboff's *Surveillance Capitalism* describes surveillance entirely as a demon—this is wrong. If we don't have eyes at all, we're totally blind.

However, if you have mass surveillance *without* First Values and First Principles, then you have totalitarianism in its worst form. *Surveillance Capitalism* is a fantastic and important book, but Zuboff forgot to explain that there are reasons why we need surveillance, which she completely ignores. She doesn't see this because she cannot articulate a vision that would enable us to have eyes *with* First Values and First Principles. Her impulse is correct, but she cannot ground it in value.

Ultimately, the answer is quite simple: **If the root cause of the generator functions of existential risk—rivalrous conflict based on win/lose** metrics and complicated, fragile systems instead of robust, complex systems—is a global intimacy disorder, then we need to evolve intimacy.

But how do we do that?

A SHARED STORY AS AN EXPRESSION OF GOODNESS, TRUTH, AND BEAUTY

Let's say you're in a couple: partners, lovers, two friends, or two people working in a group in a company. The core structure of intimacy in any couple is that they need some sort of shared story. They certainly don't have to agree on everything, but they do need what Huxley in 1944 called some kind of "minimum working hypothesis," some basic shared story about their past, present, and future.

If you don't have a shared story within a couple, the relationship breaks down. It might break down into ongoing, prolonged deadness, or the couple might actually break up. But if you want a partnership to remain a vibrant, throbbing expression and articulation of Eros, then you need a shared story. And this might mean a romantic couple that never has sex, but who are madly in love. It's not about how you do it—it's not about sex but about Eros. If you want a couple to be enamored by Eros, looking deeply into each other's eyes, deeply connected in a lasting way, then there has to be some sort of shared story. Otherwise, intimacy breaks down. **So the way you create intimacy is that you live within a shared story.**

Now, this of course has shadow versions. For example, ethnocentric nationalism in the fourteenth century was a shadow version of a shared story: *We all believe a fundamentalist, exclusionary shared story, and are therefore willing to die for each other.* Or you have a very particular version of belief in Christ that gets you to Heaven, and any other belief system takes you straight to hell. So we end up in the brutal Protestant-Catholic wars, like the Thirty Years War that ripped Europe apart over which version of the shared story is right. We're all willing to die, to kill each other, our brothers and our sisters, for this shared story.

So that's the shadow version—which also allows you to see the power of a shared story.

Despite the potential for shadow, a shared story is absolutely essential in creating intimacy. **You need a shared Story of Value, *rooted in First Values and First Principles*—it must express the Good, the True, and the Beautiful. And just as important: That story has to evolve.**

So what's the direct hit on the culture of death in the grip of a global intimacy disorder? The direct hit on the Death Star is articulating a new shared Story of Value grounded in Goodness, Truth, and Beauty. If we can do that, the story will spread, and spread quickly.

But this story cannot be *declared*, as I always said to Barbara. It can't be like, "I proclaim this story to be true; this is the new story." No, that's totalitarianism. You can't impose a story. **The story has to well up from the value structures of Reality itself.**

In other words, it has to be rooted in First Principles and First Values.

3.8

THE PATHWAY FROM NEW STORY OF VALUE TO RESPONDING TO THE META-CRISIS

If every challenge we have is a global challenge, such as the widespread intimacy disorder at the root of the meta-crisis, we can only respond with a new global Story of Value. Local doesn't exist anymore—from AI to sexual slavery, to the dead zones in the oceans, to the absurdity of dealing with a virus state by state. Do you think Covid respects state boundaries?

If you understand economics, this is how currency works as well. If we can see clearly underneath it all, we realize that it's all one currency—it's all interconnected. The notion of dealing discretely on any level today is simply ignorance.

And yet we still keep developing these ineffective micro-solutions to global problems.

- Every issue is a global issue, so we need global coordination.
- To achieve global coordination, we need global coherence, a very important concept that comes from systems theory
- To create global coherence we need global resonance—similar to musical harmony.

- We can't have global resonance without global intimacy.
- We can't have global intimacy without a shared Story of Value.

The direct hit on the Death Star—on the culture of death, on the potential death of humanity and the death of our humanity, second shock of existence—is actually a New Story of Value. I hope that sentence has a lot more resonance now.

It's not just a slogan—it's deeply grounded.

Along with many friends, colleagues, and students, I've spent the last couple of decades of my life trying to work out that story—to make this da Vinci move, this time-between-stories move, to gather the information, and read very widely. For example, I watch every Marvel movie carefully because they are each key cultural texts. To sit in the library and just read economics books (which I also do from time to time) but not understand what Marvel movies are doing, will completely dissociate you from the deep movements of culture.

Of course, we need a new economic system—it's not going to be socialism or communism, and it's not going to be classical capitalism. It's going to be something else. John Mackey made a stab at it with "conscious capitalism," but I don't think that gets us there, for a variety of reasons. **There's going to be a new economics integrating the best of the entrepreneurial spirit of innovation and the best of social safety nets—and the best of a larger sense of the commons.**

We desperately need a new, emergent economic system.

3.9

TELLING THE NEW STORY: INTIMACY IS A CORE STRUCTURE OF REALITY

Let's try and get a sense of what this new story could be. One place to start is with the two basic properties of Reality, which are evident at scales all the way down and all the way up: *synergy and emergence*.

Now, when I mention those two properties, does that honestly feel arousing? Well, next time you're on a date, just try it. "Oooh… synergy and emergence." Look deeply into their eyes and whisper: "synergy." Whisper: "emergence." It's actually crazy hot. By the end, you're never going to say, "Touch me here, touch me there." You're only going to say "synergy and emergence." [*Laughter*]

But for real, what does synergy mean? **Synergy is what moves Reality.** So, for example, a cell respirates. The *parts* of a cell don't respirate—the cytoplasm, the organelles, the mitochondria, the DNA, all that stuff. Science is driven by this insatiable, gorgeous curiosity, a drive to know, to become intimate with the structures of the physical Cosmos. And science notices something correctly: Before it's a cell, all that other stuff is not alive in a classical sense. That distinction between life and not-life is complex—

and there's much more to be said about this—but it's pointing to something that's absolutely real, obviously.

So in a classical scientific sense, the parts of a cell are not alive—**but then those parts come *together*, they synergize, *voilà*, you have a living cell.** And that cell has new emergent properties—e.g. it's metabolizes, it breathes, and all the rest. That cell then finds other cells, and it becomes a collection of cells, an organism—and eventually, a human being. That's a new emergent. Synergy means that there are invisible but demonstrable lines of allurement, accessible through the instruments of classical science.

There are vectors of allurement that move through and crisscross Reality. Those vectors of allurement are made of separate parts, which bring them together. This is what David Bohm was trying to express. He couldn't quite get it before he died, but he was pointing to that property of wholeness in Cosmos, where separate parts come together and form new wholes.

Synergy is the creation of a new whole that has properties none of the parts have.

If you had to break down Reality and strip everything aside, Reality is a movement of synergy, which is actually a movement of allurement, as separate parts are woven together—but not into new *complexities*.

Although it's partly true, that doesn't totally describe what's happening. It's the formation of new *intimacies*. What happens is that Reality is driven by this vector of allurement, animated by Eros, which brings separate parts into new wholes—new configurations of intimacy, new configurations of Eros.

The Eros that animates the four fundamental forces—which are all forces of attraction, allurement, and autonomy—moves all throughout Reality, all the way up and all the way down.

And it never stops.

3.10

REALITY IS THE EVOLUTION
OF ALLUREMENT

It's quite beautiful and quite surprising that allurement doesn't turn off. Let me ask you a question: How did you get here, reading this? What are you doing here? How did this happen?

Let's make this even more real: *Why are you here?*

You're here, I'm here, we're here because we were all somehow *allured* to be here. There's many good, logical reasons why it doesn't make sense for each of us to be where we are. But we are here, right now. **And if you check your interiority, we're all where we are because we were somehow allured**.

Allurement is also responsible for mitosis, myosis, the amazing chlorophyll molecule, the great process that generated photosynthesis… It evolved all the way up through matter, life, and mind—and then… what? It stopped at the human being? Allurement just went away? Went back home? Really?

No, allurement is *always* moving—throughout all the layers of the human experience. There's intellectual allurement, emotional allurement, somatic allurement… **Allurement is a structure of Cosmos, and every single one of us—everyone listening, everyone reading this—is here because we were allured.**

Gravity is just a word—quite an important word, but just a word nonetheless. It's absolutely essential that science has precise words, because it makes us more intimate with Cosmos. But if we get real and go big: What's underneath gravity? Nothing. **Gravity *is* allurement.** That's what it is. Gravity is allurement in the celestial sphere. Allurement playing with autonomy like it always does.

Now let's go subatomic. What's underneath electromagnetic energy? Nothing. **Electromagnetic energy *is* allurement. Reality is the evolution of allurement, interiors and exteriors, all the way up and all the way down.** That's what Reality is.

Over the last few years, I've been working with my friends Venu and Kerstin on a new way of writing science—not a mythopoetic writing of science, which is what Brian Swimme does, wonderfully, in *The Universe Story.* We're writing science, but we're not taking the words for granted.

When words are used in the scientific community, they're precise, but you sometimes forget what they're describing. So when we say gravity or electromagnetism, for example, we think we're done. But what underlies both of these forces? Electromagnetism and gravity are both dances between allurement and autonomy.

When we say even the simplest things in science, like "a cell respirates," that it breathes—it's called aerobic metabolism. But what does that mean? We're going to look at this scientifically using a couple of formulas.

The first is what I want to call the Eros equation:

Eros = the experience of radical aliveness moving towards, seeking, desiring, ever deeper contact and ever larger wholeness

This formula works across the board—in biology, economics, physics, sociology, psychology, and relationships. It's actually a little shocking.

Eros equals the experience of radical aliveness, whether it's my experience, your experience, the experience of a plant, or that of a single cell. There's obviously a massive difference between a full human being and a cell, but there's also deep continuity and a clear developmental, evolutionary trend.

COSMOS HAS AN APPETITE, COSMOS DESIRES TOUCH

Eros equals the experience of radical aliveness seeking, moving towards, desiring ever deeper contact and ever greater wholeness. It's incredible.

That's the nature of Eros, all the way up and all the way down the evolutionary chain. It's this movement, a driving towards, always seeking. But not just seeking—it's desiring.

So, for example, Alfred North Whitehead doesn't talk about desire. He talks about the "appetition" of Cosmos. And the appetite of Cosmos, to paraphrase Whitehead, is for Fuck, which he also sometimes calls Eros—I was delighted to see that.

- You could say that Cosmos is hungry and has desires.
- Desire is at the very heart of matter.
- Matter is inexplicable without desire.
- Matter desires to be God, to become music, to become moral reasoning...

So there's this process called Eros at the very heart of Reality that animates everything, all the way up and all the way down. **Eros is always seeking deeper contact.**

It wants to touch, which Whitehead called "prehension," but actually touch is a better word.

This Eros, this desire for deeper and more intense contact, generates a deeper synergy, and this brings all the parts of a cell together to generate a new emergence, a new wholeness, which we call cellular respiration.

In other words, Eros is always searching for greater intimacies.

Ervin László suggested that we shouldn't use the word intimacy. He was thinking, and understandably so, that intimacy only exists in human sexuality—he couldn't get out of that frame.

He's certainly not alone in this, but ultimately we come to see that intimacy is the very structure of Reality.

That then opens things up in surprising and beautiful ways…

3.11

THE EVOLUTION OF EROS: UNPACKING THE INTIMACY EQUATION

Intimacy lies at the core of CosmoErotic Humanism, this New Story of Value we are developing. Let's take a look at our second equation, the intimacy equation:

> *Intimacy = shared identity in the context of (relative) otherness ×*
> *mutuality of recognition × mutuality of pathos (shared feeling) ×*
> *mutuality of value × times mutuality of purpose*

Let's unpack this:

- Intimacy equals shared identity in the context of *relative* otherness because there's distinction, but there's also an ultimate True Self that underlies everything—our deeper shared identity.
- We multiply this by the mutuality of recognition, meaning that we recognize each other, and we see each other.
- Then we multiply this by the mutuality of pathos, meaning we can feel each other.

- Then we multiply this by mutuality of value, meaning the degree to which we're in a shared Field of Value.
- Then we multiply this by mutuality of purpose—we have a common goal.

Let's just check this for a second. There we are hanging out at the Big Bang. At that instant, the entire spacetime continuum emerges—and we might think that's the end of the story because *nothing* crazier could happen than that. However, all of a sudden, what emerges? These *things*. Gazillions of "things" emerge—waves or particles, or both, we're not quite sure. They're called quarks, or at least that's what we call them today.

Scientifically speaking, a quark is not nothing. There's actually only sixteen forms of quarks. In a random Cosmos, you might think there'd be a billion forms, or even "infinite" forms. Nope. There are only sixteen possible types of quark, each with very particular properties, particular codes of value, and codes of meaning. They are information personified. That's what a quark is. **At some point, the strong nuclear force, a particular fundamental force of allurement, moves quarks into becoming a new kind of thing called a proton or neutron.**

It's so incredible and so extraordinarily beautiful—if you're not fainting right now, try reading that sentence again.

In other words, three quarks come together after a certain amount of time, at the very beginning of the Cosmos—two up-quarks and one down-quark, or two down-quarks and one up-quark. One becomes a proton, the other becomes a neutron. Protons and neutrons are entirely different than a quark—**they are completely new emergents**. The synergy of allurement between quarks creates something entirely and completely new. There's just no way to even begin to describe it adequately.

- It's a completely new emergent called a proton, or a neutron.
- It's a completely new configuration of Eros.
- It's a completely new configuration of intimacy.

Then, about 380,000 years later, give or take, you've got all these protons and neutrons created from quarks in the field of allurement. They are like the size of a mouse compared to the Empire State Building, all madly allured to **each other. They're desiring** *each other*—**quite literally.**

Inexorably driven to find each other, these subatomic particles come together, moved by allurement—and along with electrons, they create an atom.

Let's go through this in light of the intimacy equation:

- There's a shared identity between the subatomic particles— they're part of an atom—but it's identity in the context of relative otherness, because the particles don't entirely lose their distinction. It's not that there are no protons, neutrons, or electrons after that. No, they're still there, though together, in different configurations; they now share an identity called an atom.
- Between the subatomic parts of an atom there exists a mutuality of recognition. It's very clear that these parts recognize each other in their new relation.
- There's mutuality of pathos. They *literally* feel each other at the subatomic level, and at the level of quarks.
- They exist in a shared Field of Value, a shared field of information, or shared field of meaning. Meaning structures live in Reality, as Whitehead pointed out, all the way down and all the way up.
- Finally, an atom clearly has a new shared function, a mutuality of purpose. Atoms can do things that their subatomic particles cannot. An atom is an entirely new world with a shared goal.

This understanding of intimacy applies to everything—to atoms, to stars and galaxies, to politics, to international diplomacy, to a couple, to a friendship. There's lots of versions of it, but genuine intimacy is not just functional. And it's certainly not mere rivalrous conflict governed by win/lose metrics, where we're mutually advantaging and just superficially calling it friendship.

Real friendship means there's intimacy between us—in some way, you're part of my identity. When that happens, it's gorgeous—we have a shared identity, but in the context of otherness. It's a gorgeous union, not mere fusion. **We can act in the field of shared identity, and recognize our distinct and unique otherness.**

Subatomic particles are governed by the same intimacy equation that a couple is. That should make you ecstatic because it means we live in one Cosmos, in one Eros, in one intimacy, and in one Reality. The same principles and values govern subatomic particles, cells, multicellular life, emergent tissues, organs, plants, amphibians, animals, humans, all the way up to any collective cultural or economic system—as well as planets, stars, and galaxies.

That's what we mean when we say that evolution is the progressive deepening of intimacies.

That's what Reality is. Does that mean it's always a cakewalk? Of course not. There's a long arc to evolution. **It's the on-going agony and ecstasy of every love story**—not some Pollyannaish romance. It's a much larger vector than what we can see in one dimension, or even in one lifetime.

So, again, Reality is both synergy and emergence—vectors of allurement, the movement of Eros, which is in fact quite a formal equation in the interior sciences. **Eros is always doing the same thing: generating and evolving intimacy as the movement of Reality itself.**

149

3.12

TOWARDS A COSMOCENTRIC INTIMACY: FALLING IN LOVE WITH REALITY

I'm going to share something beautiful. It's a love note written by my beloved lineage teacher, Abraham Kook, about a hundred years ago.

He says, "There is a one who sings the song of her soul. And in her soul, she finds it all." Beautiful. Full, complete satisfaction, egocentric intimacy. "There is a one who sings the song of her soul," and in that song is him and her, and the kids, and the dog of course. "And in her soul, she finds it all": full complete spiritual, complete existential satisfaction.

Then he writes, "And there is a one who's singing the song of the nation." Here she leaves the zone of her personal soul, which she doesn't find wide enough and not settled in ideal serenity and beauty, and she attaches herself with tender love to the totality of the congregation. And together with the congregation, she sings her song, she suffers her pain, she fulfills her hopes, she ponders high and pure ideas about the nation's past and future, and she investigates with love and the wisdom of the heart, the inner content of the soul of the nation."

The first one was egocentric intimacy.

The second one is ethnocentric intimacy.

Then Kook says, "And there is a one who widens her soul even further. She spreads her soul even further, until it expands and spreads beyond the boundary of her community, to sing the song of humanity, and her soul is continuously expanded by the genius of the human and the glory of the human divine, and she aspires towards the human being's universal purpose and anticipates the higher wholification of humanity. And from this living source does she draw the entirety of her thoughts and explorations, her aspirations and her visions."

That's worldcentric intimacy, increasing the boundary to include every human being on the planet.

He continues, "There is a one who rises even further than this, in expansion until she joins herself in union with all existence in its totality, with all creatures, with all worlds. And together with all of them, she gives forth song and she engages in the song of the universe."

That's what would we call **cosmocentric intimacy.**

Now, which one of those is right?

Kook continues, "And there is a one who **rises with all of these songs together in one union, and all of them send forth their voices, and all together they play their melodies, and each pours vitality and life into the other,** and together"—egocentric intimacy, and ethnocentric intimacy, worldcentric intimacy, and cosmocentric intimacy, "they sing a song of jubilance, a song of joy, a song of celebration, a song of rapture, a song of rejoicing, a song of the sacred, the song of the soul, the song of the nation, the song of humankind, the song of the universe, all flowing together within her at every moment, and every time and in this completeness, in this fullness, it rises to become the Song of Solomon, a fourfold song, the King to whom wholeness belongs."

Solomon wrote the Song of Solomon, and one of the key verses is "its insides are lined by allurement." Akiva, one of the lineage masters, wrote that if all of the law was not given, we would be able to govern the world based only on the Song of Solomon. **Its insides are lined with love.**

This is just a snippet of the **evolution of intimacy**.

Currently, most Westerners, most people in open societies are, at their core, egocentric in the way they act and worldcentric in the way they talk.

Most people in closed societies, like Russia and China, are egocentric in the way they act and ethnocentric in the way they talk. **But imagine what it would mean if we could all deepen into the intimacy formula and actually have shared identity in the context of otherness times mutuality of recognition, pathos, value, and purpose—not only at the egocentric level but at the ethnocentric, worldcentric, and cosmocentric levels as well.**

We're not going to save the world because we *think* we need each other. It's never going to work. We're not going to save the environment because we *think* we need the environment.

The environmental movement has fundamentally failed: It's proven time and again that we *logically* need the environment—and absolutely nothing changes.

We can't just say we need the ecosystems of the oceans and the plankton— we have to fall in love with the plankton. We can't say we need the other countries—we have to fall in love with them.

We're only going to save the world if we *fall in love* with it.

If we don't fall in love, there's no story.

Only a love story will take us home.

There's no other way.

It's actually fantastic news; Reality is a love story—not a superimposed love story, not a made-up love story—a real, Outrageous, Evolutionary Love Story.

LOVE OR DIE: *DON'T LOOK UP* AS A SERIES OF LOVE STORIES

All of Reality is synergy and emergence, all the way up and all the way down. Herbert Spencer talks about differentiation and integration. Reality is differentiating, meaning more and more autonomy. Allurement means higher integration, all the way up and all the way down. It's all a love story. **There's continuity and discontinuity, for sure, like every good love story, but at the core, the whole thing is Eros. It's all *allurement*.**

In *Don't Look Up*, Peter Isherwell says to Randall Mindy, "We've got all the data on you. I know who you are." He says to him. "I know what you are. We have eight types. We have 400,000 data points on you. We have predictive analysis of who you are and what you're going to do, because you're measurable. And you're going to die alone."

But he was totally wrong. Randall didn't die alone.

Unbeknown to even the writers of the movie, *Don't Look Up* is actually a series of love stories, and pseudo-love stories:

- Brie and Jack, the two announcers—no real love story.
- Brie and Randall—no real love story.
- Peter Isherwell—no love story. The little ten-year-old goddess says, "I love you, Peter," and he doesn't even hear it. "I've always wanted friends," he says. He dies, devoured at the end of the movie, but only after attempting to save himself.
- The President and her son, Jason—no real love story. In another scene near the end, the President says they have a ship waiting, just in case they were wrong. She calls Randall and says, "We've got room for two more. You can take either June, your wife, or Brie—your choice." And he says, "Thanks for calling, but I'll pass and good luck. I hope you and Jason are good over there." She says, "Jason?" She forgot to bring her son, who's in the bunker at BASH headquarters, the only person to survive the blast. And after the shock waves, the first thing he screams is, "Mom!" She left him behind—because there's no love story.

- Kate has these frightened eyes at first, but gradually, in her desperation, she meets Yule, who teaches her about love. In those last scenes, you see her face start to soften. She kisses Yule after he does the prayer. It's a love story.
- Randall and June, his wife—that's a love story.

The only response to crisis—the necessary response—is love.

We *must* fall in love, with the one Eros, with the one heart.

It's Love or Die.

3.13

EXAMPLES OF THE INTIMATE UNIVERSE

We saw that the intimacy equation applies to subatomic particles. It applies to couples, and it applies to friends. Let's do a few more applications.

What does it mean to know yourself? It means to be *intimate* with yourself, to have shared identity with all of your parts. That's a big deal. In other words, when I split off parts of myself, which are not part of my shared identity, then I'm not intimate with myself. **When I don't recognize parts of myself, when I can't feel them, and when some parts are dissociated from my crux of value and operating at cross-purposes with my central self—then I'm not intimate with myself.**

So, the same intimacy formula applies to subatomic particles, to cells, to a couple, and to the self.

Let's go bigger. Peter Senge, from MIT, wrote a popular book called *The Fifth Discipline*, which is a pretty good book about organizations, but his best book is called *Presence*. I recommend the opening chapter to everyone. He tells a story about being hired as a consultant for a car company, who had major overruns in their budget. And of course, no one could figure it out.

It was going to bring the company down, so they bring him in. After a long process of several years, they wind up not only eliminating the overruns but finishing their production schedule about a hundred days early, which was unheard of.

So, what happened? Like every car company, it was split between the people who made the fender and the people who did this part of engine, and that part of the engine, and the people who did the upholstery—all these different divisions of the company. Even though they were part of the same company, they were all sub-optimized and engaged in an implicit, unspoken rivalrous conflict governed by win/lose metrics, always fighting with each other, and never really collaborating. **There was no intimacy among the divisions because there was no shared identity between them in the context of otherness.**

Of course, Senge doesn't use this language, but he does describe the process, for the first time, of generating a shared identity in the context of relative otherness. **That's what *Homo amor* would look like in the business world.** He ends up cultivating a mutuality of recognition among the divisions— they can feel each other—as well as a mutuality of pathos, a deeper shared Field of Value, and a grander mutuality of purpose.

When that comes together, all of a sudden, everything changes quickly and radically.

INTIMACY AS THE BUILDING BLOCK FOR LIFE ITSELF

Next example: We've talked about cellular respiration—but that's just a word. In fact, respiration means this very gorgeous process that produces ATP, a phosphate, which is also itself a configuration of intimacy. A chemical is a compound, a relationship between atoms, a new configuration of intimacy. **A chemical reaction is how allurement takes place between atoms, or between compounds of atoms called molecules.**

Let's look at water, for example. Neither hydrogen nor oxygen are liquid at room temperature, but when they come together synergistically and a new configuration of intimacy emerges, they become liquid. In other words, **when you synergize, when there's allurement, you can create a new form of beauty that never existed before—now there's liquid water, the ground of life.**

Allurement doesn't stop at the human level. We're here because we're allured. When we come together and everyone bring their unique chemical structure of that Unique Self based on allurement, we create a new property. **That's the Unique Self Symphony, which throughout history has many times helped to create the more beautiful world that we know in our hearts is possible.**

This is structural to Reality itself. This is the way it works.

If we realize this truth, then we ground the story, then we tell the story, then we write the story. **We show the story to be true, that intimacy and Eros are part of Reality, that First Values and First Principles actually govern Reality, it's going to make the Darwinian revolution or even the Freudian revolution look like a joke.**

This changes the world.

We can show that there's no preordained system. No old, eternal values that we're trying to go back to. They're eternal *and* evolving values.

The eternal Tao is the evolving Tao.

These values are real. Intimacy and Eros are at the core, and they mean real things. They govern all systems of Reality.

THE LOVE STORIES INSIDE OF US

Let's just take a look at this video of what respiration actually looks like. This video was conceived by two leading scientists at Harvard, Alain Viel and Robert Lue.

VIDEO CLIP: "POWERING THE CELL, MITOCHONDRIA"

We see colorful, accurate animations of the dancing, complex, interconnected movements of the parts a cell, as they coalesce and come apart in constant, co-ordinated flux. It is both familiar and alien, a stunningly beautiful choreography set to epic classical music. It suggests the beautiful complexity and connection at the heart of every process in Reality.

Thirty-seven trillion of these are operating inside each of us right now. **We are infinities of allurement**—quite literally. These two scientists are trying to give us the most accurate representation of what is happening scientifically: configurations of intimacy and configurations of allurement at the cellular level.

After the death of Lynn Margulis, who was an incredibly important biologist, the person who picked up her work was James Shapiro, the leading geneticist today, who's at the University of Chicago. He talks about "natural genetic engineering." Along with an increasing number of leading scientific thinkers, his essential point is that **the neo-Darwinian synthesis, which expresses a kind of reductive materialistic world, is dead.**

This does not, however, bring us back to a pre-modern creator deity and intelligent design. It brings us to a world that self-actualizes based on its own inherent allurement and its own structures of intelligence that are everywhere. That's what we call the "LoveIntelligence" of Cosmos, which literally lives everywhere.

The Cosmos is animated by LoveIntelligence, LoveAllurement, and LoveBeauty.

Shapiro's work on the nature of Reality is actually a love story at its core. Here's the thing: **That love story lives inside each of us. We don't merely**

live in it—it lives in us. So, at this moment in the Anthropocene, we now are the authors of the story. This entire story at this moment depends on us.

That's what conscious evolution means. It doesn't mean that evolution was unconscious before; it evolved by chance, and now it happens by choice, which is how Barbara used to say it. No: Evolution was always intelligent and inherently conscious throughout the entire system. Conscious evolution means that now we're *awake* to this realization. We can now see the entire evolutionary story. We've realized that it's all literally inside of us. The love story is literally interior to us. **We're now the storytellers of the universe.**

Our stories are chapter and verse in the story of the universe—and this is an ontological truth—and we're writing the next chapter in the story.

INTIMACY ACROSS SPECIES

Let's take a look at a beautiful clip about the octopus, about water, about cosmocentric intimacy—and the evolution of love. We're in deep, tender meditation as we watch this. This is from the end of *My Octopus Teacher*, a documentary about Craig Foster, a diver who came to develop a deep relationship with a non-human being.

MOVIE CLIP: *MY OCTOPUS TEACHER*

We see mesmerizing images of undersea life and various colorful fish. Then we see Craig Foster diving, swimming, and interacting with the octopus. It's the end of the movie, and he's talking about the death of the non-human friend and teacher he had come to know over many years:

> *Craig Foster (voiceover)*: I was around for a good eighty percent of her life. Each moment is so precious because it's so short.

There was this one incredible day. A big shoal of dream fish. Fairly shallow water. Suddenly, she's... reaching up for the surface like that. Initially, I thought, "She's hunting the fish." Then I was like, "Hold on. When she hunts, she's strategic, and she's like... focused. This behavior doesn't feel predatory to me." It took a long time to actually process it.

But I couldn't help thinking, "She's *playing* with the fish." You see play often in social animals. Here's a highly antisocial animal playing with fish. It takes that animal to a different level.

She'd made me realize just how precious wild places are. You go into that water... and it's extremely liberating. All your worries and problems and life drama just dissolve. You slowly start to care about all the animals, even the tiniest little animals. You realize that everyone is very important. To sense how vulnerable these wild animals' lives are, and how vulnerable *all* our lives on this planet are.

My relationship with the sea forest and its creatures deepens week after month after year after year. You're in touch with this wild place, and it's speaking to you. Its language is visible. I fell in love with her, but also with that amazing wildness that she represented and... and how that changed me.

What she taught me was to feel that you're a part of this place, not a visitor. That's a huge difference.

He's expressing something very beautiful, but we can go a step further and realize that it's not just that we're "a part of this place"—the whole place also lives in me. It's not just, "I live *in* the intimate universe." **It's also essential to realize that the Intimate Universe lives in me.**

As we said earlier, when artificial intelligence makes rational decisions—bypassing all of the muons and all of the hadrons and all of the protons and all of the electrons and all of the atoms and all of the molecules and all of the macromolecules and all of the cells and all of the multicellular organisms and all of the organelles, bypassing the entire chain of evolution and splitting off a particular function of the neocortex separate from the music of Reality splitting the Eye of the Mind, from the Eye of the Heart and the Eye of Consciousness and the Eye of Value and the Eye of the Spirit—**that dissociation destroys the love story.**

That's why AI is an existential threat.

We can respond to this only when we get that it's a love story—when we get that the love story lives inside each of us...

- Reality is not merely a fact—it's a story.
- Reality is not an ordinary story—it's a love story.
- Reality is not an ordinary love story—it's an evolutionary, outrageous love story.

Most importantly, my personal love story is chapter and verse, literally, in the Universe: A Love Story.

There's so much magnificence in that.

CHAPTER 4

THE RADICAL PATH TO THE TRANSFORMATION OF SHAME

FROM THE FINITUDE OF SHAME TO THE CELEBRATION OF FINITUDE

4.1

A SONG OF THE SABBATH: LIVING THE DREAM

I want to introduce you to a 3000-year-old chant, "A Song of the Sabbath." In this context, Sabbath means to live the dream. **With so much outrageous pain everywhere, we can't work to fix the world, to heal the world, to liberate the world without getting bitter—unless we're willing to already *live the dream.***

Heidegger said we need to *change the mood of the world*. Just notice the mood we are in, and we can shift it. On the one hand, we're not turning away. You can step closer, you can step back, but you can never turn away. We're allowing ourselves to enter the depths of Reality. Even in this unimaginable time of existential and catastrophic risk, we're absolutely not turning away.

On the other hand, we're not becoming Doomers. **We're not losing ourselves in the collapse—rather, we're finding ourselves in it—not just with responsibility, but also with mad joy.**

There's a sense not just of urgency but *ecstatic urgency*.

In other words, we're living in the world that's already liberated, and we're also drawn towards that place—we are living the dream as we realize it.

We can also call that the Sabbath—an ancient technology for radical liberation. We talked about integrating interior technologies of the premodern, the modern, and the postmodern, and Sabbath is a powerful premodern technology. Do the math: If you live until seventy or eighty, and you spend one day out of every seven living the dream, that's many, many years spent living the dream. You're an advanced meditator on living the dream.

And remember, we're doing this **not as an individual practice, but as part of a democratized spirit**. This is not about the spiritual elite attaining special states. It's part of the fabric of culture—it's for absolutely everyone.

Rather than building a palace in space, we're building a palace in time— we're living the dream—that's Sabbath.

That's what this chant is about. In ancient Jerusalem, David wrote it as a love note to Reality, as a love note to himself, and as a love note to his son, Solomon.

CHANT: MIZMOR SHIR

Mizmor shir le'yom ha'shabbat

> [To sing a song of the Sabbath]

Tov lehodot L'adonai

> [It's good to sing with God.]

Le'hagid ba'boker chas-decha ve-emu-natcha ba-leylot

> [To speak of your love in the morning, to trust you through the night…
>
> To speak of your love in the morning, you trust me through the night…]

Through this song, **we can know that Reality is a love story filled with agony and ecstasy, with allurement and autonomy.** This is the evolution of intimacy, a love story, so therefore: *Speak of your love in the morning and trust you through the night.*

Imagine your Beloveds around the world, and know we can get through the hard times: *to speak of your love in the morning and to trust you through the night.*

Think of all the people in all of our circles who somehow got lost. We sing to them too.

How desperate we are to sing to her, to mom or dad or brother or sister, some Beloved, to be able to look at my brother, to look at my father who's passed, to look at my parents as they argued, and let them in on the dream.

4.2

SHAME IS MULTI-LAYERED AND INSIDIOUS: RETURNING TO EDEN THROUGH THE DOOR OF SHAME— FROM PRE-TRAGIC TO POST-TRAGIC

Let's first recall that Reality is one: one Eros, one love, one heart, one field. It's also many: diversity, distinction, individuation, uniqueness. *It has to be both, always.*

Reality is the creative advance of synergy and emergence, the creative advance of the new, of Eros, of new configurations of intimacy. Let's not forget that *every moment is new*. This very moment will never come again. **This moment is an infinite moment which will never happen again.**

This moment invites us inside. You know you can feel when a moment opens up. The moment opens and you can feel the Tao. You can feel the moment saying, "Open me, love me open, touch me there, not like that, open me."

Let's stay with this sense, a gentle opening of the moment, ever new, as we go deeper into the story.

EDEN AS AN ICONIC WESTERN LOVE STORY

Let's make a distinction between these three moments:

- The original time in the Garden of Eden.
- The exile from Eden.
- The return to Eden.

Let's keep this structure in mind as we go deep into the personal. We're going to look into shame. We're going to do some important exercises. It might be a rough ride down on a turbulent river, so let's proceed with care. It's scary—and exciting. And to find our way into that river, let's evoke the Universe: A Love Story.

We live in the intimate universe that lives in us: Reality, the Amorous Cosmos, the CosmoErotic Universe, evolution, the love story of the universe—all the different ways we can say it.

One of the foundational stories of Western culture is Eden. It is a love story, and sorry but it's heteronormative—you had a naked man and a naked woman. I didn't write the book, but that's what you had. There was a snake. The snake was kind of hot and tried to seduce Eve—**there was a lot of desire moving around**, but it didn't quite work out. They got thrown out of the Garden, and humanity started. That's a brief recapitulation of the story.

It's the big, iconic, original Western story. Now, here's the crazy thing in this love story: In Eden, the snake represents desire. Adam and Eve get exiled because of desire, and then the story of humanity is about trying to get back to Eden. When they're in Eden the first time, you think wow, there's no shame. They were in their nakedness, and shame never even occurred to them.

Then they're ejected from Eden and filled with shame.

This means that **to get back to Eden is to somehow transcend shame**—to "trance-end," end of the trance of shame.

SHAME ALWAYS BLOCKS EROS

The love story of the Universe is intimately connected with shame and our relationship to it. **It's wild that shame is not merely a psychological structure—it's a core structure of Reality**. Often when you hear "shame," you're like, "I'm out of here—I'm not doing that, that's hard." It's a big deal, shame. But you can't engage in the Love Story of the Universe without engaging shame, because **shame always blocks Eros**.

Now let's call Eden pre-tragic. Eden is pre-tragic sexuality, pre-tragic life. And let's call the exile from Eden—meaning our lives in all their complexity—the tragic. The return to Eden, though, is not always a regressive reversion to the pre-tragic. It can be a move *through* the tragic to the post-tragic. *The post-tragic and the pre-tragic are not the same place.*

SIMPLE, CRYSTAL-CLEAR MORAL CLARITY IN THE PRE-TRAGIC

Let's take a look at the pre-tragic, not in terms of sexuality or Eros, but in terms of viewing how the world generally works. He's in a different dimension of Reality now, but I had a little brother, David, who as I've mentioned before, was killed a bunch of years ago, in 2015, in a car accident. He was a completely lovely young man. He married my assistant, Miriam, and they had ten kids.

So David marries Miriam—and they didn't mention to me that they were going out, because they thought that I might have something to say about that. One day they told me they were getting engaged the next day. I said, "Fantastic," because there's really nothing else to say at that point. They were, they are, fantastic, beautiful people.

They took the world I grew up in, a highly Orthodox world, and they exponentialized it: They chose a very particular and intense form of belief. Any time something would happen in the world, any tragedy, he would have a verse to explain it.

He would say, "Oh, that's this verse or that's this text, and everything was clear, there was nothing out of place in the world, the world was crystal clear."

That's the pre-tragic, and I've got to tell you, it's a beautiful place to live in. You're so deep in certainty that you've removed the uncertainty. **There's no longer a mystery—there's a text to explain everything**.

Then you get ejected from that world, as I did, because you start saying, "This doesn't work for this reason and that reason."

In other words, you're seeing things a bit more clearly, and you're in the tragic mode. This is the deep awareness of the brokenness of the world, of the outrageous pain in all of its facets, as well as the very real possibility of existential risk.

At that point, it's very tempting to go back to the pre-tragic. I dearly miss the pre-tragic all the time. It's a beautiful place to live—it's actually quite rich, not just superficial. **There's a depth of text, and a depth of practice, and a depth of sexuality, and a depth of the sacred in that pre-tragic world**—it's a beautiful world.

There's a reason why sixty to seventy percent of the world still affiliates and aligns with traditional, largely pre-tragic religion. Many of us in other pockets of the world, who think we're going to heal the source code by avoiding engagement with traditional religion, are narcissistically self-absorbed.

We absolutely need to engage with the traditional, pre-tragic mode in a very deep and profound way, and we need to understand those texts and live them and breathe them.

But the post-tragic is asking: Can I face Reality and move beyond the doom, beyond the postmodern uncertainty, *and* reweave a New Story of Cosmos that integrates the orienting certainties and wisdom that comes to us from all domains—into a new story that absolutely holds the mystery at the same time?

Can you feel the difference? We must *return* to Eden. As Yeats writes,

> *When such as I cast out remorse,*
> *So great a sweetness fills my breast,*
> *We can dance, and we can sing.*
> *We are blessed by everything.*
> *And everything we look upon is blest.*

This is not the blessing of the pre-tragic. It's the blessedness of all things, of the amorous Cosmos on whose ground we stand to engage existential risk.

But to get to the post-tragic, we have to go through the door of shame. We can't engage the Universe: A Love Story, without in some genuine way going through the door of shame.

4.3

WE LIVE IN A PLANET
DRENCHED IN SHAME

B efore doing an exercise to relate to our shame, we're going to set things up. And once we've set it up, then we're going to go through three specific practice stages.

The planet drenched in shame is in some fundamental way a root cause for existential risk. I just want to point to a scene that I mentioned before in passing. In 2016, there was a presidential debate happening between Donald Trump and Hillary Clinton. An audio recording of Trump had surfaced, where he's talking to a particular figure from the Bush family, saying, "When you're famous, you can just grab them by the pussy—and they'll let you." It was an obnoxious recording, obviously, and it caused great scandal in America but in no way prevented him from being elected president, as we know.

All of the press is going after him, but then Trump's team in response assembles the four women who've made accusations against Bill Clinton, of various forms of harassment and sexuality—so those four women are sitting there. Then there's a series of internet posts talking about Hillary's ostensibly secret relationship with Huma Abedin, the woman who was her chief of staff. Abedin's husband, Anthony Weiner, had been sexting with teenagers, and he eventually lost his political office—he had an enormous political potential, and he's a very gifted man, but it didn't end well.

So all these various scenes are being piped into ninety million homes, and no one is really talking about what's happening: **a performance of shame at the very heart of culture, at the center of a Western culture, that will have a rippling, cascading effect on everything that's going to happen in Reality, going all the way back to Eden.**

Shame everywhere—a particular kind of sexual shame, a weaponizing of shame.

Much of the reaction may in some sense be appropriate. That's not the issue at play here—we're not here adjudicating Donald Trump or Bill Clinton. We're not trying to compare these stories. **We're noticing instead that at the very center of culture, you see this ejection from Eden and an utter confusion about the sexual:** a complete inability to find desire in its most potent and beautiful expressions, and various forms of transgressive sexuality disowned and split off, at the very center of this highly public event. In the extensive commentary that followed, none of this even remotely came up.

So shame is split off—and shame is always, in some sense, related to desire.

4.4

THE FOUR TANTRIC PRINCIPLES OF COSMOEROTIC HUMANISM

As we enter the field of shame, I first want to briefly introduce what we call the four guiding "tantric" principles of CosmoErotic Humanism. Of course, **tantra is an overused and often misapplied word, and it has virtually nothing to do with sexuality**. I have spent a good deal of my life on tantric texts from many different traditions—99.7 percent of them never once mention the sexual. Instead, these principles are about a set of stories of identity out of which also emerge certain implications for sexuality.

We are not doing this for our own transformation, although that may happen, that's a part of it—we are here to evolve the very source code of the conversation and the engagement with shame on the planet. That is what we are here to do.

So here are the tantric principles of CosmoErotic Humanism:

- Principle one: **Non-rejection**—nothing is off the table, nothing is rejected.
- Principle two: **Trace every experience back to its root**—you can get underneath the experience and find the source.

- Principle three: **Reality is a trickster, a joker**—not always evident, often elusive.
- Principle four: **She comes in threes**—there's always a trinity, and one and three always *look* the same, but they're not (e.g., the pre-tragic, tragic, and post-tragic; the original Eden, the fall, and the return).

We're not fully unpacking these now, just briefly naming them. They're crucial context for what's to come.

4.5

SHAME IS DIRECTLY RELATED TO OUR EARLY EXPERIENCE OF DESIRE & PLEASURE

Shame is often directly related to our experience of desire and the frustration of our desire. It's even in the original story of the West, the Eden story, represented in the snake. Shame often adheres to the sexual, not because the sexual comprises all of desire, but because the sexual is a potent expression of it. **The sexual models a greater, more fundamental Eros whose quality is desire—it doesn't exhaust Eros.** So you've got this quality of desire that is somehow frustrated. And in some fundamental way, the frustration of that quality is deeply related to the fundamental experience of shame itself.

Let's take an example I've previously used, before we get into the sexual expression, because while shame virtually always adheres to sex, it is not limited to sex.

Imagine that you're two years old. Your mother, who you love dearly, who is your entire world, has just bought a new apartment with perfectly white walls. She's in the kitchen, preparing your first dinner there. She left you in the living room, and her purse was there. As you look at this new space and at these big, beautiful, gorgeous, empty white walls, you feel your aliveness surging through you—you want to engage this white wall and create something beautiful.

So you go into your mother's purse and you find some lipstick. Oh my God, Mother loves me so much that she left me a paintbrush! Feel into the sensation of aliveness in this: You take the lipstick out, and start coloring that wall. It's so beautiful, all this bright red color!

Maybe there's more lipstick? Oh, look, she left you three because she knew that you needed to fill up the whole wall with red and pink. Now it's fantastic. This wall is so gorgeous.

And then you call out, "Mommy!"

Your entire heart is wide open.

And she walks to the door—and you know she's going to pick you up and love you and embrace you as she experiences your wild and beautiful aliveness. She's had a really hard day, and she walks into the colorful room, and all of a sudden your beautiful mommy looks at you, and she's furious. *Raawwwr!* Maybe she loses it and swears and calls you names, or storms off.

You were in ecstatic joy a moment ago. You've been rejected at the height of your aliveness. Shame is born. **At this time in your life, you cannot distinguish between your goodness and your aliveness. Nor should you be able to—because they are in fact inextricably bound.**

Your aliveness and your goodness have just been rejected by the universe because at that age the mother *is* the universe. That's why attachment theory works. The way your early caretakers—your mother, your father—attune to you is a major factor in determining the entire trajectory of your success or failure in life. This has been shown to be the case over decades of studies.

This only makes sense if the Universe is a Love Story.

If your mother loves you and holds you in a particular way, and you are attuned to Reality, then the Universe: A Love Story is incepted in your body early on. But if your early caretaker—whoever is playing that role—rejects your aliveness, and with it, implicitly, your goodness, then your life can go off the rails. **Your body tells you the universe is a love story, but then your parent tells you that your body is lying.**

So you begin to understand that you can't trust your body—this is why despotism of every kind tries to break the relationship of trust between a child and their parents, and between a person and their body.

STORIES OF SHAME: "THOMAS IN THE BATH" AND "DANIELLE KISSES ALL THE BOYS"

Before the first exercise, let's look at two other short examples. These are from actual people who Kristina and I have worked with. This first is from someone, let's call him Thomas, who remembers at age eleven or twelve the experience of taking a bath. He was immersed in the hot water and witnessed an emission from his penis. He believed this was the sperm he had read about. He could remember the feeling—it was new, he had never felt it before, and it was *undeniably good*. "A gift he had never before felt," he said. **He had never felt more alive or more at home in the world than at that moment. He was excited.**

So he jumped out of the bath and went straight to his parents' bedroom, dying to share with them the good news of his discovery. He was sure they would be equally excited—but **his words were received in stunned silence with no emotional cues. Instantly, he concluded it was not safe, nor would it ever be safe, to relay to his parents anything of his sexual nature.**

He did not recover this memory until he was in his late forties. Nevertheless, the lack of engagement by his parents was a crippling rupture. He was instantly cut off from what we're calling Eros. His conclusion: *I'm not good, I'm dangerous. My sexual aliveness will cause me to lose my place in the world*. And it had taken decades to re-access that moment of aliveness, of being fully at home in the world.

Example two: Danielle—and again, the name has been changed—remembers walking to school as a six-year-old, past a church with steep steps leading to double doors where her family never went. One day a group of older boys (strangers) stood at the top of the steps and asked her to come up and kiss each one of them. As she climbed the stairs, she remembers being aware of the sacred space. She bestowed each kiss as a sacrament, enacting a Holy Communion, the communion of holy kissing. The very next day, she kissed them again.

There was no teasing or roughhousing by the boys of any kind—quite the opposite. **All of them felt, without anyone speaking it, that something important—even sacred—was happening.** This continued for several days until someone reported it to her teacher.

Her teacher then took her to the coat closet and told her that she needed to find only one person, someone who *deserved* her kiss. "Good girls do not kiss many boys," her teacher said. "To kiss so many boys was to be a 'slut.'" Her teacher said that word with a kind of fascinated contempt that went straight into Danielle's body.

She was filled with shame. Danielle loved kissing *all* of the boys, so obviously she knew she was not a good girl. The seeds of shame were thus planted in fertile soil.

PRACTICE: TELLING THE STORY OF A MOMENT
OF "ORIGINAL SHAME"

You can do this exercise by writing in your journal, but it also works well if you have someone to share with. You can do it with a person you don't know at all, someone who is a fair witness. Or you can do it with somebody who's close to you. You might think it's best to do this with the person your closest with, which may be a good option, but you don't need to. The intuition that you may want to do this with your partner is totally fantastic. If you're in deep with them, if there's a deep trust between you two, and you've got a container together, go for it.

In your dyad, identify each other, say hi to each other with your eyes. Try and hold a genuine Silence of Presence.

If you decide this will work better by yourself, that's a completely welcome option—that's not being antisocial, it's not indicative of any DSM pathologies. You can absolutely do this by yourself with a journal—it works perfectly. But be sure to engage in the emotions, be honest, and stay with it—even if it gets difficult.

• • •

We are going to do this first step in two stages. Take a few moments, and silently sense into it. You can start writing if that helps. Try and find what I'm going to call a moment of "original shame," where you felt somehow that your aliveness wasn't received by Reality.

- This is not about blame.
- This is not about bad parents.
- This is not about trauma.
- This is not about, "Oh, I had such a difficult childhood..."

It's not aggressive like that—each one of our parents and our caretakers also had imperfect parents and caretakers, and so did their parents, and so on...

Shame is inter-generational—any shame we don't heal, we pass on to our children, or to others. The greatest gift of love that a parent can give to a child is to heal some dimension, however small, of their shame, because this dis-inhibits the generational cycle, the downward spiral over time. **And it's *never too late* to heal this.**

It's also not about whether or not you have children. When you heal a dimension of shame, whoever you are, something shifts in all of Reality.

But first we just have to notice it—that's our first step. You can write it out or sense into it silently. If you wish, you can share some stories, or some broad outlines with a partner. You might want to just take a few moments and just stay in silence until you find a time when your aliveness was rejected. Can you find and then feel the experience of the rejection of your aliveness? It may have to do with sexing—it may or may not have to do with the body.

Start with sensing, start with noticing. Take fifteen or twenty minutes, or longer if you need, to contact and feel this sense of original shame. And then write it all out or share it with your partner.

4.6

THE FOUR DOUBLE BINDS
OF SHAME

We're now going to go through a few more layers. And again, we're doing this not only for our individual healing; we're literally doing this for everyone, to heal an entire culture drenched in shame. We're identifying shame as a root cause of existential risk.

You're willing to step into the fire for your own sake, for my sake, for our sake, and for the sake of the whole thing—**be fully willing to do it for the sake of everyone, for the whole field of Reality**.

Every person has their own what I want to call invisible "shame plex" that we live inside of. We often don't even notice it ourselves, which is why the first step is just noticing. And everyone has a unique shame print which is at the very center of their shame plex.

THE ORIGINAL, DOUBLE BIND OF BROKENNESS: IF I LIVE, I DIE

What is shame at its core? **Shame is not the experience that I did something bad. It's the experience that I _am_ bad.** Our colleague Lori Galperin, one of the most brilliant clinicians of shame in the world, says that shame is the root of all evil:

- It's the experience that *I'm broken and can't be fixed*
- I didn't do *something* wrong, but I *am* wrong.

We can't begin to heal this unless we actually find it, unless we notice where and when it comes up.

We're going to go deeper now. We're going to get even more daring, further opening the space. Very gently...

Shame is not I did something wrong, but the sense that fundamentally I am wrong because my very aliveness, which is inseparable from my goodness, has been rejected.

If you experience shame, you experience a double bind. And to find the experience in your body, you have to know what a double bind is. Gregory Bateson talked about double binds when he shared a particular story about working with a schizophrenic young man.

(By the way, we're all on the spectrum here—there's no "those are the crazy people, and we've got it together." No, we're all faking it till we make it more effectively. There's a reason why R.D. Laing and his followers ran clinics where the clinicians and the clients all lived together. His point was that we're all in this together—we're all on a spectrum.)

So there's this beautiful kid, about twenty-four years old, he's got some serious schizophrenia, and is being treated by Bateson away from home. It's not a simple personality split—that's how we typically understand it—but a much deeper disorder that's clearly related to his parents. It takes Bateson weeks and weeks to finally stabilize him.

He finally feels okay, and his mother comes to visit. She walks in and says, "Oh my god, it's so great to see you!" At the very same moment, you can sense the energy from her body, and from her eyes, coldly push him away.

He immediately goes into a schizophrenic episode because he's caught in this double bind—in his body he feels:

> *I love you, I hate you.*
> *I totally care about you, I don't care about you at all.*
> *You're the most important thing to me in the world, I despise you.*
> *You're everything to me, you're a burden and in my way.*

There is intense somatic dissonance between what is felt in the body and what the world is presenting. Double binds often happen in those early (and late) experiences when shame is encoded in the body, often around desire and pleasure—but not always.

So this is the first double bind: a deep sense that we are wrong, a sense of our own brokenness, our fundamental lack of goodness.

• • •

In *Don't Look Up*, there's one character who clearly embodies shame—and as a viewer, you're ashamed just to look at him. He's the shameless incarnation of shame: Jason, President Orlean's son. The entire movie he talks about his mother as the president, and at the very end when they're in the room at BASH industries and the meteor is about to hit, Peter Isherwell gets up to leave. Then the President, Jason's mother, says, "Oh, yeah, I think I should excuse myself." Then people start realizing what's happening. Jason, her son, is locked there in his chair and the only thing he can say is, "She'll be back, she'll be back."

That's the exact phrase Winnicott uses when describing "transitional objects." When Mother leaves the room, and I can't feel her, I'm desperate to know she'll be back. Jason's eyes are glazed, and he looks back, but he never leaves his seat. Then President Orlean calls Randall and she says, "We've got a plane." Of course she has a plane. He declines her offer, and then says, "Good luck with Jason." Jason? **She didn't bring him with her on the plane because he has become representative of shame itself. Even his own mother is ashamed of him.**

ORIGINAL AND PERSONAL DOUBLE BINDS

At the depths of the original double bind there is a source of shame: *If I live, I die*. Try to feel that in your body.

If I live, I die. Can you feel that? I'm desperate for my aliveness but life means I die—that's the original ontological double bind. The shame of the animal. *If I live, I die*.

We're going to look to transform shame, but **shame is multi-layered and insidious**. Some shame you can heal. But you can't fully heal this original double bind.

In the original double bind, I experience myself as fundamentally broken or flawed because of early experiences, or because of the sense that *if I live I die*. The sexual revolution healed very little of this shame. Instead, it largely bypassed it. And then, as John Bradshaw has pointed out, the shame came back with a vengeance that was unimaginable. **You don't heal shame by getting naked**.

Now we're going to try and find our way into the heart of the whole thing. Try to stay in the body as much as you can, moving between the sexual and other experiences. It always plays out in the aliveness of the physical, in the shaming of desire. It's not only sexual desire. **As we are sexually, we are emotionally. That is the nature of your living presence— you can't split the two.**

There's a second set of double binds, which I'm going to call "personal" double binds. What happens here is a kind of recapitulation of the original double bind, *If I live, I die*. **A little later in life, we have a second set of double binds, personal double binds, where that rejection is recapitulated.**

The personal double bind of shame can take many forms, or be based on many different types of experience:

- It might be your experience of a first kiss, or a first kiss that didn't happen.

- It might be, "I went for it, and it didn't work."
- It might be, "Why didn't I go for it?"
- It might be, "He didn't choose me because I didn't attract him."
- It might be, "I used my attractiveness and gave myself to people I didn't want to."
- It could be, "The girl rejected me and I don't know why."
- It could be a particular contour of desire that seems to be bad—often we desire at night what we protest against during the day.
- Later in life, we may shame our partner's sexing.
- We may shame the contours of their desire.
- Or we may shame their lack of desire.
- We may shame their Yes, or we may shame their No.
- We shame their refusal to play in our sexual scripts, or we shame our own sexual scripts that we keep hidden from our partner.
- Or our partner plays in our sexual script, but they withhold something of themselves as a kind of slap of shame—and we feel it.
- This might be in my own sexing with myself, in my self-pleasuring, or in relationship with a partner—it doesn't matter whether it's with myself, a partner, or life itself.
- There may be a caress that I feel, but I know she or he is not really *in* the caress.
- Or I know I'm not in the caress.
- It might be an offhand, casual remark.

These are examples of personal double binds, where shame lives and is expressed.

CULTURAL DOUBLE BINDS

There's a third set of double binds: Cultural double binds, which like all double binds always refers back to the primal one: *If I live, I die.*

The way I love, the way I experience desire, is somehow wrong in the eyes of everyone I hold dear, and I desperately want their love. Yet if they knew the way I desired, they wouldn't actually love me. That can be the female voice or the male voice, but it's often coded more feminine. We'll call that the whore-Madonna double bind. I'm either the good girl, the Madonna, or I'm the bad girl, the whore.

Then on the masculine side, there's the predator-provider double bind. **As a good man, I'm a provider. But then what does that mean when I'm called a predator?** What do I do when I feel experiences of desire that well up in me and don't fit into the provider model? Desire itself is a cultural double bind.

A major *New York Times* editorial by Steven Marche from three ago criticized masculine desire for its *inherent* brutality—and no one objected. In the middle of #MeToo, at the center of culture, masculine desire was declared violent. Aspects of feminine desire were also split off. As Laura Kipnis asked, also in the *New York Times*, was there not even *one* woman in the #MeToo period who wanted to get fucked? Was there no feminine desire at all?

Obviously, sexual harassment is a total violation, and we stand completely against that, of course. But wasn't there any feminine desire at play?

So there's a split-off agency on the feminine side, and an inherent self-perception of being brutal on the masculine side. And of course, the masculine and feminine can live on both sides of the aisle. But this is generally what we mean by cultural double binds.

META DOUBLE BIND

Finally, let's go meta for a second and add these aspects of double bind:

- We're shamed for what we desire and what we want.
- We're shamed by the rejection of our desire.
- We're shamed for wanting what we can't have.
- We're shamed by our lack of desire for what we're supposed to want.

- We're shamed for our very desire in wanting.
- We're shamed by the rejection of our desire.
- We're shamed for desiring or wanting what we can't have.
- We're shamed by our lack of desire for what we do have—and we no longer trust our bodies to tell us the truth.

We're going to do our original exercise one more time, but first, let's see if we can unpack it one more level.

4.7

ENGAGING SHAME: BECOMING A SHAME DETECTIVE

How do you heal or begin to heal these layers of shame? The answer is that shame festers in the dark, so first, we notice it—we observe it, recognize it, and name it. Then in phase two, we begin to engage with the shame, being sensitive to the double binds: I look for my original double bind, then for my personal double binds, and then how any cultural double binds are playing me.

What I want to do is realize that I'm actually madly beautiful, and rediscover that aliveness is fundamentally good. I don't want to realize it intellectually or because I read it someplace—**I want to *feel in my body* the experience of the goodness of my aliveness**.

To do that, I have to tell the story of my shame.

I can tell it:

- By writing it on paper and reading it out loud to myself or to the community.
- With another person—I look at them and see them as part of the Universe: A Love Story.

So again, let's do our original shame practice. Remember: The partner who's listening, or your journal, is the amorous Cosmos, you are She, you're the Goddess. As you glance up, as you tell the story of your original double bind—*if I live, I die*—or a personal double bind, a recapitulation of it later in life, something distant or something close—you look into the loving eyes of your dyad partner, and find your goodness in their eyes. You could find it reflected back in your journal. You could imagine telling your story to a loving imaginal being. Or you could even look into a mirror.

The most important thing to remember here is that contact heals shame.

Contact heals shame. Eros is the experience of radical aliveness seeking ever deeper contact. So when I tell the story of my shame, and I can find myself in the face of my Beloved—who doesn't have to be my lifelong beloved, but the person sitting next to me as the Amorous Cosmos (there are no strangers in the intimate universe)—I experience healing.

I just look in their eyes, I feel into, and I see in their listening as I tell my story: *They're not recoiling. They're actually holding me with the loving eyes of She.* **Connection begins to loosen the grip of the shame. Again, contact heals shame.**

QUESTIONS THAT GUIDE US IN TRACING SHAME BACK TO THE SOURCE

You need to get a license in becoming a shame detective. You've got to look for shame—and shame always leaves hints and clues. There are breadcrumbs.

How do you get a sense in your shame plex of where the shame resides? What you have to do is use one of the tantric principles of CosmoErotic Humanism: Trace every experience back to source. Trace it back, and you're doing the work for the evolution of love, for the evolution of Eros. We're trying to evolve and loosen the fixity of shame, to begin to heal, and to create a way, a method, a path of healing a planet drenched in shame.

Follow the breadcrumbs, trace them back to their source to try and find: **Where did shame incept in your body?**

Here are some guiding questions that may help:

- What's the part of yourself that you hide?
- What part of yourself makes you extremely uncomfortable?
- Who's the relative that makes you really uncomfortable?
- Who do you not like to be around in your immediate family, like you just want to get the fuck out of there? You might not even show up for a key event of theirs just because you don't want to be there. It could be a brother, a sister, an uncle, a father, a child— our relationships with our children are far more complex than we might think.
- What parts of yourself do you hide, the part of yourself you hide from yourself and from others?
- Who triggers you most in your immediate circle? This doesn't necessarily mean there's something off about them, but they trigger you. Why do they trigger you?

Now think about vulnerability, how you share yourself.

- What information about yourself do you always leave out of a conversation? You've got all sorts of reasons for leaving it out, but trace everything back to source.
- What's the hidden shame?
- What secrets do you never share? (Even with those people you think you'd most want to share them with.)

You can start with distant experiences or use more recent experiences.

I'll give you another set of clues for your training as a shame detective:

- In what ways do you find yourself shaming others? How do you shame others, either publicly or (especially) privately? Do you take the moral high ground? Do you refuse to follow the thread of a conversation? Do you fail to give someone your full attention? Do you always subtly move the conversation back to where you want it to be?
- What makes you angry?
- How do you respond to feedback?
- How do you respond to critique?

We don't have to answer *all* of these questions, though notice which ones open up immediately and are easier to answer. Then notice which ones you tend to resist. We're trying to loosen the fixity, the ossification of shame. **Shame always hides in the shadows, so you have to trace shame back to its root, illuminate the corners.**

Just to give you another example, what if someone said to you, "Whenever I'm interacting with you, I always feel like I have to perform." Maybe that's because you always had to perform and took that in, and now you make everyone around you perform—and you don't even realize you're doing it. Because there's an early shame that the very aliveness of who you were was rejected unless you fulfilled very particular and very prescribed roles.

As another way into the shame plex, you can ask:

- What are the things you refuse to forgive?
- What are the ways you subtly shame your partner's fantasies?
- When do you refuse to laugh?
- What particular words trigger you?

Again, here are the three possible doors, and you can pick any one of them.

- Original shame—that was the first exercise but it's not like it's all done. **Remember, shame is multi-layered and insidious.** So you can go back and find other instances and facets of that early aliveness associated with your goodness, which was fundamentally rejected.

- Personal double binds concern the ways I like to love, the ways I like to desire, that have no place—I can't even share it with those close to me. I'm not allowed to say it out loud because everyone's face at the party goes sour. Personal double binds are a **recapitulation of the original double bind**, often from the teenage years or your twenties. They can also be more recent, involving the way you're living your life right now.

- Cultural double binds are the way **I fully experience my desire, which culture says no to**. For example, pornography is a cultural double bind. It's widely available, yet no one "signs their name" triumphantly on their porn. What do you do with the fact that you're watching pornography—bless that—but there's really no place to share it. You can't triumphantly proclaim it, and you're pouring so much energy into it. That's an example of a cultural double bind. Or the limited provider-predator standard for men. Or the whore-Madonna standard for women. The shaming of masculine desire, the shaming of feminine desire, at scale.

This practice is utterly essential. Take your time and tell the story of your shame. Unpack it all. Be a shame detective.

Through this process you can heal. You can realize that you're fully good, that you're beautiful, that you're gorgeous, that you're always held by Reality, and that your partner is the Universe: A Love Story. **But the main idea is to tell the hidden story because shame grows in the dark. Shame festers in the hidden world.**

Contact is Eros—contact begins to heal shame and begins to move something.

I don't expect you to go through all those clues that I offered in one session. This is something to work through over time, in many sessions, for a deep, gradual healing of shame.

MARC'S PERSONAL STORY: MADLY IN LOVE WITH THE TALMUD

To know yourself, to seduce yourself, you have to find your way into your own hidden shame plex. Let me share something about my own hidden shame plex. Here's a story. I'm a teenager, one of the three or four prodigies in Talmud at my academy, madly in love with the Talmud, like madly, insanely in love.

I just finished high school when I met a woman who was still in high school, a few years younger than I was. We fell madly in love with each other—deeply, profoundly.

According to the law under which I lived, there was no physical contact allowed. The extent of our contact was "teenage necking," as we call it in America. In other words, very limited—but it broke the law.

I was madly in love with the law, with the text of the law, with the brilliance of the writers of the text. The only way I could hold that sexual energy was through self-pleasuring, through masturbation, which itself was against the law.

Even back then, I knew I had the capacity—I could feel it—to reread the texts and change something. **I felt this enormous calling to heal something in the source code.**

At that point, I thought it was the source code of that religion, but how can I do it if I was always violating the aliveness of the very law and system? I was convinced that I was the only boy in that world who masturbated because clearly, no one else would do something like that, because it was such a violation of the law, and we were all such good boys.

So I broke up with that girl. She wrote me the most beautiful letter you can imagine. I received it six months later because it got lost in the mail. I was nineteen, and I cried on my bed for two hours, I couldn't stop crying, suffused with shame. Shame for the teenage necking, shame for breaking up with her, shame for the masturbation, and complete confusion over these sacred texts I loved so much—how could it possibly be that they spoke to me so deeply and yet I couldn't follow them at all?

I gave you that example just so you know that we all have experiences of shame we're working with.

No one escapes shame.

4.8

GIVING SHAME A VOICE: ENGAGING SHAME THROUGH THE PSYCHOLOGICAL INTERVIEW

The first step of this process is noticing how shame shows up in our lives and telling the story of the shame. Of course, we're touching the beginning of the process—an archetypal process to evolve the source code. We're standing as part of the Universe: A Love Story, to open the space for the healing and transformation of shame, by opening up the source code itself. In terms of each of our individual processes, it's not going to be a complete moment—it's an ongoing process.

What I want to do is walk through the entire process, which is a bit like a labyrinth.

- We did step one, which was **recognition**—we realized that we even had what we're calling a shame plex.
- Then we stepped into **engagement**—our first definition of shame was not "I did something bad," or "I did something wrong," but "I am wrong, and I can't be fixed."

- Then we went through **the double binds**. There's an original double bind—*If I live, I die.* My goodness and my aliveness are inseparable, but at some point early on my aliveness was rejected and that affected my sense of goodness. Then there are personal double binds from later in life and also more widespread cultural double binds.

The reason Lori Galperin said that *shame is multi-layered and insidious* was because we were trying for many years to bring different approaches to shame, and then Kristina (Kincaid) was in her own practice of applying various somatic approaches to shame. We've brought many of them together, working for years trying to find novel approaches to shame. **Every time we thought we'd cut off the head of shame, there it was again, like the Hydra—growing someplace else.**

"Shame is multi-layered and insidious." It's a beautiful sentence—simple, elegant, and worth remembering often as we go through this process.

In response, we created what's called the psychological interview, as well as the tantric interview.

Do you remember our first tantric principle of non-rejection, meaning nothing's off the table? In doing this process, we have to be very careful that we don't shame shame itself.

We sometimes need to give shame the microphone. Maybe shame has something to say that we actually weren't hearing completely. So we conduct what is called the "psychological interview," where **we give shame the microphone, and we allow shame to speak.**

It turns out that shame always has something to say. In other words, you think that you've got it all worked out and that shame is horrific and terrible. But then shame gets a little offended because it's interested in saying something—if anyone will actually listen.

Let me give you just a sense of what an interview looks like.

THE STORY OF VERA AND THE SHAME OF SELF-PLEASURING AND REJECTION

Here's a story from "Vera," whom we spoke to at great length. She wrote an incredible letter in which she talked about her early experience of self-pleasuring and her mother's shaming of that experience. So that looks like a classical telling of the story of the shame process. But afterwards, it didn't seem to be quite right, so we decided to give shame the microphone. We said, "Shame, okay, we really love our friend Vera here. We wonder, you can't be all that bad, and there's a principle of non-rejection, and we don't want to shame you. So, I guess we'll give you the microphone."

We did a full psychodramatic process with her. First her shame said, "Oh, thank you so much. Everyone's shaming me all the time—I'm totally rejected and no one ever lets me talk."

All of a sudden, there was new air in the room.

We said to shame, "Well, we didn't have much confidence that you would have anything to say, to be perfectly honest with you, but we wanted to at least go through the motions."

Through a series of questions, through the process, shame eventually said to us, "Listen carefully. If you actually knew the story, it would be different: Vera's mom always used to come late to pick her up from school. And sometimes, she would just forget and not pick her up at all, and Vera would be left standing there when all the other kids had gotten picked up—kid after kid after kid would get picked up, and **at least two or three times a month she'd be standing there by herself, waiting for her mother, who never came.** The unbearable truth—and I knew this because I was there—was that her mother didn't love her."

It is an unbearable truth.

Shame was protecting her from the unbearable truth that her mom didn't love her.

A STUDY ON LULLABIES FROM ALL OVER THE WORLD

As a side-note here, have you ever listened to a lullaby? In 2005, I did a three-month deep dive into lullabies from all over the world. I was shocked to discover that almost all lullabies, in every language in the world, are about horrific violence imposed by the mother on the baby... *Rock-a-bye, baby, on the tree top, when the wind blows, the cradle will rock*—and then what happens? The bough breaks, down comes the cradle, baby and all, splattered skull on the ground.

Every single language in the world has lullabies sung by mothers in these beautiful voices that are about ripping the baby apart and killing the baby. And I said, "This is weird. Why is nobody noticing this? It's creepy." I found a German version, and then a Norse version, and then I found some Chinese versions—they're all the same.

So what's this all about? **Here's the truth you're not allowed to speak. It's not easy being a mother.** All of your energy gets completely absorbed by that little demon. You had a big life, you're sexy, you're excited, you're alive, you had dreams—and now all you do is literally run around as a servant to this tyrannical being who demands every second of your time. It's been nine months since the birth, and your partner hasn't touched you since then. Everyone's too exhausted.

So lullabies are a chance to express this honest but brutal feeling. Then there's an entire sub-section of the population, people like President Orlean in *Don't Look Now*, who simply don't love their children. Simple and straight—and no one will say it out loud. Some lullabies may have this in them as well.

FIRST LEVEL OF ENGAGEMENT: SHAME AS A PROTECTIVE MECHANISM

Back to the example of Vera. What did shame say when we gave her the microphone? "I wanted to protect Vera because I knew that the unbearable pain of knowing her mother didn't love her would have ripped her to pieces—there's no possible way she could have held that. So I was a decoy. I focused her energy on sexual shame and her mother shaming her self-pleasuring. That got her completely absorbed, and she made it through her whole childhood and into adulthood without ever realizing that horrible truth."

Vera had tears in her eyes at this point, and we said to shame, thank you. Vera also turned to the shame that had the microphone and also expressed gratitude. Then we asked shame, "Do you love Vera?" And the shame immediately said, "**Oh my God, yes, I totally love Vera!**" So we asked shame, would you now be willing to let go? Would you be willing to let go of your grip on Vera now that she's an adult, now that she's powerful, now that she can hold it? She doesn't need that sexual shame anymore.

And shame said, "Okay, I'll try. It's a big habit—it's not easy, but I'll try."

So over time, the shame gradually let go. It's not that shame disappears entirely—that's not quite how it works. It's more like it moves from the foreground to the background—it no longer has the steering wheel.

That is the psychological interview of shame.

SECOND LEVEL OF ENGAGING SHAME: SHAME AS A FALSE FLAG

There's a couple of other things that shame might do when you give shame the microphone, aside from being protective by distracting attention away from what will destroy you. Let's add one more piece to it, something we noticed time and again.

First, **sexual shame in culture is often used to deflect from the actual meta-crisis of culture.** So you may notice that we're facing existential risk and catastrophic risk, and we're also in the middle of insane arguments about this or that detail of the culture war. So instead of addressing important but very difficult issues, there's this obsessive new puritanism that finds a bunch of people to crucify across the board. We focus on that crucifixion because it's easier to do—it distracts our attention from the root issues at the core of culture.

If you use that hermeneutic prism, you'll actually understand an enormous amount of why we're giving so much focus to sexual scandal, which, for example, is currently drowning out the enormous challenges of suffering brought about by existential risk. It's deployed intentionally on all sides of the aisle. **In our culture, in fact, when you give sexual shame the microphone, it often tells you it's being deployed as a decoy**.

But let's go back to the personal level. In our own lives, we often use sexual shame to avoid the deeper shame of not living our lives, of not living my Unique Self, of not giving my gift. So I actually focus my energy on the early shame—this is the third tantric move: Notice how Reality's a trickster. We just made a big shift; we just did a trickster move. We went to the principle of non-rejection.

First, we traced shame back to the root, and we just did a complete 360-degree trickster turn, and we can work it out over time. We don't have to work it out now, but just hear that voice where sexual shame uses a "false flag," a distraction, to allow me to avoid giving my gift, to let me avoid living my Unique Self.

So now there's a third level of engagement. The first level of engagement, telling the story of the shame, is very important. I would say, for example, that Brené Brown focuses all of her work on the first level, on telling the story of the shame. It's a great contribution, but it doesn't take you home. It's a very important step to tell the story of shame.

Then you go to the psychological interview—that's the second level of engagement, both parts that we just talked about, to see how shame might be being used as a protective mechanism or as a "false flag."

Let's now move to the next level.

4.9

THE TANTRIC INTERVIEW: TRANSMUTING SHAME AS A CONFESSION OF GREATNESS

Now we go to the next step, where we're trying to heal the source code of culture. We're trying to go the heart of the very source code of culture and begin to open up a new space. There's another type of interview at the next level of engagement, what we call the "tantric interview"—based on the principle of non-rejection.

We all know the phrase, "You should be ashamed of yourself"—it's a pretty universal phrase. It's often not useful, but **there is one inner voice you should be ashamed of, which can be quite beautiful: you should be ashamed when you hear yourself saying something like "I'm just not that kind of person"—very often this violates something of the full dignity, nobility, and honor of who you are.** You're *not* an ordinary peasant—you're royalty, you're a king, you're a queen.

Kings and queens hold themselves in a particular way. They don't need to hide.

So if you liberate the spark—to borrow a phrase from sixteenth-century Hebrew wisdom—from the husk, from the outer shell of the phrase, "You should be ashamed of yourself"—there's something very beautiful there: a hidden whisper, an invitation.

This is the third level of engagement with shame. We listen to the core of shame, and we can start to hear the voice: "I have a secret to tell you: You're a fucking king or queen, you're actually gorgeous, you're actually beautiful. **And because you're so gorgeous, because you're so beautiful, because you're so powerful, if you're doing that thing, or not doing this other thing—whatever your unique contribution may be—you should be ashamed of yourself."**

Not because you're bad but:

- Because you're gorgeous,
- Because you're royalty,
- Because you're wonderful,
- Because you're powerful,
- Because you're beautiful...

So we transmute the shame into greatness.

CONFESSING OUR GREATNESS

There's a dimension of shame that we have to recover, a dimension in contemporary culture in which shame got lost. That's why we cringe at Jason Orlean in *Don't Look Up*, when he's given the microphone by his mother, the President, to say a prayer to the nation—and he does a prayer in praise of stuff, material things and objects. *Has he no shame?* In other words, he's the inverse: He literally has no shame—but not because it's been liberated and transmuted and transformed.

So again, you first have to go through the first level and tell the story of your shame. To step out of your sexual shame, which is festering in the dark, you have to discover those places where you're using shame, or what shame is protecting you from.

But there are other voices of shame, which are about something else.

- They're not about sexual shame.
- They're not about the rejection of your aliveness.
- They're not about finitude, not about *if I live, I die.*
- They're actually an invitation to live.

There's a voice of shame that needs a place at the table. It's not toxic shame but a powerful, potent expression of my own nobility. If I know my own nobility, I can be skillfully, productively disappointed with myself.

That shame doesn't tell me I'm bad. It's the exact opposite of level-one shame. This shame says *you're fucking awesome, you're a king, you're a queen—so why aren't you going for it?*

This shame is a function of what we call "confessing your greatness." If you are genuinely willing to engage in a confession of greatness, it can feel like such a strange thing to do because **we're so trained in knee-jerk humility**, which in fact is anything but humble, which doesn't own our clear and inherent grandeur.

We have to own not our grandiosity but our grandeur.

The tantric interview is when I allow the expression of a different quality of shame.

Notice that these three levels of engagement identify three distinct qualities that are all called shame.

- The first level of shame is *If I live, I die*, and it goes through the four double binds.
- The second level of engagement is the psychological interview and the various ways we talked about it. We give shame the microphone.

- The third level comes through the tantric interview—we give shame the microphone, but it's a completely different story of your greatness, with a different phenomenological quality, a different quality of consciousness.

They're all called shame, and they all need to be engaged, in that order.

4.10

THE RADICAL PATH TO THE TRANSFORMATION OF SHAME: FROM THE SHAME OF FINITUDE TO THE CELEBRATION OF FINITUDE

So after doing all of this work, for many years, with myself and with others, I kept coming back to the stark realization that *shame is still there*. We've worked with it, we've healed it, we've moved it, and each one of these processes is insanely important in its own way, but in some essential way shame doesn't move.

Why? A few years ago, I realized, oh my god, there's **an entire other level of shame that's beneath that**. Here's where it gets wild and crazy and beautiful—this is where we can do the deep healing, this is where it all happens.

You can't skip any of the early stages—you have to go through them fully. Once we've done that, once you've again run into the realization that the shame is still there, after you've parsed the whole thing, you realize that there's an even deeper level of shame that I want to call the "shame of finitude." There's no bypass for where we're about to go.

THE SHAME OF FINITUDE: DISGUST AND POWERLESSNESS

Remember, we've got to get back to Eden. We were ejected from Eden, from the pre-tragic, and we've been meandering in the tragic. Now we want to get to the post-tragic, back to Eden—in a complex, non-naïve way—because that's what the love story is, integrating the greatest premodern, modern, and postmodern structures of consciousness. So how do we get back?

There's two cherubs with flaming swords at the entrance to Eden in the book of Genesis, who burn us when we try and get in. When I turn to addiction to cover up the hole, or to all sorts of excessive acting out—those are the angels with their flaming swords that burn us, on what Mark Vonnegut, Kurt's son, called in his book on addiction, the "Eden Express." It's dangerous trying to get back to Eden. There's a reason why there are two cherubs guarding the way with flaming swords.

The shame of finitude, at its core, evokes disgust. There's a dimension of our physicality that evokes disgust—what do we call it? Shit. **It's why we turn sexing and defecation into curse words**. "Wait," we might think, "I thought I was a king or queen, royalty evoking reverence, with authority, in control, virtually immortal. And now we're shitting, pissing, and fucking?" There's this level of disgust, this core shame of finitude, and it's related to a shame about our powerlessness. Some people only experience it if they develop some physical ailment, or all of a sudden if they realize that their ability to control Reality has been challenged.

When he got cancer, Steve Jobs wrote that for twenty years he'd actually experienced himself as omnipotent. All of a sudden, he was sick, and able to access virtually every advanced treatment in the world, and nothing worked. Then he realized, **"Oh, my God, look at the shame of being in a body. I'm Steve Jobs and there's nothing I can do."**

Other people experience the shame of powerlessness when it comes to money. A dear friend of mine experiences this when she has a hard time paying the rent. For some, when we're desperate about finances or health, we feel the shame of that desperation—and no one's even allowed to share it because we're so ashamed. So the shame of finitude is a shame of powerlessness, and it expresses itself in three ways.

SHAME OF OUR MORTALITY

The first is our experience of physical mortality, and we do everything we can to deny that. How much time do we like to spend with people who have a terminal diagnosis? Think about bodies rotting—because bodies do rot. We resist the experience of our mortality, which is the experience of our finitude, even if we may have a religious belief in an afterlife (which is no longer merely a religious belief—we now have an enormous amount of phenomenological information about the continuity of consciousness).

However, even if I have an deep knowing that death is but a night between two days, I still have the shame of my mortality—that *this* life is going to end, that I'm actually going to die, that this body's going to rot. There's a deep shame of mortality, related to the original double bind, *if I live I die.*

That shame of mortality is deeply connected to sexing because sexing, the little death of orgasm, is this involuntary movement of the body. In other words, we experience this abandonment of self, this loss of self, this disappearance of self.

- On the one hand, sexing is ecstatic.
- On the other hand, it's a deep reminder of death, which is why so often at the end of sexing, according to the proverbial archetypal image, the couple they roll over and go to sleep. Or they face the wall, and she smokes a cigarette.

In other words: we just faced something together, so there's a whisper of mortality. **In sexing, there's a deep reminder that we're invaded, that the body invades us—everything else is blotted out and in some small way we realize our end.**

SHAME OF MY ANIMALITY

The second way the shame of finitude expresses is in my animality. I don't mean my "animal nature"—that's way too polite a word. There's an essential animality to me—shitting, pissing, bleeding, and fucking—underneath this rational being, a separate self operating in human culture, *homo economicus* acting appropriately according to self-interest. Right underneath there's a sense of our animality, and we're shamed by it. Animals don't choose, but we humans are supposed to be captains of our fate and masters of our destiny.

There's this animality lurking underneath all of us, which is going its own way and doing its own thing. Our animality undermines and threatens the public self we're putting into the world—this enlightened self, this social self, this good citizen self, this good businessperson, or this good kindergarten teacher self, etc.

So there's an animality, the shame of finitude, and a shame over our very mortality, in our decaying bodies. And by the way, just try growing older. My friend Sally Kempton said to me a week ago, "I'm ashamed of my body." She's just about eighty years old. A beautiful woman, she did yoga her whole life—she's a beautiful being, and now she weighs about ninety pounds. One of the most brilliant spiritual teachers in the world. "I'm ashamed of my body," she says.

This is pretty universal, a common response. We all feel it to some degree.

SHAME OF MY NEEDS

In addition to the shame of finitude expressed in the shame of mortality and the shame of animality, there's an essential shame in our very experience of needing, the shame of needs. This shame also goes right back to the earliest part of my life, when I experienced myself as being humiliated in trying to getting my basic needs met.

When I can't pay the rent at the end of the month, it recapitulates the entire thread of shame, which leaks backward and forwards in time. Each experience of shame is like exploding time bombs throughout the timeline of our lives, which actually explode all the charges that were in the field.

So every time you feel shame, you feel all of the shame that explodes throughout the entire system, and you're completely stunned by why you're overwhelmed by that. Here I am this rational, good, competent being—all of a sudden I encounter shame, and boom, I'm taken out. Shame is intimately linked with needs.

We're humiliated in getting our basic needs met. On this topic, to my mind Martha Nussbaum is one of the best living philosophers in the United States today. She has a very important book called *The Language of Emotions*, which is related to the work of Kohut, Winnicott, Fairburn, and Bowlby, and other attachment theory literature that says: **if you don't heal the humiliation of getting your basic needs met, you can't be whole**.

That's the basic Western model on attachment, and that's how I would summarize all the literature in one sentence—it doesn't quite say it all, but that's the core. Here's where it gets a little crazy…

THE FUNDAMENTAL DOUBLE BIND: IT IS SHAMEFUL TO HAVE NEEDS

The Western model for needs comes from all the major spiritual traditions— Islam, Judaism, Christianity—which in various ways say that divinity is the opposite of need. That's the entire point of the entire Western canon that forms the Renaissance and beyond: **God or Infinity or Reality or Divinity has no needs**. Aquinas spends all of his time attempting to show this, and Maimonides spends the first fifty chapters of the *Guide for the Perplexed* to show that if any text seems to imply that Divinity has needs, you're misreading it. At the same time, the ultimate injunction of the Western canon is *imitatio dei,* be like God, whatever that means to you.

If you want to get out of that, then you can turn to the East. Let's go to India, let's go meditate. Let's read Abhinavagupta, a major source for Osho. Let's turn to the Buddha. What's the point of Buddhahood? **Buddhahood is the shift to True Self awareness, to move beyond needs and desires, which are obviously closely correlated, tightly linked.** God doesn't have needs and desires, nor does the Buddha. In the core Buddhist texts, the Buddha has transcended all needs and desires.

This is the fundamental double bind now:

- On the one hand, Western culture tells me that to be a whole human being, I have to overcome one of the three core aspects of the shame of finitude: the essential humiliation of getting my basic needs met.
- On the other hand, whether my model is Buddhahood or *imitatio dei*, both Eastern and Western visions of enlightenment say that needs are a violation of wholeness.

So need and desire, on both sides of the aisle, East and West, is a violation of wholeness—**it's a double bind at the very heart of culture.**

It took me many years to see this clearly. It's gorgeous, in its own terrible way. At the very heart of culture, to be whole, you have to overcome the humiliation of getting your basic needs met. And the model of need is such that only the anti-divine has needs, the ungodly has Eros, the un-Buddha has desires. **This double bind literally lives inside of us.**

I was contemplating and considering this for a long time, and it just kept burning in me until slowly—the Goddess is not always willing to immediately reveal what's happening—after more and more time passed I realized, oh my god, there's this double bind underneath all first three dimensions of shame—the shame of finitude, mortality, and animality. **This is the humiliation in trying to get my basic needs met as a child, which culture tells me I need to become whole—but I've got no model of wholeness, divinity, or Buddha, because they have nothing to do with needs.**

4.11

HEALING OUR ESSENTIAL NARRATIVE OF SHAME AND DESIRE: INFINITY DESIRES FINITUDE

The only way to heal this core shame of finitude—and this is where it gets so beautiful, so hopeful, and so wondrous—is that **we need to heal our essential *narrative* of shame and desire**. The story we tell of shame and desire is an old story that's found its way into Western literature and culture. But what if we realized something else?

What if we go to the root of it all and ask the question, why are we here? **We're here because infinity desired finitude.** We are here because infinity is not just the empty absolute, but what we call the "Infinite Intimate"— these two apparent opposites are joined at the hip. Working with this in terms of narratives of shame, it's crucial that we engage it in our bodies, that we take this Dharma into its own embodied space. It has to reach the cellular level of the body.

Infinity desires finitude, and at the core, we must realize there's no distinction between need and desire. The distinction between need and desire is a false distinction—when your consciousness is clear, you see that your needs and desires are the same. **You need what you desire, you desire what you need—not surface desire or need, but clarified.**

Infinity desires finitude, meaning
Infinity desires us, Infinity needs us.

In other words, the world exists because Infinity was hanging out and basically wanted to have lunch with somebody. Infinity desired intimacy, or said differently, Infinity actually *needed* intimacy. In other words, deep within the very heart of the Infinite are needs. **Infinity is not without the experience of need—there's an experience of need in the very heart of the Infinite. Infinity needs intimacy.**

What this means is that Infinity is so powerful that he/she/it/the field/the Real allows itself to need. Meaning: If I'm powerful enough, I can surrender power. To surrender power means I'm willing to love you so fucking much, that I need you, *The Universe: A Love Story.* I love you so infinitely much, so insanely much that I'm willing to need you ontologically—I actually need you. I'm desperate for you. **Infinite Divinity desires desperately to be incarnate in the manifest.**

How do you know? *Because here we are*

Infinity desires. Desire and need are ontologically identical at their core, so Infinity needs finitude. It's shocking that there's a string of need/desire in the Infinite, that Infinity yearns for and needs intimacy. This is the basis for what we call the manifest.

All of a sudden, I begin to understand that if I'm genuinely powerful, I can also experience myself as powerless. **And then the shame of finitude just begins to dissipate—because Infinite Power was willing to make itself powerless as an expression of ecstatic love.**

This is the beginning of the new narrative of need and desire that can start to heal shame.

RECLAIMING OUR VISION OF DESIRE

Now let's take it even further. So here I am—I'm a baby and desperately want to be held by my mother. I want to be held, I want to be kissed, I want to be caressed, and she never does it quite right, or it's not quite enough. I never experienced myself as *truly* being held, and so I never have the experience that my need is dignified. **I'm humiliated in trying to get my needs met.**

My needs are sexual, but by sexual I don't mean penetrative sex. I mean the need to be touched, to be held—we're using sexual in its broadest sense—to be nourished, to be kissed, to be touched, to feel that fundamental experience of the Universe: A Love Story alive in me. The embrace of my aliveness, the holding of me in that core way—where can I heal that? **I can heal that when I reclaim my vision of desire itself.**

SHAME AND SEXUALITY IN POPULAR CULTURE: *STAR WARS*

The narratives we have of desire in our culture recapitulate the original double bind. As an example of a cultural double bind around sexuality, let's look again to *Star Wars*, where Jedi Knights are not allowed to marry. They have no Eros—they're only in service to agape. When was the last time you saw Obi-Wan Kenobi making out with someone? In fact, in the first three movies, there's only one scene of a desirous person, Jabba the Hutt, whose desire is ugly and disgusting. In the scene, he forces Princess Leia to dress in a bikini, chains her up, and she's displayed in the most degraded possible way—he's not doing it with any beauty whatsoever.

In the second trilogy, there's one person who engages in the sexual, Anakin, who falls madly in love with a woman named Padme. He then goes to the wise Jedi Knight Yoda to talk about his experience of desire, and Yoda gives him some terrible advice. He doesn't dignify the desire, he doesn't recognize it, he doesn't honor it at all. Anakin knows his baby with Padme is a blessing—he knows that is true in his body. But Yoda says get rid of those attachments—they lead to the dark side. But it was actually Yoda's advice that led him directly into the arms of Palpatine, to the dark side.

You might think this is a hidden, esoteric story, or an old church story. No, this is from *Star Wars*, the major cultural enterprise of our era, and it's filled with the shame of finitude. The Jedi Knight essentially represents a fundamental split between Eros and agape. The shame of desire.

About a year and a half ago, I was at a sports bar with my son, because he wanted to see the Super Bowl. I hate football, but I love my son. So we're watching the game, and in this insurance company commercial there are multiple forms of love being named. "Okay, wow," I say. "This is good, I like football, we'll watch this." It goes through the different Greek words for love. There's Eros, the uncontrollable urge, and you see this hint of a sexual scene, but then there's the "great love," which is agape, represented by a young teenager washing the body of an old person. It's an utter split at the heart of culture, between Eros and agape, the shaming of desire in the middle of the fucking Super Bowl—right after two quite well-known and beautiful women just did a major half-time show in which they were essentially performing quite striking public orgasms on stage.

So you watch these public orgasms, which were quite beautiful, as public orgasms go, and then you see this commercial that promotes this huge split between Eros and agape. Eighty million people were watching this.

This is the double bind at the heart of culture. This is the narrative of shame and desire we have to heal.

HEALING OUR ESSENTIAL NARRATIVE OF SHAME AND DESIRE

Among our sexual narratives, we have "sex negative," which gets you in a lot of trouble these days, saying sex is dangerous, bad shit—though there is some truth to it. The "sex neutral" narrative says sex is kind of like having lunch—that one doesn't work either. You've got "sex positive," quite a bland word for the sexual, it's positive, which is great, but is certainly not complete. And there's "sex sacred," which is a beautiful way to create babies.

Those four narratives obviously don't exhaust our experience with sexual. We have no good story for one of the most powerful forces that exists in Reality—the only story we have for it is a shaming story. **At the very heart of culture—the Super Bowl, *Star Wars*—is the story of the shame of finitude**. We're humiliated in getting our basic needs and desires met, and yet desire itself is fundamentally shamed.

- We have to heal the narrative of desire.
- We have to heal Eros itself.
- We have to engage deeply with the phenomenology of Eros itself, in all of its beautiful forms.

Why are we here? We're here because desire is at the heart of Reality. So let's call that not sex sacred because it creates babies, nor sex negative, sex positive, or sex neutral—let's call it sex-erotic. **In other words, the desire that moves in me is the very same desire, the same Eros, that courses through all of Cosmos.**

That urge in me is not a violation of my goodness but the very *expression* of my goodness—and my aliveness and my goodness are inextricably one.

We can begin to talk about the goodness of our "Fuck," though it may be a strange word to use in this context. We can hold it lightly. The goodness of our Fuck doesn't argue for who we should fuck, or when—and it's not about polyamory or monogamy or celibacy. We each have to work out the ethics question—that's not our conversation here.

---

*The desire that moves in me is
the expression of my Goodness.*

Our conversation is about the essential goodness of desire itself. When desire moves in me, it's interpreted through the frame of my best read of Reality, the mediating prism for my experience. **So we have to realize that Reality is a love story, and it's not a chaste love story or a virginal love story—it's rooted in desire.**

In our society, a woman is prized because she hasn't had sex—for being a virgin. What an insane thing to do. This is the shaming at the heart of culture. So we need to evolve the very source code of desire because this shaming of desire is the root cause of breakdown.

Here's the big sentence: *Every single collapse of ethics is a collapse of Eros.*

My friend Daniel Schmachtenberger has said this is the only ethics he's ever found to be legitimate, the only real ontological basis for ethics. **All failures in ethics are not because you couldn't follow the rules, but because *there was a breakdown in Eros*, in my experience of my aliveness. If I'm filled with Eros, then I act out of the goodness of my Eros.** When there's a breakdown in my Eros, when I'm in emptiness, I fill that emptiness with every manner of addiction, with every manner of acting out.

All breakdowns in ethics result from prior failures of Eros. And these failures are never just personal—they're at the very heart of culture, which has collapsed Eros.

- What would it mean to recreate a culture of Eros?
- What would it mean to have a politics of Eros?
- What would it mean to fully reclaim the goodness of desire itself?

When I pleasure myself or turn to my Beloved in sexing, filled with my needs, and then my Beloved turns to me, whether that's me and my body or someone else, and says, "Your need is my allurement"—then shame is healed. My mother couldn't hold me, caress me, kiss me, care for me in the way I needed, so I experience a fundamental humiliation in the meeting of my basic needs. **When I'm filled with the urgency of my need in sexing,**

and I know that my need is your allurement, then the humiliation and the shame begin to release.

Later in life, it all opens up because this possibility is recreated in the most stunning way. I'm filled with those same urgent needs—emotional, physical, sexual, sensual. I look into the eyes of my Beloved, and they don't even need to say it: I can hear it in every cell in my body. I can hear Reality whispering, *your need is my allurement.*

When need becomes allurement, existential risk will disappear.

When need becomes Fuck, there'll be no more hungry people in the world.

What does that mean? For virtually all of the open societies in the Western world, the experience of *your need is my allurement* is egocentric. Me, my kids, my partner, a couple of friends, some extended family perhaps: That's my circle of care and intimacy. The love story stops at that boundary of allurement. The universe is not a love story, except for those thirteen people, and even then it's often governed by rivalrous conflict based on win/lose metrics, often hidden and papered over in a family context.

For closed societies, your need is my allurement is often a bit more ethnocentric. Places like China, Russia, much of Asia, Turkey, the Philippines, Brazil on a bad day or decade. In these societies, the need of the whole nation is prioritized.

But then imagine that your need is my allurement includes every human being on the planet. Then when global need becomes Fuck, there'll be no more hungry people. Then imagine that this includes the entire animal world, from a cosmocentric level of intimacy. At this level, we can start to heal the shame of animality. We've healed the shame of finitude in terms of needs, and then I get to animality and I realize animals don't have choice.

Let me ask you a question, what's the nature of choice?

We pretend we're choosing everything. We pretend that we're *homo economicus*, rational actors, separate selves in a materialist Cosmos making rational choices, and so we're super annoyed by sexuality that disrupts our public-facing social selves.

Animality tells us it's not true because animals are driven by instinct; they don't make choices. But what if instinct became a lower limit? What if I realized the reason we're here is not because we chose to be. We said, "She comes in threes," so maybe choice has three levels:

- Level one, no choice at all.
- Level two, I absolutely am able to choose.
- Level three means a type of refined choicelessness where I'm living through my *clarified* allurements—in fact, allurement guides my entire life.

That's the soft animal Mary Oliver was writing about: clarified allurement directing my life.

DESIRE IS A QUALITY OF ETERNITY

When I experience sexing not as sex negative, sex positive, sex neutral, or sex sacred, but rather as sex erotic—as the Eros of Cosmos moving through me—then sex is not death. **Sex is actually eternity itself**. This is why, in the final scene of *Don't Look Up*, right before the end of the world, Yule turns to Kate and says, "desire." In that moment of desire, the fear of death disappeared because desire itself is not against eternity.

Desire is a quality of eternity.

When we make love and scream the name of God, we've actually transcended death already, we're tasting the timeless time and the placeless place—it's fully available right here.

Suddenly, the shame of finitude dissipates before us:

- The lack of choice of the animal became the beauty of choicelessness.
- Instinct became allurement.

- The humiliation of basic needs becomes *your need is my allurement.*
- Death and sex merge to become eternity, screaming the name of God.

This is the way of the Universe: A Love Story.

You can't heal shame without retelling the very story in which we live, but this is not some fanciful retelling or conjecture. Of course we have to support every sentence we're saying, with footnotes if necessary, and we have to steel-man the opposition. We have responses for all the objections that people typically raise.

This is not New Age spirituality or fundamentalism—those will not take us home.

By healing shame, we can evolve the very source code itself. In fact, we may have no other option.

Can you imagine if we could tell the new story?

CHAPTER 5

THE LEADING EDGE OF HUMAN IDENTITY

5.1

THE BIRTH OF UNIQUE SELF

In this chapter we're talking about Unique Self, and to start, I'll share some backstory.

In 2001, I wrote a book called *Soul Prints*, which was well publicized and became a bestseller in the United States—though I was living in Israel at the time. PBS made a documentary special about it. There was even an auction for it among all the big publishers. Simon & Schuster bought it, and they thought I should spend six months touring the book in America. I had a strong sense that a tour was not what I should be doing.

At that time, my focus was on changing the fabric of Israeli culture, and that was what I was going to spend my life doing. I was doing a TV show in Israel that was like Israel's Oprah show, which became the highest-rated show of that genre in the country. So I was busy and refused to go to America and tour *Soul Prints*. Needless to say, Simon and Schuster got quite angry at me.

Then this book got to a well-known American philosopher named Ken Wilber, who said it was "sweet"—and on some level he was right—but that this thing about uniqueness is ridiculous. He thought I didn't understand enlightenment: "Any uniqueness is separate self," he said, "so you must transcend and enter True Self, beyond all uniqueness." Basically, the very warm and sympathetic look in his eyes was such that said, "If only Marc actually had some realization, he'd get it; so instead I've got to find him on his own level, talking about how nice and sweet *Soul Prints* is."

This is a common idea in spiritual circles: "Uniqueness is a property of separateness, and you've got to get beyond your story." You've got to rest in the groundless bliss of cosmic consciousness and *Be Here Now*—then you will ultimately, automatically respond to Reality in the best way.

I knew that wasn't the case, or at least wasn't the whole story, but I couldn't quite explain it the right way. Over the next few years, I went to Oxford and wrote a 1,500-page work called *Radical Kabbalah*. I sent it to Ken, who read it in three nights, marked it all up, and wrote me ecstatic emails all through it.

Ken's marked-up version of the manuscript was circulated around Boulder, and a young man named Zak Stein read it—that's how we met.

The basic argument, grounded in 1,500 years of lineage teachings, is that who you are is actually something called Unique Self—which is not the same as separate self at all, and even goes beyond True Self realization— and only the experience of this enlightened quality, which is available to every human being, can give a person the experience of being at home in the universe.

All of the therapy, which is important, and all of the processing, which is important, and all of the pharmacology, which is sometimes important, won't actually give the person the core experience of being welcome in the universe, of being the hero of their own life.

Everything depends one way or the other on responding to that question: Are you welcome?

Do you know that you're welcome in the universe?

In some sense, you might say that The Universe: A Love Story that we've talked about is the first piece of the New Story of Value.

The second piece of the New Story—and they go together, they're completely integrated—**is the story of identity, or what we might call the Dharma of Unique Self.**

Let's look at these now.

5.2

THE SELF-ORGANIZING UNIVERSE: COMPLICATED VS. COMPLEX SYSTEMS (EROS, INTIMACY & ALLUREMENT)

When we talk about existential risk, what are we really saying? Let's go through several steps, six in total.

One, we clearly have a culture of death—represented by the Death Star from *Star Wars*.

Two, the task is monumental, daunting—as the rebels, we have a seeming inability to respond to the entire culture of death. It's too massive and overpowering.

Three, our only possibility is a direct hit: something that can change the source code of the whole system, that can change everything.

Four, we understand that the direct hit is a **New Story of Value**.

Five, a new *global* Story of Value is the only direct hit possible because only this can respond to the global challenge of existential risk, according to our formula:

- Global challenge requires a global solution.
- Global solution requires global coordination.
- Global coordination requires global coherence.
- Global coherence requires global resonance.
- Global resonance requires global intimacy.

Six, this is why we're saying it's a global intimacy disorder at the source, and that global intimacy can only emerge out of a shared story that we live in. The core of that shared story is The Universe: A Love Story, the Eros story we've been telling this week, and the story of Unique Self identity.

But now let me say it differently, from another angle. Let's weave the strands together. Here's a kind of subtle—but exciting—idea. Once we get it, it changes everything. Here it is: **The world itself is a complex system**. Remember the distinction we made between a complicated and a complex system? The difference between the Brazilian rainforest and a Ferrari. The complicated Ferrari is fragile, doesn't take care of its own waste, etc. The complex system is anti-fragile, regenerates itself, and takes care of its own waste. There's an integral relationship, like a cell, in which all the parts breathe together. What organizes a complex system is an interesting question.

The world is exponentially complex. In other words, the world of matter, the physiosphere, and the world of life, the biosphere, are not complicated systems—they're complex systems.

Underneath the cellular level, there are about twelve layers of depth in the subatomic world. If you look at videos of an E. coli bacteria, for example, it's so gorgeous, so beautiful. It is the simplest bacteria. **So how does this entire system not go complicated—why is it complex?**

One of my favorite human beings in the world is Alan Turing, who cracked the Nazi codes during World War II. He's this young British gentleman, brilliant beyond imagination, and his genius was turned to cryptography. After the war, he worked at Bell Labs. He died tragically in 1954 because the

British arrested him for being gay and soliciting sex. They pumped him full of horrific chemicals in order to "fix" him, and he apparently committed suicide not too long afterwards—it's not clear.

In 1946 or 1947, Turing was in contact with Claude Shannon, who was developing information theory, and Turing wrote this amazing essay called "Morphogenesis." If you read that essay, you have to be prepared for bliss. It's quite hard to read—bliss is not cheap! But that essay changed the world.

It took about thirty years for people to even begin to get what he was saying, but Turing is describing the way **exponentially dazzlingly complex systems self-organize** through simple first rules and first principles. If you have a simple first rule and first principle, and you exponentially repeat it, again and again and again, it will generate a certain result. It's beautiful, so elegant and clear.

So I'm looking at an E. coli video, and realize that there's exteriors and interiors all the way up and all the way down in Reality. And if there are exterior First Values and First Principles, there must be interior First Values and First Principles. Remember: If we want to change Reality, we can't superimpose change from the top-down; we actually have to go into the source code itself.

That's where we started talking about evolving the source code, meaning that we must articulate the intrinsic First Principles and First Values of Reality.

5.3

FIRST PRINCIPLES AND FIRST VALUES AS A STRUCTURE OF REALITY—ANSWERING THE BIG THREE QUESTIONS

It is very important to discuss how we can even talk about value because much of society today assumes there's no such thing as value, that there are no intrinsic first values.

Let's bracket that question for now. For now, let's just say that there are simple First Principles and First Values in the interior of Reality, and **those First Principles and First Values are encoded in a *Story* of Value**. No one really likes to watch documentaries. Between a documentary and great drama movie, which one do you enjoy watching more? With a documentary, you want to get educated. That's great, but we love stories more.

We think in stories. God loves stories.

So not only do you need First Principles and First Values, but you need a way for them to become part of the structure of Reality—and that happens through story. In fact, and counterintuitively to much of culture these days, **story itself is *not* a human creation. Story is a First Principle and First**

Value of Reality. Stories began way before humanity was on the scene. Stories mean something, and there are stories all the way up and all the way down, at every level of Reality.

So we realize that stories are needed to change Reality. When we're looking at this exponentialized, complicated world system, which is generating existential risk, how do we change it? Xi and Putin suggest that a totalitarian closed society is the only way. It's got to be a command-and-control top-down system. Xi says there's no other way to run China, and he's actually quite a thoughtful man.

There's absolutely an alternative to closed societies, but open societies quickly fall apart if there's no set of simple First Principles and First Values that cohere it together.

Let's look at the problem more deeply.

The current dominant cultural script of postmodernism says that First Values and First Principles are impossible, as truth is "relative." We're also going to address that soon. But for now, let's just say that you can actually find and identify basic, authentic First Values and First Principles within the structure of Reality itself—which are themselves the plotlines of the story of Reality.

This is where it gets crazy and beautiful. **Those First Principles and First Values are answers to three simple questions.** It's simple, but it's a second simplicity, not first simplicity—it's the simplicity that comes after you've experienced, moved through, and accepted complexity.

The three questions are: where, who, and what? These structural questions or phrases live in every language. They are structures of Reality.

> **WHERE?** Where do I live? Where am I? That's what we call in our language, *The Universe: A Love Story.*

> **WHO?** We look in the mirror and ask, who am I? It's what we call our narrative of identity.

WHAT? What is this? What's there to do? It's dependent on a deeper set of questions: What do I desire? What do I want? What do I need? Only from clarified desire can we know what we should do.

In fact, everyone lives inside those three questions, and everyone is operating with an implied set of answers to those questions, which form the hidden script of our lives. Those scripts are almost never self-authored. They're generally unconscious, sloppy, plagiarized, inaccurate, badly written, filled with inaccuracy. Yet, they dominate culture. They are the hidden contours of our mind, and it's hard to fight an enemy who has playgrounds in your mind.

So in order to play, we've got to make the subject an object; we have to objectify the hidden assumptions and scripts in our mind that we can't see. We all have to answer these questions, and we'll do that both implicitly and explicitly. For now, we're focused on critiquing the current narratives of culture.

To answer them, we can't declare an answer, as we've said already. The answer has to be intuitive and true. We've got to be able to give an answer that will survive not the peer-review process of some hijacked society of academic professionals, where many peer-reviewed journals are funded by external sources with their own agendas.

Rather, it has to survive the peer-review process of culture itself.

In other words, you have to support these values by addressing and steel-manning all objections—you can't make them strawmen. Often in spiritual teachings, you set up objections as strawmen and you easily kill the strawmen. However, whenever I think of something new, I try to steel-man the objections by calling three or four credible people who can tell me why I might be wrong about the new idea. *You need those people in your life.*

· · ·

So we're going to try and respond to Where, Who, and What.

We've already found a response to the Where question: The Universe: A Love Story. So now we've got to talk about Who and What.

Let's frame it this way: In order to turn the complicated system that governs planet Earth into a complex system, we need all parts to be intimate with each other. How does this happen? They have to live together in a conscious, shared story.

In the world of matter and the world of life, the physiosphere and the biosphere, the conscious shared story is just being there—intimacy is automatic. There's a shared Story of Value between subatomic particles as they come together to become atoms because there's intimacy—there's no disorder. Let's check again with the intimacy equation:

- There's shared identity as atoms.
- There's a context of otherness, as distinct subatomic particles.
- There's mutuality of recognition in their relation.
- There's mutuality of pathos—they can feel each other.
- There's mutuality in a shared field of information or value.
- There's mutuality of purpose when they become more structurally complex as atoms—and eventually molecules, and beyond.

So there's clear intimacy at the atomic level, but at the collective human level, we have an intimacy disorder.

What humanity needs to do—which is the clear but implicit movement of Cosmos, Infinity desiring a new dimension of itself in finitude—is awaken to conscious evolution. But conscious evolution doesn't mean, as it used to, that evolution was materialist and just happening by itself, and now suddenly we're choosing the direction.

No, evolution was always conscious, in its own inherent way. But we've now come to this point in Reality in which we're actually awakening to the entire evolutionary story. **We realize that Reality lives in us—as it always**

has—and we need to consciously articulate a shared Story of Value rooted in First Principles and First Values that will allure us to each other.

We can only heal Reality if we fall in love with all of its dimensions. The evolution of intimacy is the continual extension of the boundary of who and what we're willing to fall in love with, and in a complex system, there's a lot more allurement among all the parts.

So what generates allurement? *Value.*

The experience of value generates allurement, while the violation of value generates outrage.

For example, we're currently in the middle of the Covid pandemic. All of the liberal communities in the United States are clearly, for lots of good reasons, in support of (sometimes mandatory) vaccinations. Overall, there's been huge disruptions to society, much horror and fear of death. But then a police officer named Derek Chauvin put his knee on the neck of a guy named George Floyd, and his knee stayed there for nine fucking minutes. It's all being recorded, Floyd's calling for his mother, saying he can't breathe. And then that video goes around the world, and everyone bursts out of their houses. Fuck Covid! Fuck the fear of death! **There's this huge explosion of beautiful, sacred outrage, which fueled Black Lives Matter in the United States.** It's a complex organization, requiring a nuanced conversation—but the impulse is clearly sacred.

Why did this mass protest happen during a pandemic? Because we saw intrinsic value being violated.

Whatever our postmodern position may or may not have been, regardless of our views on whether value fundamentally exists or not, for so many people it was a clear violation of value. We were allured by this, so we rose up in an explosion of outrage. Of course, without expressing clear and explicit First Principles and First Values, this type of protest can't fully develop into what it needs to be to transform society. That's not our point here, but rather more basically: *Value allures us.*

When there's no value, we're not allured.

Value is Eros, and Eros is value; there's actually no difference between those words, there's no split between the two. We can even combine them into ErosValue.

Eros is the experience of radical aliveness seeking, desiring—because desire is incepted in the very core of Cosmos—ever deeper contact and ever greater wholeness. That's what Eros says. **Eros is already in relationship with the other, and in that relationship, in that seeking and desiring of contact, is the value of Cosmos.**

Desire *is* value.

Separate parts becoming larger wholes through contact is a core value of Reality. So when we say God is Fuck, what we mean is: God equals Reality, Fuck equals Eros. **Reality is Eros, which really means Reality has value.** "God is Fuck" is a much more fun way to say it, but you get the idea. It's another way to say that Reality is Eros, which means that Reality is Value.

THE STORY OF REALITY IS THE EVOLUTION TOWARDS GREATER UNIQUENESS

With that as our context, we can begin to answer and approach the question: Why? The answer is that Eros is the structure of the story of the universe. Remember:

- The universe is not merely a fact, but a story.
- It's not an ordinary story, but a love story.
- It's not an ordinary love story, but an Evolutionary, Outrageous Love Story.
- Stories have plotlines, and if Reality is a story, it has a plotline.

We're just sketching the contours here—these sentences could be paragraphs, even whole volumes.

The plotlines of Reality are the First Values and First Principles of Reality. It's so gorgeous. That's what Turing was reaching for in the exterior world. The plotline of Reality is made up of its First Principles and First Values.

What is Reality reaching for? How do you find plotlines of Reality? We need to just look at what's happening. I've mentioned this before, but I remember talking with Ervin László, and I said, "Reality is a plotline." He wrote a brilliant book on systems theory in 1972. So in response he said, as a great systems theorist would, that "Yes, Reality is moving from simplicity to complexity."

Okay, but how does that make you feel? "I need more complexity in my life"—just feel that in your body. More complexity. Don't only think about it. You've got to feel it. Does that feel like something you want?

Let's go a little deeper: What is complexity? Complexity means more interconnectivity. Reality is moving to more interconnectivity. That's on the exterior, while the interior of interconnectivity is intimacy—more and more intimacy. Okay, now we're getting somewhere.

To have more and more interconnectivity and more and more complexity, something else is happening:

- More and more creativity.
- More and more care.
- More and more uniqueness.

That's one of the major plotlines of Reality, without which Reality is inexplicable. Reality is moving to more and more uniqueness. **You can actually tell the story of Reality as the evolution of uniqueness.** In that sense, Unique Self is quite properly the explosive climax of the love story. It is not an aberration, nor is it a contrived category.

Reality moving towards more uniqueness is a description of the most evolved, most stunning expression of the inherent plotline of The Amorous Cosmos, of The Universe: A Love Story.

So what happened in the esoteric lineages? What happened to Hebrew mysticism? To Buddhism? To Kashmir Shaivism? They got something wrong in the plotline. They got a lot of things right, clearly, but they got something wrong, for lots of cultural, socio-economic, historical reasons, which we're not going to get into at the moment.

5.4

THE FIVE SELVES & UNIQUE SELF THEORY: BIRTHING THE NEW HUMAN

Intimacy means more and more shared identity in the context of relative otherness, as well as mutuality of recognition, mutuality of pathos, mutuality of value, and mutuality of purpose. So to be more intimate with myself means having a wider and wider identity within myself. **Unique Self is an expression of the intimacy formula because it's a wider and wider shared identity with myself that also honors the various parts.**

What the great interior sciences realized was that if you say "I'm a separate self"—this is how virtually all of Reality in Western consciousness describes themselves—you will experience suffering. That's the common answer to the question of who? This is the simple first-principle answer given by society to the question of *who am I?*: I am is a separate self. That's who I am.

Actually, according to modern Western culture, to not know that you are a separate self is to be somewhat insane. It's in the DSM. To not know you're a separate self is psychiatrically considered an expression of pathology.

SEPARATION IS AN OPTICAL DELUSION OF CONSCIOUSNESS

The interior sciences have known for a long time that this wasn't enough, and the interior sciences are matched by the exterior sciences. The notion of being essentially a separate self, Einstein writes, is an "optical delusion of consciousness." In fact, the interior sciences understood that we have to awaken from the slumber of experiencing ourselves as separate. **If I'm only a separate self, I experience myself essentially as a puzzle piece looking for the whole puzzle.** Then you try and cover up the weirdness, fill in those little weird holes, and then you desperately look for the puzzle, for your wholeness.

The only thing is that, in our postmodern culture of materialism, everyone claims there's no puzzle. And if you challenge that and claim that there is intrinsic value, that there is a larger puzzle, you are diagnosably mentally ill according to the DSM. That's an intense response for asking the simple question of who you are in terms of First Values and First Principles.

Being a separate self is crazy-making. I'm a puzzle piece, looking for the puzzle. But apparently there's no puzzle. How does that make me feel? I can't find the puzzle—no greater meaning and value—and they tell me there's no puzzle there at all, so I can't understand why I have this inconsolable yearning for a larger puzzle. I must be fucking crazy! The Western experience of separate selfhood creates insanity and pathology, which we then treat with medication. It's a vicious circle.

Thankfully, the interior sciences come along and, in lots of different versions, say that I'm not merely a separate self. My truer being is that **I'm inseparable from the field of awareness**.

That's absolutely true and a great first step—I am inseparable from the field of consciousness. Any separation there is just an illusion. There's lots of jokes about it—the Zen monk who orders a hot dog, saying, "Make me one with everything." We get it. There's a whole literature and a whole set of technologies and practices, from many different lineages, that allow us to access that realization.

It's insanely important to do this work, and it's actually the beginning of true sanity. **If I had to say what enlightenment was in three words, I would say "enlightenment is sanity"—and sanity is knowing who I am.**

Sanity is the movement from separate self to True Self.

TRUE SELF IS AN INCOMPLETE REALIZATION

Eventually, if you're lucky, you get a realization of True Self. This is the opposite of separate self: True Self is not a single puzzle piece, but the whole puzzle. The issue is this: When you look at the puzzle, you see that there are clear lines between all of the pieces. See those lines? Your teacher says they're just an illusion. There's only the whole puzzle: Oneness. Unity. If you think there's lines separating the pieces, just keep sitting on your cushion, keep meditating, and you'll see right through all that.

But the teaching of True Self can become just as crazy-making as the separate-self delusion of consciousness. Separate self is crazy-making because I'm a puzzle piece looking for a puzzle, but **True Self says the *only* Reality is the Absolute, the whole puzzle.**

A friend I do frequent dialogues with ran the most significant American expression of True Self wisdom for many years. He called his organization the Impersonal Enlightenment Fellowship, where the point was that separate self is locked in personality. Accordingly, he argued, we must get beyond the personal and into the impersonal field of awareness. Most of the major teachers in Europe and the United States today still teach some version of this. Those were my early conversations in the Integral world as well, which had basically adopted a Buddhist position. It's what's generally taught in enlightenment teachings all over the world: You have to move beyond the personal, beyond the story, and identify with the impersonal, the field of awareness. That's who you really are, they say.

The only problem with that is, those lines between the puzzle pieces are not just an illusion—I can actually feel them, and it's completely crazy-making to tell me they're only illusory expressions of separate self.

CONSCIOUSNESS PLUS DESIRE

Then you begin to come alive and realize that beyond True Self, there's a higher individuation. She comes in threes. We're not separate self, and we're not just True Self, not just the field of awareness. Neither of those are entirely true. True Self is not the field of awareness, and it's not the field of consciousness. **True Self is the field of consciousness *plus* desire. It's the field of *allured* interconnectivity.**

It's the field of intimacy, and all intimacies are expressed as unique nodes interfacing on the system. So I'm not merely True Self or awareness. I'm a *unique expression* of the field of True Self—and the field of True Self is the field of Eros.

We can say that consciousness is just another word for Eros—and it's the field of ErosValue. Buddhistic metaphysics that say everything's relative completely misunderstand True Self. True Self is the Field of Eros and value, and awareness (of awareness) is an expression of both Eros and value. I'm a unique configuration of ErosValue.

This is a truth you must experience in your body.

How does it feel to be one with awareness? It's not bad. You can sink deeply into it, and it's beautiful. But that's not what you're really sinking into. **When you actually sink into real True Self meditation, you're filled with Eros, you're filled with aliveness.**

You're not just filled with awareness—you're filled with a sense of the Ground of Being *and* the Eros of Being.

It fills you up, and it fills you up *uniquely*.

There's a seamless coat of the universe, which is True Self. However, **while that coat of the universe is seamless, it's not featureless. Its unique, distinct features are me and you and everyone else.**

UNIQUE SELF: THE FINITUDE DESIRED BY INFINITY

My Unique Self is not my separate self. It's the unique configuration of Eros, intimacy, and desire that incarnates and individuates in me, as me, and through me—that never was, is, or will be ever again, other than through me. God (or Reality) has an experience of shocking self-recognition when looking in and through my eyes. *There I am!*

This is the finitude desired by Infinity.

There's a set of mystical texts, which you can find in Sanskrit and Aramaic—as far as I know, they haven't been translated yet—that understand all of Reality as divine *sha'shua*, **God making love to Herself/Himself, in order to have more God-ness.**

That more God-ness is *you.*

So She/He/It, the Infinity of Intimacy, the Infinite Intimate, literally desires *you.* **That's what it means to be welcome in the universe.** It's quite a profound and shocking idea.

Let's look at it from another perspective. When you go into your mind, into the inner space, what do you think about most of the time—just between us? Is it World Peace? A Deep Silence? Pure Eternal Awareness? Let's just cut the bullshit, what do you think about most of the time, for real? *You think about yourself*—just be honest. That's what most people are thinking about, most of the time.

Now, is this because we're all flaming narcissists? No. Enlightenment teaching will tell us that we're thinking about ourselves all the time because we're stuck on separate-self identity. That's not it—and this view is actually destructive.

You're not thinking about yourself all the time because you're a narcissist, and it's not because you're egoically stuck in separation. *It's because you're eavesdropping on the divine conversation that's always thinking about you.* It actually brings tears to my eyes, just to even feel it.

You're eavesdropping on the divine conversation that's about you all the time.

It's shocking, and this realization changes the way we see everything.

I'm not thinking about myself because I'm on the savanna, and only if I think about myself all the time will I survive. Even this evolutionary perspective misunderstands survival. Evolutionary psychology clearly has some important insights, but the hidden cognitive distortions are shocking. They reduce all of the incredibly important human dimensions and say they're just drives based only on survival. But what does survival actually mean? Why do I even *want* to survive?

I want to live, survival is life, and I want my unique life to perpetuate itself. That's Unique Self. It's not a reductive, evo-psych, materialist, separate-self understanding. No—there's a *telos*, an inherent drive to perpetuate my unique life, in all of its vibrant dimensions.

So I'm thinking about myself all the time because I want to *fulfill* life, because the current of the life force inside of me—uniquely individuated in me, as me, and through me—understands that *I am the self-recognition of eternity itself.* So I think about myself all the time because I'm eavesdropping on a conversation of Infinity. **Finitude has the capacity to eavesdrop on Infinity—and all of a sudden, I realize I'm *always already* welcome in the universe.**

It's insanely destructive to teach that the reason I'm thinking about myself all the time is because I'm trapped in a narcissistic loop that I can't get out of—**this is essentially like saying everyone's broken and can never be fixed. As we know from the last chapter, that's a recipe for shame.**

You see how it all begins to fit together?

Shame means I'm broken and can't be fixed. Teaching that any experience of my uniquely individuated self can only be an expression of separation before I've realized enlightenment is the ultimate shaming proposition. It's actually quite brutal.

YOUR UNIQUE GIFT IS NEEDED BY ALL-THAT-IS

Infinity desires finitude, and finitude eavesdrops on that desire—and that desire is unique. It's not a meta-desire. Infinity desires every single individual person in their radical, irreducible uniqueness. In other words, Infinity desires your exact unique expression, so Infinity is giving you an answer, implicit in the very structure of the Cosmos, to the question of who you are.

Let's put it all together. Who are you?

- You're an irreducibly unique expression of LoveIntelligence—The Universe: A Love Story.
- You're an irreducibly unique expression of LoveDesire—Infinity desiring finitude.
- You're an irreducibly unique expression of LoveBeauty.
- You're an irreducibly unique expression of the LoveIntelligence and the LoveDesire and the LoveBeauty that is the initiating and animating Eros and value of All-That-Is, that lives in you, as you, and through you, that never was, is, or will be ever again, other than through you.
- Not only do you have a unique perspective, but a unique quality of intimacy.

These aspects all come together to foster your unique gift that is absolutely needed by All-That-Is, and which can be provided only by you. **Giving your**

unique gift—which cannot be identified by any guru or any teacher—is the inherent categorical imperative of your life. To live your Unique Self is to give your unique gift, which addresses a unique need in Reality.

Because Infinity needs, because Reality desires, your gift addresses a unique need in your unique circle of intimacy and influence. And your unique circle of intimacy and influence is not at all coincidental—it's webbed together by the allurement of the entire Cosmos itself, which birthed you in this time.

You think you're such a powerful separate self? Well, who decided where you should be born? Who decided which structure of society you should be born into? Who desired what DNA code structure you should have? You? I don't think so.

You and I are being lived by a vast, interconnected web of allurements.

I have a unique gift to give to my unique circle of intimacy and influence, which can be given only by myself. When I realize the truth of that, I locate my Unique Self in the context of the allured, webbed evolution of intimacy that lives in me, as me, and through me. **I'm not just Unique Self, but I awaken more intimately to the entire evolutionary process as conscious evolution—I'm Evolutionary Unique Self.**

I realize that I'm made up of atoms of music, and I begin to play my instrument in the Symphony of Unique Selves. I begin to experience myself not merely as *Homo sapiens* but as *Homo amor*.

Homo amor is The Universe: A Love Story in person, which is an answer to the question of *Who*.

Now, you might rightly ask: How are we going to explain that to everyone? Well, how did we explain democracy to everyone? A thousand years ago, modern democracy did not exist as a structure of Cosmos. It's a far more complex idea to explain in terms of governance. Yet, every eight-year-old in the Western world has some sense of democracy today, and we all feel the violation of value when we hear about how democracy is increasingly being undermined by the categorization, surveillance, and control perpetrated by the TechnoFeudal order, by the tech plex.

- We have to communicate this notion of Unique Self as a source code notion, together with Eros, together with *Homo amor.*
- We have to communicate it in every language, at every level of complexity.
- We have to communicate it academically as Unique Self Theory.
- We have to communicate it in popular writing.
- We have to communicate it in movies.
- We have to communicate it in alternative forms of expression— imagine a rock opera on *Homo amor.*

We need all of it because that's how you shift culture. We must create a culture of Eros, an ecology of Eros, the core of which is Unique Self and Unique Self Symphony.

It's all one story.

5.5

THE PERSONAL BEYOND THE IMPERSONAL: LOVE AS THE UNIQUE SELF EXPRESSION OF YOUR INFINITE PERSONHOOD

———————————

Before we go to an exercise, let's look at the personal more deeply together. We commonly think there's the personal and the impersonal—and that's it. But above the impersonal, you actually have the personal again. In other words, **Unique Self is the infinite *personhood* of Cosmos—quite literally, not metaphorically or mythopoetically— signing its name as you.** It's infinitely personal.

That's why it's another corrupting mistake—one as bad as the one we talked about before when we think about ourselves as narcissists, as separate—to describe Divinity only as the Infinity of Power.

Divinity is not just the Infinity of Power but the Infinity of Intimacy. Divinity is intimate personhood. But intimate personhood doesn't mean some dude in the sky hanging out pulling the strings.

Divinity is way more personal than even you and me—and we're part of that personhood.

There's a quality of Cosmos which is not just objective third-person. It's also not just the first-person living in me. **There's an infinite second-person relationality to Cosmos, to Divinity, which is why we fall in love. You fall in love with someone when you see their Unique Self.**

Falling in love can be called Unique Self perception.

When you watch Robert Redford in the movie *The Natural*, he's this incredibly talented baseball player who gets shot before he starts his first season, and then he comes back at age thirty-seven. I won't tell you the whole story, but in the last scene when he goes up to bat, he probably shouldn't because they're afraid his system will collapse if he swings again.

But he just has to do it.

You see him there, and you hear the music—he's got the bat, and you just fall madly in love with him. You can't help it because he's totally living his Unique Self.

If you want to create true Eros in any kind of couple—friendship, marriage, business partnership—you actually have to live your Unique Self. **If you're not in your Unique Self, you don't have the capacity to fall in love.**

- As separate self, you're desperately covering over the emptiness and therefore parasitizing off of everyone around you, and ultimately just moving the pieces around.
- As True Self, you lose all sense of unique distinction, and there's no context whatsoever for relationship.
- Only as Unique Self can you fall in love as part of the field of consciousness, of awareness, *and* as your particular expression of the Divine.

So love is a Unique Self perception of what? Of your infinite personhood, of the personal beyond the impersonal. It's re-telling your personal story as *the Universe: A Love Story*

• • •

Here's an exercise so we can practice this. You can do this with a partner or by writing in a journal. I want to throw a sentence at you. In order to get this notion of being Unique Self, what I have to do is be able to re-understand my life and move my self-understanding from being a victim to a player. We've talked a lot about the difference between victim and player—it's a very important distinction. Another way to put it is that **I've got to move from a sense of living a traumatic life to living a mythic life**.

The way to do that is to sense into this phrase: **Mythologize, don't pathologize**.[7]

Generally, we sit around and look at our lives as victims: Our lives *happened* to us. We read a popular book called *The Drama of the Gifted Child*, by Alice Miller, which explains how you are a victim of your childhood, and how all the misattunements work. Then you work out all the terrible victimization in your life—which is often true, by the way. Attunement in childhood is quite hard, raising children is hard, mistakes are made all the time. Life is hard—and gorgeous.

But then later in life, we keep going over that story, using it to explain how I became this person. "I'm so broken in these quiet ways that I don't admit to everyone. If people really knew who I was, what I was thinking about, they'd pathologize me." All those voices live inside me, which means I end up self-pathologizing.

The way to shift this is to mythologize instead—to realize that I actually live in The Universe: A Love Story, and that allurement guides my life. We can realize that I was born in the right place, at the right time, to the right people.

My life is a great and wondrous myth.

---

[7] For more information on this process, refer to the series of oral sense-making essays from the 2019 Eros Mystery School, *Mythologize, Don't Pathologize: Living Your Sacred Autobiography—Your Story is Chapter and Verse in the Universe: A Love Story* (World Philosophy and Religion, 2024).

Let's say, for example, I was born as Princess Leia, in Utrecht, to these particular, imperfect parents, in a small home that was actually a castle in disguise. The difficult, imperfect parents were the first of many heroic trials of my life. But the Universe rejoiced at my birth, because Princess Leia was born. The Universe understood that in order to emerge as the great princess that I am, I needed to undergo trials, like every prince and every princess does.

So I begin to **mythologize my life**, experiencing my life for what it is—a great mythic life—in order to emerge as the prince or princess, the king or queen, that I actually am.

I mythologize—I don't pathologize.

I realize that I'm already—and have always been—living a mythic life. This completely changes my self experience, and this is an accurate understanding of my life: I'm living a mythic life.

CONTEMPLATION EXERCISE: WRITE YOUR SACRED AUTOBIOGRAPHY

First, spend ten or fifteen minutes narrating or writing out either the basic thread of your life story—or even better, a particular piece of your life story—which up until now you might have understood as a story of victimization, which created pathology in you, and that has been a disaster.

Next, move from victim to player, transform that fate into destiny, turn that pathology into mythology. Not in the sense of false imagination, not mythology in the sense of make-believe— but mythology in the sense of the great myth of Reality, meaning the great story of my life and your life. Take ten or fifteen minutes to speak or write that out.

*Take a particular incident that you have up to now understood as a victim incident, as a pathological incident. Transform from a victim into a player, and turn that narrative into a mythological story. In other words, **mythologize, don't pathologize**.*

Take your time to outline the contours of your story. Get the main shape and arc and themes.

Use the examples and prompts given above to fully inhabit your story, and see it from a "God's-eye" perspective.

Fill in the details as necessary—this may take many days or weeks.

Fully honor this process as an important step in your journey, in order that you can be an Outrageous Lover for the sake of the whole.

Mythologize, don't pathologize.

5.6

SIX CORE UNIQUE SELF NEEDS

Let's do a quick history lesson here. There once was this dude named Abraham Maslow, who spent his final days at Esalen. He's writing in the 1940s. His major work is being done in the middle of World War II, during the Holocaust.

Maslow famously came up with what he called the "hierarchy of needs." So all of a sudden, when we hear the word "need" remember that Infinity desires and needs finitude; and we remember that *at the higher levels of consciousness, needs and desires are one.*

At a lower level of consciousness, they're separate—these are my needs, and those are my desires. But that's actually a product of an unclarified consciousness, pointing only to superficial needs and superficial desires. **When my consciousness clarifies, my needs and my desires become fully aligned.** So Maslow's whole self-actualization hierarchy—where he talks about the need for survival, then safety, then belonging, then self-esteem, and then self-actualization, that famous pyramid—addresses only the separate self. **The entire Maslow Pyramid is about separate self.**

That's because Maslow himself experienced the world as separate self. It was only in the last couple of years of his life, when he was at Esalen, that he got a sense of True Self, as he writes in his diary. He makes this distinction at the end of his life between his hierarchy, which he calls "deficiency needs," and another set of needs he calls "self-transcendence needs." For him, however, as for many spiritual types, self-transcendence means to transcend your separate self into the one—which is true but partial.

What would it look like to talk about **Eros needs**?

I want to tell you something painfully beautiful and shocking. A story about a British officer who goes into Bergen-Belsen, the concentration camp, and sees men and women who are barely alive. You may have seen the pictures of these survivors, who are emaciated, barely there, and they're trying to nurse them back to health. Then someone from the Red Cross opens this huge case of lipstick. The officers weren't sure why. He opens the case and somehow the lipstick gets out, and all of the women who are survivors are putting on the lipstick. You suddenly realize what Maslow got wrong.

Maslow says you always first take care of the basic level of the hierarchy—survival, safety. But these people wanted lipstick immediately, before any of that had been figured out. He describes emaciated women with no breasts, barely a body—you can hardly recognize a feminine form. Then he describes seeing women who didn't live to see the next day, seeing dead women in the water wearing lipstick. He describes the enormous beauty of those days, claiming what genius it was from the Red Cross to send lipstick. There's fundamental need there.

TO BE INTENDED, CHOSEN, RECOGNIZED, ADORED, DESIRED, AND NEEDED

As we conclude this section on Unique Self, **let's review the six core Unique Self needs**. These are not separate-self needs. This is why Maslow's hierarchy, as important as it is, doesn't take you home. After separate self, I have to move to True Self, but I cannot stay there. I have to move to Unique Self, and then to Evolutionary Unique Self. Then I want to be playing my instrument with others in the Unique Self Symphony.

We're going to go through the six Eros needs of Unique Self. They barely need explanation, but there could also be a full book written on each one.

All six of these needs are fully accounted for in the New Story. If we actually realize the Amorous Cosmos—we realize that the answer to the question *Where are we?* is that we live in The Universe: A Love Story.

The next big question: *Who are we? Who am I?* I'm an irreducibly unique expression of the LoveIntelligence and LoveBeauty and LoveDesire of All-That-Is, that lives in me, as me, and through me.

Finally: *What is there for me to do?* As Evolutionary Unique Self, I realize the Deepest Heart's Desire of Reality in me, as me, and through me, by giving my unique gifts that address unique needs in my unique circle of intimacy and influence. **All of a sudden, we move from a top-down, closed society to an open, bottom-up, self-organizing structure of Unique Self Symphonies. In this way we can engender, through simple First Values and First Principles, a planetary awakening in love.**

In this vision, in this New Story, all six of these needs cannot be met by someone else. You cannot export these needs. You cannot say, "When I meet that person, they're going to fulfill them all." That's a disaster. They are needs that can only be met by Reality itself. They are structural.

Here are the needs:

- One, there's a need to be **intended**. We want somebody to remember that it's our birthday, for example.
- Two, there's a need to be **chosen**. Remember grade school, playing soccer, when everyone lines up—the best player is chosen first, and then second person's chosen, and the third. There's a deep need to be the chosen one. That's not pathological—it's a beautiful and fundamental need.
- Three, there's a need to be **recognized**. To be seen. To be heard. To be felt. To be met.

- Four, there's a need not just to be loved, but to be **adored**. So much so that I'm going to make up new words to describe our love every time it reaches a new depth.
- Five, there's a need to be **desired**. We all need to be wanted, to be the object of desire.
- Six, we all need to be **needed**. We must feel like we are honored for what we offer, that our gifts are given in service of the whole. We all need to feel needed, to feel necessary.

We often pathologize some or all six of these needs, so they're off limits to many, unknown or simply inaccessible.

Next, to the extent that we do recognize and honor them, what do we often do? We outsource them. We make them dependent on that person, that guy, that woman, that friend.

- If they desire me in that way, if they choose me, need me, I'm okay. If they don't, I'm definitely not okay.
- If they intend me, recognize me, adore me—I'm okay. Otherwise not at all.

That's actually a fundamental mistake.

In fact, I'm always already intended, desired, adored, chosen, recognized, and needed by *all* of Reality. Reality is thinking of me—finitude can eavesdrop on the conversation of Infinity. I am born of the intentional allurement of Cosmos, through a process that has never stopped, which has brought together an entire set of unique propositions that manifested an irreducibly unique expression emergent from the field called me.

I didn't choose where or when to be born—I was intended. So just feel that in your body, don't think about it in your mind. I was intended by Reality, chosen by Reality. I'm the one. In this sense, *Dune* got it right. I'm literally chosen by Reality to play my instrument in the Unique Self Symphony, and that instrument changes the entire Symphony.

I'm recognized, as in the intimacy equation—there's mutuality of recognition. The Intimate Universe recognizes me, and the Universe doesn't just love me, the universe adores me. The universe sends me scents and sounds. Do you know that there are 100,000 unique DNA markers in your body? That DNA has 100,000 unique dimensions inside of you? The interior of your body is filled with explosions of irreducible uniqueness: **thirty-seven trillion cells being breathed in Eros every second.** Reality is Fucking me open, Fucking you open, uniquely, every second. Not to realize that is to be asleep. You're literally being adored!

Reality desires me, because Reality is itself the movement of desire. I don't outsource my desire to one person who likes the curve of my hip. That's pathological.

Finally, I'm needed; my unique gift is needed by All-That-Is.

All of these needs are always already met by the Infinite Intimate, by Reality itself.

CHAPTER 6

TOWARDS A NEW UNIVERSAL GRAMMAR OF EVOLVING VALUE

6.1

BLESSING OF THE FATHER: CALLING US TO RECLAIM THE FIRST PRINCIPLE OF VALUE

We've been invoking the mother in Janie Orlean, the President in *Don't Look Up*, and her son Jason, who is traumatized by the mother. At the end of the movie, she gets on a plane and simply forgets about her son. The mother is an expression of the intimate universe, an expression of being welcome. If there's no intimate universe, then I'm not welcome.

I'm not welcome, there's no mother.

This is why Camus starts his book *The Stranger* with the line, "Mother died today, or was it yesterday?" Because it doesn't matter. In other words, for Camus, as for so many of the existentialists, there's no Intimate Universe, nothing of ultimate value. And if there's no value, you can write things like "Mother died today, or was it yesterday?" And Janie Orlean can get on a plane without her son, leaving him behind. "Oh, where's Jason?"

Of course, mothers are gorgeous. What mothers do is unimaginable. And— this is a big *and*, a shocking *and*—the inherent goodness of the mother needs to be trained and exercised, honored, and valued—not misunderstood as a mere survival mechanism. Inherent goodness is not natural goodness. Inherent goodness needs to be exercised, but most importantly, goodness itself needs to be recognized as a value.

There's two ways not to recognize goodness. One way is to say goodness lives only in my ethnocentric context, only for my people, or that there's no redemption outside my church. Because evil is what happens when we default to the lowest common denominator of the human being who hasn't realized their true identity, or Unique Self.

We are inherently good, and it's very clear that the structure of Cosmos is transformation. That's the Evolutionary story—Reality is a series of transformations, and we participate in that transformation. So goodness, like the other values, is both inherent *and* it needs to be trained and developed.

Why is Reality structured that way?

Don't ask me. Anyone who tells you they know why is lying. But that is the structure of Reality—a series of transformations in which we participate and cannot avoid. Either you transform or you don't. **When we don't transform, we don't become neutral. We become a beast. When we don't transform we're confronted with the unbearable intimacy of existential risk.**

On this crowded planet, if we don't have a system of First Principles and First Values, when we don't become angels, we become demons and beasts. We're seeing that today, quite literally.

We've been talking about the mother. We've invoked the invitation of the mother which welcomes us.

Let's now go to the father and write an invocation or blessing of the father. We all want the blessing of the father. Can everyone feel that in reading that sentence? **We all want the blessing of the father.** We first look for the blessing of the father from the biological father. The biological father is not some chance coincidence—the Intimate Universe allured each of us to this particular place, so you can't dismiss the biological father. There's real work to be done with the father.

But the blessing of the father is not dependent on our dads—the blessing of the father is the blessing of the father writ large.

Let's invoke the blessing of the father with this beautiful duet performance between a father and a son.

SONG: "FALL ON ME," ANDREA BOCELLI AND MATTEO BOCELLI[8]

I thought sooner or later, the lights up above
Will come down in circles and guide me to love
But I don't know what's right for me, I cannot see straight
I've been here too long, and I don't want to wait for it
Fly like a cannonball, straight to my soul
Tear me to pieces and make me feel whole
I'm willing to fight for it and carry this weight
But with every step, I keep questioning what is true

Fall on me
Ascoltami
Fall on me
Abbracciami
Fall on me
Finché vorrai

I close my eyes, and I'm seeing you everywhere
I step outside, it's like I'm breathing you in the air
I can feel you're there

---

[8] You can view this performance at: https://www.youtube.com/watch?v=ChcR2gKt5WM.

Fall on me
Ascoltami
Fall on me
Abbracciami
Fall on me
With all your light
With all your light
With all your light

Just stay with the words for a second. "I thought sooner or later the lights up above will come down in circles and guide me to love. But I don't know what's right for me. I cannot see straight. I've been here too long, and I don't want to wait for it." This is the blessing of the father. It's about value.

In the video, you can see the father's face when his son started singing. There's both love and a demand here. How much they practice that. How much demand the father made.

How hard it must be to be Andrea Bocelli's son, with his voice trying to find its way. In any other world it would be a stunning voice. But under the shadow of his father...

If you watch this performance carefully, you see the whole dance of the father's blessing. You see the power of it. It's different than the embrace of the mother—it's a different demand. It's something else. It's the demand for value.

When we remove the father from the story—not the male father, we're completely beyond gender, but the principle of the father—we can forget about the importance of value. **When, for example, the human potential movement talks about the embrace of the mother and subtly writes the father out of the story, they're writing the principle of value out of the story.**

But love should be unconditional *and* conditional—a strange sentence, perhaps. We talk so much about unconditional love, which is beautiful and essential, but love also sometimes makes demands—the demands of value. That's the blessing of the father, which has a different quality than the blessing of the mother.

In some sense, the flash mob orchestra in Italy shows **the blessing of the mother: embracing the utter joy of Reality.** You're in the square and the music seduces you open. And you realize, "Oh my God, it's all so radically beautiful…"

- It's always already good.
- There's nothing you need to do.
- It's there, it's here, it's available.
- You can taste it; you can access it right now, always.

But the taste of the father's blessing is different. You can feel that distinction. Listen to the words: "I thought sooner or later the lights up above will come down in circles and guide me to love." But then I don't know value, I don't know what's right for me: "I've been here too long. Fly like a cannonball, straight to my soul, tear me to pieces. And make me feel whole. I'm willing to fight for it. And carry this weight."

This is the weight of value. The weight of the challenge. **This is the call to responsibility, the call to value.** "And carry this weight, but with every step I keep questioning what is true."

What is true? It's very easy to miss this in the song. And the critics of the song all missed it. It's so much more subtle, and so much more of a dance. *With every step I keep questioning what is true.*

And then he asked the father to also be the mother at the same time.

He says, "Fall on me with open arms. Fall on me from where you are. Fall on me with all your light, with all your light, with all your light." Father, would you be the mother? The father and the mother come together in, divine marriage, in *hieros gamos*.

They embrace in this together, so tenderly.

PRACTICE: TRANSMITTING THE BLESSING OF THE FATHER

In Silence of Presence, let's practice giving the blessing of the father. Go inwards, as in a prayer, and invite someone in your life who you have accepted as they are, to now step up to value, to step up to become the person they're meant to become.

It's a different motion than the blessing of the mother founded in unconditional acceptance. It's both an invitation and a demand. The father says, "I trust that you're going to show up. I'm calling you to show up. And I believe in you. And I'm holding you even as you stand independently."

The blessing of the father is: I don't know what's right, but I want to know what's right, and I'm willing to go *all the way* to make it right.

Of course, there are multiple perspectives—but there's also a right way. And the right way is not dogmatic. It cannot be imposed from without—the right way is always the invitation from within the moment.

It's the standard that lives in us, as us, and through us—that which holds us, the invitation that calls us. That is the blessing of the father.

6.2

VALUE AS THE FABRIC OF REALITY

A couple of months ago, I was at the airport and I didn't have cash to tip the guy who helped me with my luggage at the check-in counter. He wouldn't take a credit card, so I promised I would go and find a cash machine and bring him back a tip. This has happened to me two or three times because I keep making the same mistake. When you actually go and find a cash machine and come back and give the person $20 or $25, their eyes pop open—they didn't dream that you were going to come back.

Something changes in that moment—the world becomes, for that person, more trustable. This wasn't a moment of win-lose metrics. There was a demand made, a commitment made. It was important. The world became more trustworthy.

He told that story to everybody around him. They said: "Wow. Unbelievable."

But this is not some special occurrence—this the fabric of Reality. Sometimes, though, we forget. When we lose track of this fabric of Reality, we've lost our way. When we've lost the story, we've lost the thread, we've lost the value.

So what we want to do now is step back into value.

STORY = VALUE = EROS = DESIRE

We're going to go deep into two different dimensions: story and value. Ultimately, what we're saying is that **story and value are real.** We began with a citation from what we called "uncontaminated material," a pure reflection of the Zeitgeist: Harari's book *Homo Deus*. He tells the story of the Crusades, about this kid in England who's called to arms after Saladin sacks Jerusalem and the Pope launches the Third Crusade. He tells the story about this kid in England who was convinced he's going to go straight to heaven if he slaughters Muslims.

Harari—partially inappropriately, partially appropriately—mocks this. It's appropriate to mock because it's a wrong belief, a bad story. But it's inappropriate because Harari's conclusion is that all stories are therefore only just *made-up stories.* He later writes about a kid 600 years later, from the same part of England, who's working for Amnesty International, and who goes to *help* Muslims instead of killing them. He concludes, and somewhat understandably, "And now we think that kid who's working for human rights is great," but he says, "a 100 years hence, our belief in human rights might look equally incomprehensible." That's his give-away line.

Harari believes that these are actually *both* just stories. He's saying that **any notion of value is a figment of our imagination, a "fiction," a social construction.** In other words, Universal Human Rights and the Crusades are just fictions, and there's no way to compare them because there's no intrinsic basis for evaluating them.

Although he doesn't relate them directly, he's treating them both as fiction, citing the basic postmodern move that suffuses much contemporary culture, which is the belief that no grand narratives can be true. Of course, *that* story should be honored as true—a real performative contradiction at the heart of the culture. **According to Harari, there's no ground to compare or evaluate stories because all grand narratives are just fictions. As such, all values are just stories, and there's no intrinsic basis.**

This means there's no blessing of the father, no guiding hand on the son's shoulder. For Harari, that's an illusion—there's no underlying value to that, or anything else for that matter.

. . .

Now that we have a sense of where culture is at, I want to look deeper into the notion of story itself, and I want to put forth a potentially very subtle idea. **This idea is another equation: *Story equals Value equals Eros equals Desire*. There's actually no distinction between them. They're all equivalent.**

It's a complete mistake to distinguish between them. They're all saying the same thing. Eros equals Desire equals Value equals Story—and all four of those are ontologies.

- Of course, there are surface versions of all of them.
- Of course, there are pseudo-versions of all of them.
- Of course, there are counterfeits of all of them.

The proposition we're making is not some mere tentative proposition—it's as sure to me as the fact that I'm sitting right here. **It's just true, a given in Cosmos.** You just have to see it and experience it. And then once you see it, it's like, "Oh. You didn't even say anything interesting, that's just self-evident." That's what real truth should be. It's not persuasive. It's like, "Oh, of course."

I'm going to go for an "of course," and I'm going to go one step at a time.

Here's the "of course," and it's a big one: **Story is not a human creation.**

Story actually doesn't emerge with human beings. The assumption in historiography is that language comes into being, and then language generates story. Seems plausible, right? In fact, language is largely understood. According to many evolutionary psychologists and historians, it's simply what allows you to hunt better because it gives you a survival advantage. For more perceptive historians such as Harari, language is also a story. It must be. **In fact, stories—which for Harari are mere fictions— are not a uniquely human capacity.**

If you look over the course of history, historians notice that those old stories people were willing to die for are often now considered ridiculous. Likewise, we now have new stories, but of course we're going to consider those equally ridiculous, eventually. And Harari's view has been endorsed by Obama, Gates, Bezos, and many other power players in culture. This view is at the very center of culture.

If this view is true, there's no blessing of the father—nor the mother, for that matter.

Thankfully, it's not actually true.

STORY IS INFORMATION AND MEANING IN REALITY

If you look at the structure of Cosmos, you realize that Reality is story all the way up and all the way down. The word story here is no different than information, but we don't mean bits and bytes. We don't mean it the way Claude Shannon, the founder of information theory, quantitatively defined the word. As Howard Bloom correctly points out, Shannon got the math right, but the metaphor wrong. **Information doesn't mean bits and bytes—it means Reality is coded with meaning.**

So, story is the same as information—or meaning—and information is the same as value. What information means is that there's a set of values at play that guide the action, so value is the same as meaning. This means there are structures in which this or that move creates something new—and that newness has its own field of meaning or self-understanding. Its own field of operation.

As an example, remember that we looked at that moment when three quarks come together into a single new configuration of intimacy? Three quarks become a neutron or a proton, based on their spin—every single person is constituted by those quarks, as is all of Reality. Those quarks are things.

As we pointed out earlier, language actually holds and discloses Reality. Wittgenstein wasn't wrong about that. The Hebrew word for thing is *davar*, meaning "word," or Logos. The word is the Logos. In the beginning there was the word, the Logos.

What's incepted into Reality after space, time, and speed? Things. *Davar* is the word, or the Logos, or meaning. Scientifically speaking, a thing is code for value and meaning. *A thing is a Story of Value.*

It's shocking. We're talking about the structure of Reality now. To cite our friend Howard Bloom—the unofficial, behind-the-scenes guru of the space program at NASA, "When you put three quarks together, you get something that will someday make the solidity of a hand, the substance of a brain, and the churning heart of the stars." The three quarks are intertwined together so tightly that it's almost impossible to tell there were ever three individual quarks at all. And yet, of course, they retain their distinct quarkhood. Remember that intimacy equals shared identity *in the context of otherness.*

Bloom continues: "The result of these three quarks coming together is something so fantastical that this Cosmos has never seen its like before. The three quarks have transformed into a proton. **This is much stranger than the merely weird.**" Indeed, it should be impossible. "It's the equivalent of laying out three apples on your dinner plate and getting a woolly mammoth. Three quarks simply *can't* become a proton. It just can't happen."

And yet it does. Inevitably they come together in these new configurations of intimacy. I'm describing me, I'm describing you, all things—I'm describing the substance of Reality here. **When all new configurations of intimacy come together, they disclose a new code of meaning and value.** It is literally a new *Story* of Value, a new structure of information, a new structure of meaning.

That proton has a new attention space and new capacities. It has purpose. It has direction, or *telos*. And it has desires. Protons have desires—it turns out that 380,000 years after the Big Bang, these protons and neutrons will be yearning for each other, in a kind of incessant desire for deeper intimacy.

They're looking for something that the three quarks didn't have:

- A new set of values.
- A new set of desires.
- A new configuration of intimacy.

This new wholeness, this new value, this new Story of Value, this new intimacy is called an atom. So it goes, up through newer and more complex forms of intimacy: molecules, cells, organisms, lifeforms, collectives, etc. This is the structure of Reality—this is how Reality works.

I told Howard that I love his woolly mammoth example, but that we have to actually formulate this much more clearly. Here's the proposition: You can look at the specific properties of story and yet find there's something of the actual constituent structure of Cosmos that changes your relationship to it.

At the end of the conversation, Howard said, "Even I could only call that spirit."

THE FOUR DIMENSIONS OF STORY: THE TELEROTIC UNIVERSE

The first dimension of story implies *telos*, a direction. Every story has a threaded action, meaning it's not just a series of coincidences that happen next to each other. David Hume called that "constant conjunction," events happening one after the other with no intrinsic relationship between them.

But there actually is a necessary connection, a causality, if you will—one thing causes another thing, which causes another thing… So a story has action threaded by causality. Or said differently, there's a *telos*—it's going somewhere.

The second dimension of story implies value and desire—there's a desire for value that guides the story. In other words, the story *wants to accomplish something*. It goes for this value and not that value. It very clearly chooses a path of value. There's a set of values, which is why our intimacy equation necessarily includes mutuality of value.

So, if we're playing together in the story, there's a shared value—it's going somewhere, which also means there's desire. This means I want a value that I don't have—I'm alive with desire. We can see this on the personal level: My basic need is not only to be desired, which is crucial, but to desire. If I don't desire, I'm alienated from the structure of Reality itself, which is what constitutes me. Desire is not just this weird thing that messes up the presentation of my clean civic personality—**desire is the structure of Reality itself.**

If I deny desire, I'm in denial of Reality, which means I break down, which means I pathologize. This is creating a mental health crisis all over the world. One plausible explanation for depression as the fastest growing illness is that we're increasingly alienated from our own constitutive structure—we're not truly honoring our inherent desire.

Desire at the very heart of matter means: I'm desiring a *value*, and this guides the story. There are what you might call "guiding values" that direct the story.

The third dimension of story implies a necessary degree of freedom. If there's no freedom in the story, then you're reading a tech manual. If there's no freedom in the story, it's not a story. We know the difference between the two. Reading a tech manual is not that exciting—and it doesn't align with the structure of Reality.

There has to be some dimension of freedom for it to be a story. Both Richard Feynman, the physicist, and Stuart Kauffman, the cosmologist, have shown how this works in an enormously complex series of mathematical moves, which we're not going to review right now, but it's quite interesting and important. Basically, what they're pointing out is that **there's a dimension**

of freedom all the way up and all the way down. Even at the subatomic level, there's a type of proto-freedom.

Now, freedom doesn't mean, "Should I be with this person or with that person? Should I make this career choice? Should I do this to develop my..." It's not exactly that kind of freedom—but that kind of freedom is not what you think, either. The kind of freedom that you think is the rational choice of *Homo economicus* is itself a structure of allurements.

When you go a bit deeper, you realize there's this dance between choice and choicelessness. There's freedom, there's choice, but the choice is to be me. The choice is to fulfill my deepest nature, my deepest identity. I can go astray when I become alienated from my allurement.

And my allurement calls me back.

So this notion of choice is inherent in story.

The fourth dimension of story is that there's a crisis that needs to be resolved. This dimension is sometimes there and sometimes not. In most stories, but not all, there's an issue. So, we say crisis is an evolutionary driver. Crisis births action. All crisis, at its core, is a crisis of intimacy. For example, the so-called Great Oxidation Event occurred after the development of photosynthesis, and the resident single-celled organisms initially didn't know what to do. The environment was changing rapidly—it was a crisis of intimacy between an over-abundance of oxygen and the elements.

Over a very long period of time, the single-celled organisms resolved this crisis by becoming multicellular structures. Prokaryotes became eukaryotes. **They created a new configuration of intimacy in response to a crisis of intimacy—a new Story of Value.** Howard did the science for all of this—he has better intuitions than I do. I can read it and explain it for ten hours, but he *feels* it in a different way. He's got the math, which makes a big difference, and he validated this across the board.

This also means there's an evolution of story. We might move from unconscious to conscious evolution, and conscious evolution might be a

269

new relationship to story, which we'll talk about a little later. And between the levels of evolution, there's continuity and discontinuity.

So, there's story all the way up and all the way down, and the story has value: the value is what we desire. Eros means there's desire for value, and that's what a story is. Recall our equation: Eros equals Desire equals Value equals Story. They're actually all the same thing.

When desire is at the heart of matter, it means there's a *telos*. *Telos* and Eros come together. **So we can say that we fundamentally live in a Telerotic Universe—a universe animated by Telos and Eros, all the way up and all the way down.**

The Universe is animated by value—you can't escape it. That's the nature of Reality itself.

Because we live in a Telerotic Universe, this also means that value evolves. And story evolves as well.

6.3

A META-CRISIS OF INTIMACY YIELDS THE FOURTH BIG BANG: DEMANDING THE BIRTH OF *HOMO AMOR*

We said that Reality is not a fact but a story. But what does that really mean? It means that Reality has a narrative arc, and the plotlines we just pointed to.

Let's start with a story. Let's look at a narrative arc starting from the beginning, with the First Big Bang. The emergence of matter, of the physical world. The birth of the physiosphere. This is the story of the universe, which no one was able to tell 200 years ago—**and the evolution of story itself allows us to tell the story that we're telling right now.**

This story certainly wasn't able to be told by cells or protons, nor by plants or animals. But it also wasn't accessible by humanity until the last couple hundred years, and really just the last few decades.

So the first piece to understand is the evolving nature of story—this was not a story that existed until very recently.

Let's follow it. What happened to the world of matter? It got more and more intimate, with wider and wider shared identities. We can go through all the levels.

Imagine it. There you are, at the moment of the First Big Bang, the singularity, the most unimaginable burst of energy, and you emerge as one of the gazillions of quarks that filled the universe. Then you eventually start configuring into new wholes: protons and neutrons. After some time has passed, you come together and create an atom. And the atoms come together and create molecules, and molecules create macromolecules...

There's a **constant intensification of physical intimacy** over billions of years of allurement. It's not dead, empty space for billions of years, as is written in all the history and science books. No, it's actually subatomic particles in a process of constant, dazzling allurement. So, rather than a lifeless void, we have a many-billion-year-old love story, as macromolecules intensify their intimacy—intensifying and intensifying and intensifying, and then, *voilà*, you have a new emergent. You have a cell.

Remember the videos of the cell we saw? This entirely new configuration of intimacy called life. This is the Second Big Bang, the emergence of the biosphere.

So, in the plotline of Reality, the Cosmos seeks more uniqueness, more creativity, more value, more Eros—and triumphs into an important new chapter of the story: the biosphere. There's not just one Big Bang, but a Second Big Bang in which matter triumphs as life. **But it doesn't leave matter behind. Life loves matter, it needs matter, it desires matter. So it includes all of matter with it.** It triumphs as cellular life. James Shapiro, one of the leading geneticists in the United States, claims that every single cell is irreducibly intelligent—they quite literally edit their own gene structure— including all thirty-seven trillion of them moving you right now.

Intimacy deepens again, and we go from single-cellular organisms—by way of the oxygen crisis, where they can't breathe the abundance of oxygen—to multi-cellular organisms, from prokaryotes to eukaryotes. Multi-cellular life is the beginning of life as we know it. Then we go through the entire biosphere, to greater and greater intimacies, more and more uniqueness.

We can follow another plotline of Reality: the advancement towards more and more consciousness. **It's always creating more and more conscious value, more and more meaning.** A plant has much more intimate and complex meaning structures than a proton. So, we develop through plants, invertebrates, fish, amphibians, through the reptilian nervous system, the mammalian nervous system, and the frontal cortex of the great apes.

Then a big shift occurs: We've got these neo-cortexed, frontal-lobed apes walking on the savanna in Africa. The Third Big Bang. Humans begin to have this deeper, wilder depth of self-reflection, a marked qualitative shift. They start making art in new ways, engaging in trade and developing new capacities for self-reflection. There's an entirely new emergent: the world of thought and culture.

So we've moved from cosmological evolution, the First Big Bang, to biological evolution, the Second Big Bang. And then life triumphs as self-reflective human consciousness and cultural evolution, the Third Big Bang.

THE STORY IS NOT OVER—THERE ARE MORE BIG BANGS TO COME

For the last 4,000 years we've not been able to say this. We haven't been able to see that this is the same story—that there's actually been three Big Bangs. Now, as we become awake as conscious evolution, we realize for the first time that we can tell this story, which follows a set of plotlines:

- More and more Uniqueness.
- More and more Eros.
- More and more Intimacy.
- More and more Wholeness.
- More and more Value.
- More and more Meaning.

- More and more Creativity.
- More and more Consciousness.

Here's where it gets crazy: **the essence of the new story we're trying to tell is that the story is not over.**

There's not just three Big Bangs. If you look carefully at Reality, you realize that there's an inexorable logic. It has a plotline—it's not just a fact, but a story. Just like matter triumphs as life, and life triumphs as self-reflective mind, self-reflective mind is going to go through all of its levels of consciousness, and it's going to evolve cultural evolution in all sorts of beautiful ways, and all sorts of technological ways.

What always happens? Crisis always changes the story. Crisis always evolves the story.

After all our evolution, what's happened is that we have another crisis, but this one's called the meta-crisis. That's not a surprise, though. You get how hopeful this is?

There's always a crisis, which is one of the four elements of story. That's what drives story—and every crisis is a crisis of intimacy.

The root cause of existential risk is what we call a global intimacy disorder. So, what are we doing? We're telling a New Story—with the best and latest science, in all domains, both exterior and interior—and weaving them together.

It's not like after the Third Big Bang goes through all of its stages, self-reflective mind just rides off into the sunset, and the story is over. The end.

Not at all. There are in fact two broad outcomes here:

- Either the story self-terminates due to our global intimacy disorder, which is what we described in the first chapter, where the inherent plotline terminates and ends the story. That's existential risk.

- Or the global intimacy disorder births a new Reality, a New Human and a New Humanity. *Homo sapiens* becomes *Homo amor*. A new phase shift, a new big bang.

The Third Big Bang had vectors of enormous, unfolding beauty. The evolution of intimacy gave birth to so many incredible aspects of civilization—but there was a gap between interior and exterior technologies, which exploded in the Renaissance, in modernity. **Interior technology stopped after the declaration of Universal Human Rights. We didn't quite know why we declared them—and we failed to root them in real, authentic value.**

However, exterior technologies kept exponentializing and getting more powerful. The story shifted from interior to exterior technology, and then to exponentially destructive technology, potentially in the hands of rogue, non-state actors. We came face-to-face with existential and catastrophic risk, and we've already shown how that risk is rooted in the global intimacy disorder.

So, the current meta-crisis of intimacy yields the Fourth Big Bang.

That's the inherent logic of all this.

CHANGING THE VECTOR OF HISTORY WITH A NEW STORY OF VALUE

We've never been able to tell this story in this way before. Matter triumphs in life, which triumphs in the self-reflective human mind and cultural evolution—same plotline. More and more uniqueness, more value, more intimacy, more Eros, more consciousness—and of course, more and more complexity.

Our crisis is a birth. Crisis is an evolutionary driver—and the evolutionary driver at this point demands a New Human and a New Humanity. Otherwise, just like the single-celled organisms that went extinct by failing to generate a new configuration of intimacy, we will extinct ourselves if we don't generate a new configuration of intimacy. But that's not a tragedy—this is the beautiful post-tragic realization: *That's just how it works.*

It's our turn, our moment. We actually have the capacity for *Homo sapiens* to become *Homo amor*: the realization of this grand, unfolding story and our unique, individual places in it. **Homo amor is the realization that the universe is a love story, and those are the plotlines of the story, and that story lives in me.**

I'm a unique expression of the Universe: A Love Story.

Who am I? I'm a Unique Self, an irreducibly unique expression of the LoveIntelligence, LoveDesire, LoveBeauty, LoveStory of All-That-Is, that lives in me, as me, and through me. We all are the Universe: A Love Story in person. *Homo amor* has a deep, intuitive, reflective self-awareness of this. **For the first time in human history, *Homo amor* has the self-awareness of being the CosmoErotic Universe in person, the intimate universe in person**—it all lives in each of us. We realize we are the leading edge of Evolutionary Love itself. That's who we are.

Most people in the world do not have the luxury of becoming awake to this. The fact that we're able to tell this story, that we're able to articulate this vision—that's what places us in Florence. Da Vinci was alive at a time when the Black Death was still a memory. In other words, as plague and war are ravaging medieval Europe, most of Florence is doing what Florence is doing. But there are 1,000 or so people who know—deep down—that a new story is desperately needed because **only new stories change the vector of history.**

Just like da Vinci and Ficino and all the rest, we need to articulate the story, and we need to get it right. If they had simply put it up online in order to get the most views, that wouldn't have made it work. They had to get it absolutely right first. But today the stakes are exponentially greater because we're talking about the potential for *no future*. The death of humanity.

We're not turning away. We're turning towards. And we're filled with hope, because we can actually do this. **We can tell this new story.**

The first thing we need to do to tell the new story is to realize that we're not pre-tragic. After we've fully faced the tragic, we can shift into the post-tragic because this is the movement of history. **Nothing we're saying is moving against history—this is how history moves.**

We're in the right place, at the right time—and that's insanely exciting.

THE MESSIAH IS THE NEW HUMAN AND THE NEW HUMANITY

The idea of Armageddon is pretty scary: the end of the days when it all blows up. The vision that all religions have that it's all going to end—that's Armageddon. But there's another important word that exists in the great traditions: Messiah.

The popular public idea of this is that someone's going to come and save everyone, but the deeper, more accurate, and more hopeful idea in the sacred texts is: **The Messiah is actually the emergence of the New Human and a New Humanity.** The great traditions have intuited this all along.

In our language, Armageddon is existential risk, and Messiah is *Homo amor*.

In the past, the religious authorities didn't know how to say it, so they hijacked *Homo amor* for their ethnocentric agendas: "Oh, *Homo amor* is going to be *my* dude messiah-ing, ushering in a New Age for humanity, for Christ consciousness, for Buddha consciousness, for Allah consciousness..."

They got trapped in an ethnocentric prison.

They understood that it was either going to go Armageddon, existential risk, or it was going to go Messiah, but then they hijacked Messiah for an ethnocentric context.

So we're trying to liberate that idea of Messiah, of *Homo amor*, from its historical ethnocentric context. We're saying: ***Homo amor* is all of us**.

Homo amor is actually the New Human and New Humanity.

6.4

COSMOEROTIC HUMANISM INTRODUCES "EVOLVING PERENNIALISM"

So, here's the problem. It's an argument Howard Bloom basically makes in his book *The Lucifer Principle*—a very powerful argument used to destroy value. Harari even cites Bloom as one of his sources to express the classical argument against value, against the great religions' idea of value as real.

The simple version of this argument is that if value is real, it must be eternal—because the real is the realm of Being, eternal and unchanging. But, so the argument goes, everybody knows that value cannot be eternal, nor can it be unchanging—because it absolutely changes. It's taken as a given that everybody knows and believes this argument. Therefore, value cannot be real.

A major book from a few years ago—*Revolt*, by Nadav Eyal—says that in response to our current crisis, we desperately need liberal values. The liberal world order is really important. He's a great reporter and a great storyteller as well. His assumption, which he shares with so many others caught up in postmodern culture, is that there's no real basis for value. "Everybody knows that there are no preordained eternal values," he claims. That's just ridiculous. The last chapter of his book is called "A New Story," and his new story is basically what we would call an "infrastructural" response. Since you can't talk about intrinsic value, or a "superstructural" response, what can you change in the infrastructure to make it better? That's also where Harari lands, and where Obama is coming from. What else can you do if you take it as a given that value's not real or fundamental?

In *The Lucifer Principle*, Bloom says something similar: "Well, you say love is eternal, and love is a value… Okay, fantastic. So, what did love mean 2,000 years ago? As a simple example, 2,000 years ago, if I was a Chinese patriarch and my wife disobeyed me, by law, she deserved to have her hands chopped off. But I'm a loving husband, so I just beat her—because I'm a great lover. When someone does that today, we arrest them and send them to prison, as we should—because that's not the way you love. But that's what *they* said love was. And they're both using the same word. So love is obviously a ridiculous word. It doesn't really mean anything. You're just calling it love. But actually, there's no substance, there's no eternal value that carries across time."

That's the core argument of modernity, and especially postmodernity. It's pretty powerful, and it started with David Hume. Where we're going next gets really interesting, and it's insanely beautiful—but it's subtle.

THE ETERNAL TAO IS THE EVOLVING TAO IS THE ETERNAL TAO

Modernity rebelled against the great medieval thinkers—Aquinas, Maimonides, Avicenna, and Averroes, the great scholastic traditions of knowledge—who understood value as an expression of eternal being. Meaning: being with no needs and no desires, that which never changes. In other words, the value that comes out of a world of eternal being—if it's real, if it's a true value—must be eternal and unchanging.

Postmodern thinking says that if we see that this thing called love is changing all the time, then it can't be real value because that's not how value is supposed to work. Value is an expression of the intrinsic nature of the eternal unchanging being of Cosmos, as expressed by Buddhism, Judaism, Christianity, Islam, et cetera.

But, as we've already noted, that that's not quite how Cosmos works. **Infinity also has desires. Infinity desires finitude.**

---

*Infinity is not only a depth of being
but also a wave of becoming.*

In other words, Infinity is not merely a fact, but a story. A story has *telos*. A story has desire. What is the story of desire? Value. Infinity wants more and more value. That's one of the plotlines of Cosmos, along with more and more meaning, consciousness, and the rest.

So, yes, love is eternal—*and* love also evolves, clarifies, gets deeper, gets wider.

There's the Tao, the word they use in Taoism to refer to what I would call the Field of Value, the being that is eternal. But crucially: **The Field of Value is both being *and* becoming. The Field of Value is both eternal and evolving.** So, there's something fundamental called Eros. And Eros also evolves.

From twelfth-century England to twentieth-century England, there's an evolution of love. We've moved from egocentric love to ethnocentric love, to worldcentric love, to cosmocentric love, at the leading edge of consciousness each time. But just because it evolves, we can't say that love is therefore meaningless. So what's the eternal being of love? Love *always* means connecting, caring for, protecting, and nurturing.

So, here's the sentence: **The Eternal Tao is the Evolving Tao.** There's absolutely no split between those two.

When I said this to my friend Art Green, who's the premier scholar of certain kind of mysticism in the world, he said, "We can't go back to perennialism. That's what we need, but no one's going to go back there." And I said, "it's an *evolving* perennialism." He just stopped. "So, that's a contradiction, isn't it?" Then he thought about it a bit more, and in an instant, he got it.

The perennialists had some great insights, but they were a bit confused. **Aldous Huxley concluded that perennial truths are eternal, unchanging truths. This is partly true, but also why perennialism was rightly rejected—because truth is not only eternal and unchanging—it's also evolving.** If you actually root perennialism in a denial of evolution, you're fucked. This is postmodernity's reasonable critique.

"You're going back to perennialism? Fuck off. Ever heard of evolution, buddy? Let's not even have that conversation." This is why the entire New Age bypass doesn't work, why New Age spirituality has not succeeded in changing the world.

Making a progressive/regressive move back to premodernity? You can call it Mythic, Magic, Shamanic… Well, nicely done. I'm glad you had a good experience. You drummed very well. That's great. And by the way, I love the Mythic, Magic, and Shamanic—and drumming too. It's essential, but it's not going to restore the source code on its own, unless you weave it together with modern and postmodern insights. You don't leave this out— you sometimes need to drum—but it's got to be part of a much larger story.

In a truly intimate story, you include every piece—so you don't leave out the Shamanic. You don't leave out drumming. You don't leave out the Magic or the Mythic. That's all necessary, but it's part of an inclusive and evolving story. *To be intimate is to be intimate with all chapters of the story.*

So, for example, in your own personal story, **if you start ripping out pages in your own book of life, you become non-intimate with yourself. If you start ripping out pages from all the epics of world history, we become non-intimate with Reality.**

Reality is a story—an evolving story— and all the stages of the story have value.

Culture has forgotten that there is a Tao, a Field of Value, so we first have to remember that. But then we need to realize that the Tao is also evolving, integrating the great modern and postmodern insights.

The Eternal Tao is the Evolving Tao is the Eternal Tao—if you can't say that, then you can't create value in the world. For example, TechnoFeudalism assumes that value isn't real. So, for example, the value of personhood, irreducible uniqueness, and the right I have to my own attention are all assumed by the tech plex not to be real.

When Shoshana Zuboff, who wrote *Surveillance Capitalism* to critique the tech plex, can't quite find the ground from which to launch the deep critique that is necessary, she settles on a goal of "arousing astonishment and outrage." **But you can only arouse astonishment and outrage when there's been a *violation* of value.** If value's not real, then there simply can be no astonishment and outrage—and therefore no real political will. If there's no political will, we can't actually create transformation.

Value is eternal *and* evolving. There's no contradiction between those two.

The reason the classical modern thinkers couldn't envision this is because they all viewed Reality as eternal being. That's why there's an anti-sexual bias in most of the great traditions—because sexuality is not about being. It's about becoming. They couldn't accommodate this in their system of value.

Sexuality is not the spacious bliss of being—although it has dimension of that on a good day.

It's about ecstatic urgency. It's about movement.

It's about change and transformation. Evolution is a series of transformations. **The Cosmos is a sexual Cosmos, an amorous Cosmos, an erotic Cosmos.**

We traditionally viewed Reality as eternal, unchanging being, and value was therefore only an expression of that eternity. But then we see that values change all the time, so we—somewhat reasonably—say, "Well, that's not an expression of the real, so the real itself must be an illusion. Value must be just a social construction, just a story, just a fiction."

But when we start to look deeply into this, we realize it's not just a fiction. Story itself is a First Principle and First Value of Cosmos. And what does the story, by its very nature, do? It transforms—*it evolves.* **Story has a vector, a plotline. And it matters, if you will, all the way up and all the way down.**

It's the desire for more and more value.

INFINITY PLUS FINITUDE EQUALS MORE INFINITY

Let me say it one more way, perhaps the most dramatic you can say it: "There's more God to come." That is the essence of the whole thing. **There's more God to come.** That's the realization of Infinity desiring finitude.

Here's another equation: *Infinity plus finitude equals more Infinity.*

It's quite fucking shocking—this is the essential realization that lives inside all of us.

This is something that Schelling talks about in his later writings. It's gorgeous: There's more God to come. Just get that equation: Infinity plus finitude equals more Infinity.

That's essentially what *Homo amor* means, what *Homo amor* knows: There's more God to come.

6.5

INFINITY + FINITUDE = MORE INTIMACY

HOMO AMOR = MORE GOD TO COME

As we said, Infinity plus finitude equals more Infinity. Infinity desires finitude, but finitude is really more and more of itself. And Infinity experiences a shocking self-recognition when looking in your face. That's what it means to be a human being. What it means to be **Homo amor is the realization that I'm the incarnation of** *more God to come.*

We call that Apotheosis: The human being who became God. But it's not the cheap grace of the New Age people who declare, "I'm God, or I am a God." It's so much more subtle, deep, beautiful, gentle, and true.

Apotheosis—that's the great story, the human being becoming divine. That's the plotline of the story.

Infinity plus finitude equals more Infinity.

There's more God to come.

Of course, the Mystery is always there—and always will be. There's uncertainty, and there are 1,000 things we don't understand. There's dark matter and hidden interiors and exteriors all over the place. But we can discern the general plotlines, because they live in us. We recognize them, and then we can realize, "Oh, my life matters." The perpetuation of my uniqueness matters. I've got a verse to write in the Book of Life. I'm irreducibly unique, and my story matters—it's not just a function of my pathology. **There's a new coming-together, a new way to be human, a new possibility—because Reality is the Possibility of Possibility.**

So, we're at that moment of crisis. The meta-crisis of intimacy is a birth, an evolutionary driver. The only response to the global intimacy disorder that allows us to transform existential and catastrophic risk is a new order of intimacy within ourselves, allowing us to realize that we're God. Apotheosis.

Not to realize that is to be non-intimate with my own nature.

In other words, genuine intimacy is shared identity with the Divine—but always, of course, in the context of otherness, because each of our unique individual expressions still exist.

Intimacy is Apotheosis, becoming God.

Let's go back to the intimacy equation to expand this. It's a shared identity with the Divine in the context of unique human otherness.

We have a mutuality of recognition—we recognize each other.

We have a mutuality of pathos—we feel each other. We live in the same Field of Value, which is why Abraham can challenge God and say, "You're not doing it right."

And there's a mutuality of purpose—we're aligned with the Real, with the Infinite Intimate, towards our goal.

In other words, intimacy is Apotheosis.

Let's hold Silence of Presence and just breathe for a second.

CHAPTER 7

BLESSINGS OF THE FATHER AND BLESSINGS OF THE MOTHER

AM I WELCOME IN THE COSMOS?

7.1

UNIQUE SELF SYMPHONY AND THE NEXT BUDDHA

If there's one principle we've stood against for over a decade, again and again, it's the guru principle. **Unique Self is an affront to the guru principle.** In other words, there's True Self, and then the guru says: I've got more of that than you do, so listen to me.

Unique Self says: No, there's no teacher who can have more Unique Self than you—it's not possible. So by definition, Unique Self and Unique Self Symphony say it's not that we don't want builders and we don't want teachers. We even might want strong teachers, builders, and strong expressions of *Homo amor* in politics and business.

Those are all important.

It's not that the next Buddha is a Sangha—with all due respect to Thich Nhat Hanh, he got that somewhat wrong. **The next Buddha is a collection of sanghas *and* buddhas, all working together.**

It's a self-organizing Unique Self Symphony, in which everyone plays their specific role as part of the whole tapestry, and where everyone is also always at the center.

7.2

YOUR UNIQUE SELF MEETS THIS UNIQUE, ETERNAL MOMENT— WHAT CAN WE OFFER EACH OTHER?

Let's do a simple practice that has two steps. The first is a Unique Self pointing-out instruction: How do you access the quality of Unique Self? Imagine for a second a number of people in your life: friends, family members, neighbors, partners, children, even celebrities—people you know well or not so well.

- Are you confused between any of these people?
- Are you confused between their inner and outer qualities, insofar as you know or imagine them, their minds and their hearts?
- Are you confused about who any of those people are?

Take a few moments with a few of them, and now try and access each one. Don't think about them, just access their taste.

Unique Self is a taste—it's a quality.

In Zen, you would quite simply say, "Violets are blue." Of course they would never say "Unique Self," but that's what "violets are blue" means. It's the specific quality of a person, place, or thing. You're not confused about the unique taste of a person. You don't say: "Oh, that's someone else." And even if they're not doing or saying anything, the quality of their silence, the quality of their presence, is totally unique.

Part two: Try and find your own unique taste.

It's not so easy to find your own. But Unique Self is the unique taste of a person.

Now apply it to time. This is an advanced tantric exercise, so don't get frustrated if you can't do it immediately. But go back and see if you can, for a moment, collect the taste, the experience of reading Chapter One, where we talked about seduction, the three selves, and celebration. **We talked about only being able to change the world if you're willing to already live in the world that's already changed.**

Then see if you can find Chapter Two on existential risk and the general structure of the whole thing.

Chapter Three unfolded The Universe: A Love Story.

Chapter Four was all about knowing and healing shame. Try just for a moment to sense into that quality of shame, moving through and beyond it.

Chapter Five was on Unique Self.

And the last chapter, Chapter Six, was about the New Story and First Values.

Each of those chapters has a completely different taste, not only in the Dharma. Each one featured different characters, various gods and goddesses—and each chapter engaged different aspects of yourself.

Now feel into this moment here—it has an entirely unique taste, a different quality of time that has never existed before. Here I am, and my unique taste meets this unique moment. Then I ask the moment a question, and the moment asks me a question…

Listen.

We're now showing up; we've got to wake up, we've got to grow up, and we've got to show up. I ask the moment a question, and the question I ask the moment is the ultimate inquiry question.

It's not *Who Am I?* Although that's an essential foundational question we ask along the way.

This time, I ask the moment, **What do you need from me?**

It's a conversation with the moment. What do you need from me? What do you desire from me? This moment—alive, breathing, and pulsing—is an invitation. It turns to you, to me, to us, and says: **This is what I need from you, and I have a gift for you as well—because you need something from me.**

There's something in this moment in time that I have to give you, that will never be here ever again.

The reason we're so often broken is because we're never actually in the eternity that resides in *this* moment—we're lost in the pathologies of the past or lost in the anxieties of the future. However, we can only ever find full healing in this expansive moment.

Remember that we're engaging with all this not only for our own healing and transformation—**we're here to heal and transform culture together, as part of a Unique Self Symphony.**

Now, gently, quietly—between you and the moment, between this moment and you—in the interior depths, gently ask: "Hey, I'm right here. What do you need from me?"

And then listen. Just listen. Hear what the moment whispers back to you:

This is what I need from you...
I need your full, powerful attention and presence and love.
I've got a gift for you.
And that gift is going to unfold itself over time.

We're in eternity now. In this moment, there's no past and no future.

There's just the eternity that resides in the quivering present.

Sometimes, you have a painful moment. I actually had a painful moment this morning. I discovered something that made my heart and body scream, something incredibly challenging that happened to someone close to me. I sent them blessings and called them. But just for now, I let that moment go. I let the future go, and I let the past go.

From the utter depths and utter delight of this present, on behalf of eternity, *welcome to this very moment.*

7.3

THE BLESSING OF THE MOTHER

We're going to start with a song, one of my favorites—we're going to have the Mother hold us. We're going to finish with the blessing of the Father, so we're going to open here, with Sinead O'Connor and the Blessing of the Mother. The Welcome of the Mother. So, if we can, try to fully relax and open your hearts tenderly, gently.

SONG: "THIS IS TO MOTHER YOU," BY SINEAD O'CONNOR

This is to mother you
To comfort you and get you through
Through when your nights are lonely
Through when your dreams are only blue
This is to mother you

This is to be with you
To hold you and to kiss you too
For when you need me I will do
What your own mother didn't do
Which is to mother you

All the pain that you have known
All the violence in your soul
All the wrong things you have done
I will take from you when I come
All mistakes made in distress
All your unhappiness
I will take away with my kiss, yes
I will give you tenderness
For child I am so glad I've found you
Although my arms have always been around you
Sweet bird although you did not see me
I saw you

And I'm here to mother you
To comfort you and get you through
Through when your nights are lonely
Through when your dreams are only blue
This is to mother you

This is the Blessing of the Mother: "This is to mother you. This is to be with you. To hold you and to kiss you, too. For when you need me, I will do what your own mother didn't do."

So we not only have to be fathers to each other—we not only give each other the Blessing of the Father and encourage us deeper into value—but we must also give each other the Blessing of the Mother.

We welcome each other.

We have to welcome this moment, and we have to welcome each other, again and again and again and again. We welcome the people in our lives. We hold each other in every second, even when we're apart. We hold everything dear. **We've got to hold the moment, and then the moment**

will hold us. Let me feel you. Let yourselves totally feel each other, your loved ones. We welcome each other. That's what the mother does.

- The father puts his hand on the shoulder and says: "Come my child, stand, and I'll stand with you. I'll stand behind you. But stand you must—I'm calling you to value."
- The mother says: "Welcome home! You're always already home, but welcome home again. Every moment needs to be welcomed home."

Right here, right now, let's welcome the moment. Let's open it up and love it open. That's what Unique Self Symphony does. Let's give each other the blessing of the mother.

> *For child, I am so glad I found you.*
> *Although my arms have always been around you.*
> *Sweet bird, although you did not see me, I saw you.*
> *And I'm here to mother you.*
> *To comfort you and get you through.*
> *Through when your nights are lonely.*
> *Through when your dreams are only blue.*
> *This is to mother you.*

Right now, there is no source code, there's no history, there's just this moment. Although we're doing it every second for the evolution of love, right now we're only focused on this. There may be so much violence in the world, and perhaps in our souls, and yet She's here holding us. We can actually feel that and know it.

CONTEMPLATION EXERCISE: BLESSING OF THE MOTHER

Let's breathe it in. Let's express and share this blessing. If you're with people who you're able to share this with, either explicitly or implicitly, please do so. Either now or sometime later, you can gently turn to someone else and give them the blessing of the mother—the blessing of welcome, of acceptance—and then, either implicitly or explicitly, try to receive it yourself.

Feel this blessing coming from Reality herself—and know that it is always available.

You can imagine doing this with someone close to you, or with a figure who's important to you. Or you can even do this physically with yourself.

The blessing of the mother: I am welcome—I'm always already welcome.

This can be a beautiful practice to do every day. As always, if you wish, it can be powerful to also journal about the ways you are welcomed, the ways that you can feel this blessing of the mother.

7.4

THE POWER AND GIFT
OF BLESSING

If *Homo amor* means anything, it means that no human being—literally, no one—does not have a mother who holds them. Often our biological mothers were unable to always hold us, and often our mothers didn't themselves have a mother to always hold them. But actually, we're at a moment where we transcend and include: we move beyond biological family, which we fully honor. We honor our biological families in all the ways that we must—we're fully loyal to them, as opposed to certain versions of the Christian story, which say if you believe in Christ, you must turn your back on your family.

No, we honor our families. We love our families.

We also understand that we also have affinities to other groups. Whoever your various tribes are, we're not only connected to our biological families, but also to our evolutionary families.

- In our evolutionary families, we are actually each other's fathers—we can give each other the Blessing of the Father.
- In our evolutionary families, we are actually each other's mothers—we can give each other the Blessing of the Mother.

When I say "brothers and sisters," it's not just a folksy manner of speaking. I mean: *Oh my God, holy brothers, holy sisters, holy beloveds, holy Outrageous Lovers, holy sons and holy daughters, holy fathers and holy mothers.* I don't know if there's a mother-in-law in there, but we're an evolutionary family, for real.

We can give each other blessings.

***Homo amor* has the power to give blessings. We need to take the power of blessing back. It doesn't only live with the priests, gurus, or kings.**

- Those of us who feel the flutter of evolutionary communion in our hearts.
- Those who feel the call of the future world.
- Those unwilling to turn away.
- Those willing to welcome every moment.
- Those of us willing to take responsibility for our own arousal.
- Those willing to seduce every moment open.
- Those of us willing and able to let every moment seduce us open.

We step into the world as Unique Self Symphony, and we have the power of blessing. You have the power of blessing. Every single person you meet, in every interaction—even someone whose name you don't know—can be blessed. **You're pouring blessings into the world wherever you go.**

You're not *waiting* for your mission; I'm not waiting for my mission. Our mission is always already right here, right now—at every airport, at every restaurant. In every interaction, we're pouring love into it—*we're loved and being love.*

There are no strangers in the world—they don't exist.

I know that things are often hard when you have to take responsibility for your own arousal, and maybe you're a bit sick, a bit tired, the kid's been waking up early—it's not always easy to pour blessings into the world. I know lots of us are wrestling with physical challenges, and I want to totally honor all of that. It's not easy, but there is absolutely always a way through it.

Again, never take the moment for granted. Because there's a pregnancy in this moment, in every moment.

There's a birth to be born that hasn't yet been born.

And know that the power of blessing exists completely within every one of us.

7.5

HOLY SEDUCTION: BEYOND THE CONTRADICTION OF RANDOMNESS AND DESIGN

There's a gorgeous ancient Hebrew text, a 450-word document, that reads, *sofannah utz b'hitekhelatenn, ve'hitekhelatennah utz b'sofann*—"the end of the conversation is in the beginning, and the beginning of the conversation is in the end."

This is the *Book of Creation*, the first Hebrew mystical text we know of, a book that changed history—it defined the Renaissance in many important ways. The key words in the book are *sipur*, which means story, and *sefer*, which means book. We're talking about being written in the Book of Life. What it says about story, and about any conversation—**the beginning of a conversation is in the end, and the end is in the beginning. That's how you know it's a real conversation.**

But what does that mean? It's a bit cryptic and strange. I thought about it for a couple of decades, wondering if it's really all that interesting. But then I had a flash, a moment of insight. What it means is that there's a plotline to the story; the story has a plotline. **Reality is a story**. The end is in the

302

beginning and the beginning is in the end—*and yet it's fully free along the way.*

That's the paradox. In other words, from an evolutionary perspective, the world is contingent, full of surprises—and yet not random: there's a thread, there's a plotline.

This is hard to figure out by reading the classical evolutionary thinkers, because the evolutionary model is insufficient.

I'll give you an example. I'll mention one person, a key figure in the development of education in America We've been meeting once a week since about 2009, and I've never in my life ever prepared for a meeting with her.

And yet, there's a rhyme and a reason and a thread and a fabric and a recognizable conversation. You would think that we must have designed this pattern. This must be designed—it's so intimately clear, and the designs and the threads come back and forth, and forth and back, and back and forth. Look at all these perfectly patterned threads—but of course, we didn't design any of it. How can it look like it's completely designed but not be? That's actually the biggest question today in the evolutionary world: How can it look completely designed, but also not be?

Because there's a *plotline.*

There's certain First Principles and First Values that organize the story. So we're free in the moment to play and weave patterns. When we talk, we're completely free—we can talk about anything we want. But we're also operating within an overall storyline.

We don't have to prepare, and yet when you read the transcripts over some twelve years, you can discern an elegant, unfolding design. A Christian Intelligent Design person would say: God must be directly making each conversation happen. But in fact, God lives within and as the inherent, infinite, living, divine First Values and First Principles that organize the whole system.

So our topic is seduction. That's just how the Dharma organized itself. All of the pieces fit together that way because we have this commitment together. So if you want to design your life, you don't necessarily hire a coach who intervenes into your separate-self sphere and simply gives you a bunch of tips. No, you want someone who will actually work with you from the ground up, someone who will help you access First Principles and First Values that begin to create a new set of guiding plotlines. Then your life can beautifully, dazzlingly unfold.

But let's go much deeper and ask:

- **What are the values you'd be willing to die for?**
- **What are the values you know to be true within your body, anthro-ontologically?**

Those values are the plotlines of your life, and those are the values that will design your life.

Again, the entire contradiction between design and randomness is inaccurate. In fact, contingency, which means radical surprise, is the context of a non-random universe, and the non-random universe allows for complete freedom. Is that not wild?

This solves an apparently major problem in evolution: the relationship between randomness and contingency. When I was working through this, I thought about the math, I read Stuart Kauffman, and I thought about it logically.

This was necessary, but I was only able to really work it out when I thought about doing sessions with this person. I started looking back and I said, wow, these are all somehow perfectly designed. We must have spent all week preparing for each one, because they all fit together perfectly. Or there's a God external to these sessions, who was obviously writing the script. How else could they be so perfectly designed? **It's due to the inherent First Principles and First Values that are plotlines manifesting as new elegant order, as they call it in physics.**

Our final topic is seduction—and we're going to look at a bunch of movie scenes. We're going to briefly unpack each one for a couple minutes, little two-minute dharma capsules to introduce entirely new insights along the way.

7.6

THE FOUR DOUBLE BINDS OF SHAME IN *STAR WARS*: THE ULTIMATE ALIENATION FROM EROS OF VALUE AND STORY

We're going to dive deep into *Star Wars: Episode III: Revenge of the Sith*, which is the sixth *Star Wars* move made. Let's recall: In first three movies, episodes four to six, we meet Luke Skywalker, who gradually becomes a powerful Jedi Knight. However, he's actually the hidden child, we find out, of the villain Darth Vader, who was originally called Anakin Skywalker, and as a young Jedi Knight his teacher was Obi-Wan Kenobi.

The first three movies are about Luke Skywalker, and they climax with the exploding the Death Star, which we've already referenced—the old Empire collapses. In the next three movies, episodes one to three, we're going backwards.

This story centers around Anakin Skywalker: how he's born, how he meets Padme when she's a senator, and how he grows up to be the most powerful of Jedi Knights. There's actually a prophecy about Anakin, who in *Star Wars* language has more "Midi-chlorians"—meaning the Force energy, creativity, potential—than even Yoda, that little green guy who's ostensibly the most powerful Jedi Knight. The prophecy is that young Ani Skywalker will grow up to balance The Force.

Obi-Wan Kenobi takes him on as an apprentice and soon becomes very close to him; he's his young "Padawan," or apprentice. By the third movie, Anakin is the most powerful Jedi Knight by far, but he's imbalanced, young, and impulsive.

The first hour of Episode III is all about seduction. Palpatine, the Sith Lord who represents the forces of anti-value—the dark side of the Force—is trying to seduce the powerful young Anakin. It's a total seduction story. We will watch how he does it. Palpatine is the Sith Lord, but no one knows this—he's the head of the Senate, because Sith Lords always hide in surprising and sometimes deceptively obvious places. Even powerful Jedis like Yoda and Mace Windu are looking all over for the Sith Lord, and they can't find him—but he's right there in front of them; they are interacting every day. This is a good reminder: *what you're looking for is always right in front of you.*

We're going to trace this thread of seduction by following a series of conversations from the movie. There's three conversations between Palpatine and Anakin, and three conversations between Anakin and his teacher, Obi-Wan. Then there's three conversations between Anakin and Padme, and there's one conversation between Anakin and Yoda. There's a deep, intuitive structure here that we will track.

Our focus is on the relationship between holy seduction and unholy seduction. Unholy seduction is when I try to get someone to break their own appropriate boundary of value—not for the sake of a higher value, not for the sake of their need, but for the sake of my greed, or my greedy need.

Because remember: if the universe is a love story, if Reality is a love story, which it is, then **the currency of Reality is seduction**—seduction is moving through Reality all the time. Everyone is seduced; there's no one who isn't. The question then shifts from whether I'm seduced or free from seduction, to:

- What am I seduced by?
- Can I choose my seducer?
- Can I know when I'm being seduced?
- When should I allow myself to be seduced, and when should I not?

But remember, allurement moves my life. It's not merely the rational choice of *Homo economicus*—that's only one of the qualities at play in seduction. But seduction is a deeper quality: allurement.

- How do I trust my allurement?
- How do I clarify my allurement?
- How do I know who to listen to and who not to listen to?

Palpatine is powerful, and he realizes he needs to seduce young Anakin Skywalker into becoming Darth Vader, towards the so-called dark side.

We're going to go through these conversations quickly, with some commentary after each one. And remember, watching these sacred texts requires a loving placing of attention, a **placing of the heart**.

MOVIE SCENES: *STAR WARS EPISODE III: REVENGE OF THE SITH*

1—UNHOLY SEDUCTION

In this first scene, Dooku represents the bad guys, and he has ostensibly captured Chancellor Palpatine. But actually, Palpatine is the powerful Sith Lord, and Dooku is *his* assistant, under his power. It looks like Palpatine has been captured by Count Dooku, but it's a set-up. Watch Palpatine's face throughout this scene—as we know, face shots in movies are critical. The Jedi Knights Obi Wan and Anakin Skywalker have come to rescue Palpatine—who looks like he's the head of the Senate, they don't realize he's the Sith Lord—from

Dooku, who represents the dark side. A great saber battle ensues between the two Jedi and Dooku, while Palpatine watches.

As the battle proceeds, Anakin's arm is cut off, and he grows stronger and angrier. Dooku declares, "I sense great fear in you, Skywalker. You have hate, you have anger, but you don't use them."

They continue their intense fighting, and Anakin cuts off Dooku's hands. Dooku stumbles to the floor as Anakin holds two lightsabers to his neck. Palpatine is grinning as he watches Dooku's defeat.

Palpatine: Good, Anakin, good. I knew you could do it. Kill him. Kill him now!

Anakin: I shouldn't...

Palpatine: Do it!!

Anakin cuts off Dooku's head, and an explosion somewhere deep in the ship rattles everything.

Anakin: ...I couldn't stop myself.

Palpatine: You did well, Anakin. He was too dangerous to be kept alive.

Anakin: Yes, but he was an unarmed prisoner. I shouldn't have done that, Chancellor. It's not the Jedi way.

Palpatine: It is only natural. He cut off your arm, and you wanted revenge. It wasn't the first time, Anakin. Remember what you told me about your mother and the Sand People.

While Palpatine heads for the elevators, Anakin rushes over to Obi-Wan and tries to pull him free from a console that has fallen on him.

Palpatine: Anakin, there is no time. We must get off the ship before it's too late.

Anakin: He seems to be alright. No broken bones, breathing's alright.

> *Palpatine*: Leave him, or we'll never make it.

> *Anakin*: His fate will be the same as ours.

The crucial moment here is when Palpatine says, "Kill him." It goes against the Jedi Code to kill an unarmed prisoner, but Palpatine wants him to violate the value that he stands for. The second he gets him to violate that value, the unholy seduction has begun.

Of course, Palpatine has set up this whole scene because he's actually done with Dooku. He's manipulating everything behind the scenes because he wants a new apprentice: Anakin. **He has to seduce Anakin, so he says there is no value. That's what he begins to whisper in his ear: value doesn't exist, the Jedi way doesn't exist**. He gets him to violate his value. He says kill him, he's too dangerous to be left alive. We'll notice this scene referenced again in few minutes. Anakin will hear that sentence again, at a key moment of seduction.

At the end of the scene, Obi-Wan is hurt, and Anakin goes to see if he's okay. And Palpatine says, we've got to go, let him go. Then Anakin looks up—remember to look at the faces—and he says, "His fate will be the same as ours." He saves his friend and mentor, and you realize he's not fully seduced yet. Even though he was shaken, even though he transgressed by killing Dooku, Anakin's still a Jedi and still has some sense of value.

In this scene, Palpatine also says it was *natural* what he did, and it's natural to want revenge. Then he reminded him of his earlier shame when he says, "You've done this before when you exploded in rage when you lost your mother." Indeed, **the entire Anakin story is about the fact that he doesn't have the blessing of the mother.** He came too late to get the blessing of the mother. His mother is killed—he couldn't save her. He left her early in life to go become a Jedi Knight. The Jedi aren't really that concerned with the mother; they're actually more of the order of the father in a lot of ways.

Early in the first movie, young Anakin leaves his home planet to train as a Jedi, and in this powerful scene, you see the mother standing there, left behind. If you watch it carefully, you realize the Jedi do not really honor the mother. Anakin then later has this vision that his mother's being hurt. He ignores it because he's got to do his duty. When he goes to save her, it's too late, and he fails to receive the blessing of the mother. After she dies, he explodes in rage and kills the whole tribe: men, women, and children. That's what Palpatine was reminding him of in this scene.

When Anakin tries to reclaim his value, Palpatine reminds him that he's violated his values before—he evokes his shame—because it's natural. But then Anakin finds himself because he's got this other force drawing him to value: Obi-Wan. And at that moment, you can see the beauty on his face.

2—GENERAL GRIEVOUS TALKS WITH LORD SIDIOUS: MANIPULATION OVER STRATEGY

In the next scene, a hologram of Sith Lord Sidious (Palpatine) is talking to General Grievous, who's one of his two major henchmen. Grievous asks about the loss of Count Dooku, and Palpatine says it's fine, a necessary (and calculated) loss. That's always how it is: **Holy seduction employs strategy, while unholy seduction deploys manipulation.**

Manipulation and strategy might sometimes superficially look the same, but they're absolutely not.

- Strategy means: I'm omni-considerate for the sake of the whole, I feel the whole, I'm acting for the sake of the whole; I see and feel the parts moving, and I try and help them move towards a conclusion for the sake of the whole.
- Manipulation means: I'm interested in my part, and I manipulate the parts in order to achieve my narrow goal, which ignores the good of the whole; I sub-optimize for my own greed instead of the whole.

That's the great distinction between strategy and manipulation, and the grand manipulator and unholy seducer Palpatine is setting this all up. At the end of this scene, he says, "I'm going to soon have a new young apprentice"—Anakin Skywalker.

3—THE BLESSING OF THE MOTHER

This next scene is strangely distorted and disorienting. Padme is on a table in an alien medical chamber. She is giving birth and is screaming for Anakin and saying that she loves him. Then she suddenly dies. Inside Padme's apartment, Anakin awakens in a panic, covered in sweat. He looks over and sees Padme sound asleep next to him. Breathing heavily and weeping, he puts his head in his hands, and then walks onto a large veranda. Padme joins Anakin on the veranda, taking his hand, but he doesn't look at her. Here is their dialogue:

> *Padme:* Anakin, how long is it going to take for us to be honest with each other?
>
> *Anakin:* It was a dream.
>
> *Padme:* Bad?
>
> *Anakin:* Like the ones I used to have about my mother just before she died.
>
> *Padme:* And?
>
> *Anakin:* It was about you. You die in childbirth…
>
> *Padme:* And the baby?
>
> *Anakin:* I don't know.
>
> *Padme:* It was only a dream.
>
> *Anakin:* I won't let this one become real, Padme.

> *Padme*: Anakin, this baby will change our lives. I doubt the Queen will continue to allow me to serve in the Senate, and if the Council discovers you are the father, you will be expelled from the Jedi Order.
>
> *Anakin*: I know...
>
> *Padme*: Anakin, do you think Obi-Wan might be able to help us?
>
> *Anakin*: He's been a father to me, but he's still on the Council. Don't tell him anything!
>
> *Padme*: I won't, Anakin.
>
> *Anakin*: I don't need his help... Our baby is a blessing, not a problem.

It's an incredible clip. Padme is the girl who became a senator when Anakin was a boy. He grows up, and they fall in love. Because he's a Jedi, he's not allowed to love an individual person—**the split between Eros and agape lives very strongly in *Star Wars*.** He's not allowed to be with her—no one knows they're living together.

Padme is the Mother—both his woman and his Beloved. But often our Beloved also says, "You're my baby," when it's a real relationship. She's also the mother of his baby, so **she's the connection he has to the blessing of the mother**. The last time he had dreams like this, they were about his mother, and because of his Jedi honor, he didn't respond and got to his mother too late to receive the blessing.

Now he's having these same dreams about Padme dying. She says go to Obi-Wan, but Anakin can't talk to Obi-Wan because he represents the Jedi Order, and won't understand this relationship. It's not allowed, and it's not comprehensible. But what does Anakin say to Padme? He says, "Our baby is a blessing." **He feels and knows in his body that the baby is a blessing, that Padme is a blessing.** Yet, he wasn't able to save his mother, the Mother.

The mother for him now is Padme, and he's having the same dreams in his body, about losing Padme.

That's the exact place where unholy seduction can happen. Unholy seduction is not some good-looking guy, some sexy woman—whatever that means—who comes and seduces you. That's the most boring form of seduction I can imagine. Seduction is so much more interesting, multi-leveled, and subtle. The point is that Anakin is now open to being seduced—through his relationship with Padme, and based on his shame over his own mother.

So if you want to get someone to break their inappropriate boundary, it could be holy or unholy seduction, by finding their weak point. Now, if it's beautiful, mad-love holy seduction, then that action is gorgeous and beautiful. But if it's unholy seduction, manipulation, then I'm trying to get you to open to a place where you're going to be vulnerable so I can get you to cross your appropriate boundary.

In this case—it's unholy, all for Palpatine's gain, coming from pseudo-eros, not Eros. How is he going to get Anakin to cross his boundary? Through his relationship to the mother.

We have no idea who Anakin's father is. That's one of the great mysteries of *Star Wars*—it's a very important fact that he doesn't at all have the blessing of the father. You have a series of surrogate fathers: Yoda, Palpatine, and Obi-Wan—they're all trying to be his father, and there's actually a struggle amongst them, over him.

Palpatine is going to step in and forcefully say, "I'm the father." Obi-Wan has more integrity but refuses to take on the role of the father, which is his big mistake—he plays big brother instead. But Anakin doesn't need a big brother—he needs a father.

Unfortunately, Yoda can't quite feel him, so Palpatine is the person who finally steps in to give blessing of the father—but does so from a place of pseudo-eros, not Eros.

4—YODA FAILS TO HONOR EROS AND LIFE

In the next clip, Anakin goes to see Yoda at the Jedi Temple, after having that dream, and after having that conversation where his last words were: "Our baby is a blessing."

Yoda: Premonitions... premonitions... Hmmmm... these visions you have...

Anakin: They are of pain, suffering, death...

Yoda: Yourself you speak of, or someone you know?

Anakin: Someone...

Yoda: ...close to you?

Anakin: Yes.

Yoda: Careful you must be when sensing the future, Anakin. The fear of loss is a path to the dark side.

Anakin: I won't let these visions come true, Master Yoda.

Yoda: Death is a natural part of life. Rejoice for those around you who transform into the Force. Mourn them, do not. Miss them, do not. Attachment leads to jealousy. The shadow of greed, that is.

Anakin: What must I do, Master Yoda?

Yoda: **Train yourself to let go of everything you fear to lose.**

Yoda blows it big time in this scene—he does not understand. Anakin walks in with premonitions of Padme dying, and the master can only say, "Fear of loss leads to the dark side." He essentially says: anyone you love, let go of them, because that's actually attachment, which leads to greed and jealousy. Did you see the false wisdom on Anakin's face in the end?

This is a classical double bind. In the scene right before this one, Anakin says, "Our baby's a blessing," and he knows that to be true in his body, anthro-ontologically. But Yoda can't feel that blessing—he can't feel the blessing of Padme, or access the value of those premonitions. He says that fear of loss leads to the dark side, and only liberating from attachment sets you free. **The teaching of the Jedi Order is a teaching of agape, which belittles and demonizes Eros.**

Seduction always plays with a truth that already lives inside of you. Seduction accesses that truth and you say, "Oh, they're right, I know that's true." Then seduction twists that truth in a different direction. Palpatine is going to play with this fabric, but—and this is why it's unholy seduction— it's the worst violation of someone's integrity to access that which lives appropriately as a truth inside of them, but then you hijack that truth—not for the sake of their need, or a higher need, but for the sake of your greed, which is exactly what Palpatine is going to do.

However, Yoda, and the entire Jedi order, helped set all this up. Does Yoda really know anything here? No—and I think the filmmakers got this, either intentionally or not, because in this scene, Yoda is literally in the dark, in a dark room. Yoda can't see. He *thinks* he's in the light. He *thinks* that dark is light, but it's not. At the end, when you look at Anakin's face, you realize Yoda doesn't get it at all.

So now Palpatine is now going to step in, and now the action is going to pick up. And the way you seduce someone in an unholy way is that you break their relationship to value. When you break a person's relationship to value, you shame them.

We can say that **shame is alienation from value**.

Shame is alienation from value, and remember that value and story are the same. So when you alienate a person from value, they step out of their story, and they can be seduced to another story. So Palpatine has started to alienate Anakin from value, and then seduce him away from his story, which is to become the greatest Jedi Knight and balance The Force.

5—PALPATINE SEDUCES ANAKIN BY CORRUPTING VALUE

In the Chancellor's office, Anakin stands with Palpatine at a window overlooking the vastness of Coruscant City. Several buildings have been destroyed. A brown haze hangs over the landscape. They walk as they talk.

> *Palpatine*: Anakin, I've known you since you were a small boy. I have advised you over the years when I could... I am very proud of your accomplishments. You have won many battles the Jedi Council thought were lost... and you saved my life. I hope you trust me, Anakin.

> *Anakin*: Of course.

> *Palpatine*: I need your help, son.

> *Anakin*: What do you mean?

> *Palpatine*: I fear the Jedi. The Council keeps pushing for more control. They're shrouded in secrecy and obsessed with maintaining their autonomy... ideals I find simply incomprehensible in a democracy.

> *Anakin*: I can assure you that the Jedi are dedicated to the values of the Republic, sir.

> *Palpatine*: Nevertheless, their actions will speak more loudly than their words. I'm depending on you.

> *Anakin*: For what? I don't understand.

> *Palpatine*: To be the eyes, ears, and voice of the Republic... I'm appointing you to be my personal representative on the Jedi Council.

> *Anakin*: Me? A Master? I am overwhelmed, sir, but the Council elects its own members. They will never accept this.

> *Palpatine*: I think they will... they need you more than you know.

Here Palpatine is using the value of trust—he hijacks and weaponizes it. You can see that Anakin doesn't quite trust him, but he says, "Of course I do." Palpatine says, let's appoint you to be a master on the council. So he plays directly to Anakin's sense of not being recognized, which we've seen in other scenes, and he's drawing him closer and closer. It's clearly a seduction scene. Next, we have one of the most important early seduction scenes in the movie.

6—THE SEDUCTION DEEPENS BY PLAYING ON REAL VALUE

In this scene, Anakin is summoned to join Palpatine at the Opera House, where he's watching a performance of "Squid Lake"—a collection of large, shimmering, bulbous, bioluminescent spheroids moving beautifully and slowly throughout the space, set to a low ambient drone. First, Palpatine ingratiates Anakin through flattery:

> *Palpatine*: I would worry about the collective wisdom of the Council if they didn't select you for this assignment. You are the best choice by far… but, they can't always be trusted to do the right thing.

Next, Palpatine continues the seduction by appearing to let him in on some secrets.

> *Palpatine*: You must sense what I have come to suspect… the Jedi Council want control of the Republic… they're planning to betray me.
>
> *Anakin*: I don't think…
>
> *Palpatine*: Anakin, search your feelings. You know, don't you?
>
> *Anakin*: I know they don't trust you…
>
> *Palpatine*: Or the Senate… or the Republic… or democracy for that matter.

Anakin: I have to admit my trust in them has been shaken.

Palpatine: Why? They asked you to do something that made you feel dishonest, didn't they?

Palpatine: They asked you to spy on me, didn't they?

Anakin: I don't know… I don't know what to say.

Next, there is a rich discussion about ethics and the Force:

Palpatine: Remember back to your early teachings. Anakin. "All those who gain power are afraid to lose it." Even the Jedi.

Anakin: The Jedi use their power for good.

Palpatine: Good is a point of view, Anakin. And the Jedi point of view is not the only valid one. The Dark Lords of the Sith believe in security and justice also, yet they are considered by the Jedi to be…

Anakin: …evil…

Palpatine: …from a Jedi's point of view. The Sith and the Jedi are similar in almost every way, including their quest for greater power. The difference between the two is the Sith are not afraid of the dark side of the Force. That is why they are more powerful.

Anakin: The Sith rely on their passion for their strength. They think inward, only about themselves.

Palpatine: And the Jedi don't?

Anakin: The Jedi are selfless… they only care about others.

Palpatine: Or so you've been trained to believe. Why is it, then, that they have asked you to do something you feel is wrong?

Anakin: I'm not sure it is wrong.

Here Palpatine is seducing Anakin through values:

Palpatine: Have they asked you to betray the Jedi code? The Constitution? A friendship? Your own values? Think. Consider their motives. Keep your mind clear of assumptions. The fear of losing power is a weakness of both the Jedi and the Sith.

Then Palpatine's seduction continues through the story of the Darth Plagueis the Wise:

Palpatine: He was a Dark Lord of the Sith, so powerful and so wise he could use the Force to create life... He had such a knowledge of the dark side that he could even keep the ones he cared about from dying.

Anakin: He could actually save people from death?

Palpatine: The dark side of the Force is a pathway to many abilities some consider to be unnatural. He became so powerful... the only thing he was afraid of was losing his power, which eventually, of course, he did. Unfortunately, he taught his apprentice everything he knew, then his apprentice killed him in his sleep. Plagueis never saw it coming. It's ironic he could save others from death, but not himself.

Because of his recent dream, Anakin is clearly very intrigued:

Anakin: Is it possible to learn this power?

Palpatine: Not from a Jedi.

We could take an hour to go through each line of this incredible dialog—there's so much here. But at the center of the scene is value. "Good is only a point of view," claims Palpatine: the Sith and the Jedi are identical in almost every respect. Anakin believes only the Sith use their passion, because like all Jedi he's demonized Eros. And if the Sith are accessing passion and Eros, Eros is on the Sith side. The Jedi are selfless, which is a caricatured version of agape. That obviously can never be true with anyone, because everyone's complex. **So there's a caricatured view of agape, represented by the Jedi, against a demonized view of Eros, represented by the Sith.**

Palpatine appeals to this deep knowing in Anakin, although he can't articulate it yet, that Eros actually is holy. How does he know Eros is holy? Because of Padme—he absolutely knows that it's sacred, even though Yoda has said it isn't.

At the beginning of this scene, he plays with the jealousies and power drives of Anakin. Palpatine says, "Search your feelings." So Anakin finds a feeling, but he doesn't understand that we actually interpret our feelings. We think the feeling is the interpretation, but it's not. **So the manipulator accesses the true feeling that's already there, but then subtly provides an interpretation which is false. That's how unholy seduction works.**

Then he says, "It doesn't matter because good and evil are only points of view." That's the point: value is exploded. Anakin pushes back and he says, there is value.

The conversation resolves when Palpatine just plants his ideas in the space, lets it go, and then shares the legend of Darth Plagueis the Wise, who, of course, was Palpatine's teacher—because Palpatine is Darth Sidious. So Palpatine murdered his teacher in his sleep, having absorbed all of Darth Plagueis the Wise's knowledge. But what he now says is: he has the capacity to save the ones we love. If you follow the *Star Wars* story, this turns out to be false. Actually, the Sith don't have that capacity—the only one who does is Yoda, who shows it to Obi-Wan Kenobi.

The main point of this scene is: in unholy seduction, you play on already existing values to warp someone, to manipulate them for your own ends.

7—ANAKIN CAUGHT IN A DOUBLE BIND OF DESIRE

Now we return to Anakin and Padme, in the living room of her apartment. The mood is a bit tense between them.

Anakin: I feel… lost.

Padme: Lost? What do you mean? You're always so sure of yourself. I don't understand.

Anakin: Obi-Wan and the Council don't trust me.

Padme: They trust you with their lives. Obi-Wan loves you as a son.

Anakin: Something's happening… I'm not the Jedi I should be. I am one of the most powerful Jedi, but I'm not satisfied… I want more, and I know I shouldn't.

The seduction is starting to work, and he's very confused. What does he want? He wants more power. What does Palpatine say the one real issue at play in the world is? Power. Now go back to the scene in *Don't Look Up* where Kate is talking to Yule on the roof, wondering why the General at the White House would charge her for a snack. "I guess it's all about power," she says.

Both of these scenes are reflecting what culture at large is saying: that there is no value, and underneath it all is just a power game. The only apparent alternative to this Foucaudian, postmodern position is the Jedi/religious position of agape, which says that passion is outside of the story—it's only about being selfless. This creates a caricatured version of a desiccated person, which doesn't reflect Reality—someone who has disowned Eros, and who violates their own sense that, for example, "Our baby is a blessing," which Anakin knows deeply. That's the double bind. We're reading culture directly here. Next, we're coming to the key scenes of seduction.

8—"GREATER IS THE LIGHT THAT COMES FROM DARKNESS": PALPATINE PLAYS WITH ANAKIN'S TRAUMA

Palpatine's patient seduction throughout this movie is starting work on Anakin, whose deep sense of Jedi values is strong. And of course, much of what Palpatine says is true. Here we see a dramatic turn:

Palpatine: It's upsetting to me to see that the Council doesn't seem to fully appreciate your talents. Don't you wonder why they won't make you a Jedi Master?

Anakin: I wish I knew. More and more I get the feeling that I am being excluded from the Council. I know there are things about the Force that they're not telling me.

Palpatine: They don't trust you, Anakin. They see your future. They know your power will be too strong to control. Anakin, you must break through the fog of lies the Jedi have created around you. Let me help you to know the subtleties of the Force.

Anakin: How do you know the ways of the Force?

Palpatine: My mentor taught me everything about the Force... even the nature of the dark side.

Anakin: You know the dark side?!?

Palpatine: Anakin, if one is to understand the great mystery, one must study all its aspects, not just the dogmatic, narrow view of the Jedi. If you wish to become a complete and wise leader, you must embrace a larger view of the Force. Be careful of the Jedi, Anakin. They fear you. In time they will destroy you. Let me train you.

Here Anakin's sense of value continues to hold:

Anakin: I won't be a pawn in your political game. The Jedi are my family.

So Palpatine plays his trump card:

Palpatine: Only through me can you achieve a power greater than any Jedi. Learn to know the dark side of the Force, Anakin, and you will be able to save your wife from certain death.

Anakin: What did you say?

Palpatine: Use my knowledge, I beg you...

Anakin: You're the Sith Lord!

Palpatine: I know what's been troubling you... Listen to me. Don't continue to be a pawn of the Jedi Council! Ever since I've known you, you've been searching for a life greater than that of an ordinary Jedi... a life of significance, of conscience.

Anakin: You're wrong!

Palpatine: Are you going to kill me?

Anakin: I would certainly like to.

Palpatine: I know you would. I can feel your anger. It gives you focus, makes you stronger.

Anakin raises his lightsaber to Palpatine's throat. There is a tense moment, then Anakin relaxes and withdraws.

Anakin: I am going to turn you over to the Jedi Council.

Palpatine: Of course you should. But you're not sure of their intentions, are you?

Anakin: I will quickly discover the truth of all this.

Palpatine: You have great wisdom, Anakin. Know the power of the dark side. The power to save Padme.

It's a gentle and fierce scene—quiveringly tender, but insanely fierce. First, is Palpatine completely wrong? No, he says one of the wisest sentences ever spoken: you need a wider view. You actually have to be able to embrace both the dark and the light to feel the full power. But of course, he gets it wildly wrong. For Palpatine, as for many in our culture, light and dark are neutral—they're equivalent because the only issue is power.

In a genuine vision of *Homo amor*, we would actually adopt a version of Palpatine's sentence. There's a text in the Book of Ecclesiastes, written by Solomon, the great master of Eros. It reads: *Mai'terron ha'or min ha'khoshech*, which can mean, "Greater is light than darkness." That's a Jedi reading, which makes an absolutistic split. But let's read it differently—the hidden texts say: **Greater is the light *that comes from* the darkness.**

In other words, the capacity to access the energy of the dark side is utterly necessary for blessing.

There's a story about the Baal Shem Tov, who is called to a village to tend to a very sick baby. There's this distraught couple, their baby is dying, his skin is pale—it's the middle of the night. In desperate cases like this, you usually ask for ten righteous people and they pray, but the Baal Shem Tov instead says, "Bring me ten criminals—I'll pray with them. The ten worst thieves, I can only pray with ten thieves."

The parents are madly in love with their child, and they think he's out of his mind. But they've got no other recourse. They find the ten thieves in town who no one talks to, and bring them home. The thieves pray all night, and as morning comes, they hear crying, and color returns to the baby's cheeks. The parents turn to the Baal Shem Tov and they ask, "What did you do?" He says, "I saw that the gates of heaven were already sealed. The were closed, so I needed thieves to pick the locks." It's beautiful. **In other words, sometimes you need the energy of the dark side to find the light.**

So Palpatine is not entirely wrong that the energy of the dark side needs to be integrated into the light—indeed, the reason Palpatine is so seductive here is because he's actually saying something true and important. But he ultimately hijacks that insight only for his own power, by playing with Anakin's sense of personal loss. He's becoming the father Anakin never had. He's promising to heal Padme. He's playing with Anakin's sense of having been passed over, his own egocentric traumas. That's how unholy seduction works: It plays with our traumas, and it inserts truths that are potent and powerful.

Anakin then realizes that Palpatine is the Sith Lord, but now he has a new double bind, a second double bind: If I kill him, I kill the only person who's told me they can save Padme.

9—ANAKIN CAUGHT IN THE DOUBLE BIND

In the Jedi ship hangar, Anakin approaches Mace Windu and three other Jedi, who are preparing to go to Palpatine's office.

Mace Windu: What is it, Skywalker? We're in a hurry. We have just received word that Obi-Wan has destroyed General Grievous. We're on our way to make sure the Chancellor returns emergency powers back to the Senate.

Anakin: He won't give up his power. I've just learned a terrible truth. I think Chancellor Palpatine is a Sith Lord.

Mace Windu: A Sith Lord?

Anakin: Yes. The one we have been looking for.

Mace Windu: How do you know this?

Anakin: He knows the ways of the Force. He's been trained to use the dark side.

Mace Windu: Are you sure?

Anakin: Absolutely.

Mace Windu: Then our worst fears have been realized. We must move quickly if the Jedi Order is to survive.

Anakin: Master, the Chancellor is very powerful. You will need my help if you are going to arrest him.

Mace Windu: For your own good, stay out of this affair. I sense a great deal of confusion in you, young Skywalker. There is much fear that clouds your judgment. If what you told me is true, you will have gained my trust, but for now remain here.

Next we see intercut scenes of Padme alone in her apartment, thinking of Anakin, and Anakin alone in the Jedi Council Chamber thinking of Padme, tears in his eyes. He recalls the words of Palpatine, "If the Jedi destroy me, any chance of saving her will be lost."

Anakin cannot wait in the council chambers any longer. He desperately needs Palpatine alive, or else Padme will be lost—the mother will be lost, again. Anakin does not stay in the chamber; he goes to interrupt Palpatine's arrest.

10—ANAKIN CANNOT FIND WHERE TRUE VALUE LIES

Anakin lands his speeder and arrives to see Jedi Master Mace Windu and the Sith Lord Palpatine fighting over a precipice. They stop as Mace forces Palpatine to drop his sword, and Palpatine attempts to save his life by appealing to Anakin:

Palpatine: Come to your senses, boy. The Jedi are in revolt. They will betray you, just as they betrayed me. You are not one of them, Anakin. Don't let him kill me. I am your pathway to power. I have the power to save the one you love. You must choose. You must stop him.

Mace Windu: Don't listen to him, Anakin.

Palpatine: Help me! Don't let him kill me. I can't hold on any longer. Ahhhhhhh…

Mace now moves closer, as the Chancellor's face begins to twist and distort. His eyes become yellow as he struggles.

Palpatine: I can't... I give up. I am weak... I am too weak. Don't kill me. Help me. I'm dying. I can't hold on any longer.

Mace Windu: You Sith disease. I am going to end this once and for all.

Anakin now appeals to Jedi values:

Anakin: You can't kill him, Master. He must stand trial.

Mace Windu: He has too much control of the Senate and the Courts. He is too dangerous to be kept alive.

Palpatine: I'm too weak. Don't kill me. Please.

Anakin: It is not the Jedi way. He must live...

Palpatine: Please don't, please don't...

Anakin: I need him...

Just as Mace is about to slash Palpatine, Anakin steps in and cuts off the Jedi's hand holding the lightsaber. As Mace stares at Anakin in shock, Palpatine springs to life. The full force of Palpatine's powerful bolts blasts Mace. As blue rays engulf his body, Mace is flung out the window and falls to his death.

Palpatine: Power! Unlimited power!

His face has changed into a horrible mask of evil. Anakin looks on in horror. Palpatine cackles.

Anakin: What have I done?

Palpatine: You are fulfilling your destiny, Anakin. Become my apprentice. Learn to use the dark side of the Force.

Anakin is in shock, somewhat numb. The seduction has succeeded:

Anakin: I will do whatever you ask. Just help me save Padme's life. I can't live without her. I won't let her die. I want the power to stop death.

Palpatine: To cheat death is a power only one has achieved, but if we work together, I know we can discover the secret.

Anakin: I pledge myself to your teachings. To the ways of the Sith.

Palpatine: The Force is strong with you. A powerful Sith you will become. Henceforth, you shall be known as Darth... Vader.

We see Yoda wincing and shaking his head—he clearly feels a disturbance in the Force. Back in his office, Palpatine puts on a dark cloak: he is now fully Darth Sidious.

Palpatine: Because the Council did not trust you, my young apprentice, I believe you are the only Jedi with no knowledge of this plot. When the Jedi learn what has transpired here, they will kill us, along with all the Senators.

Anakin: I agree. The Jedi's next move will be against the Senate.

Palpatine: Every single Jedi, including your friend Obi-Wan Kenobi, is now an enemy of the Republic. You understand that, don't you?

Anakin: I understand, Master.

Palpatine: We must move quickly. The Jedi are relentless; if they are not all destroyed, it will be civil war without end. First, I want you to go to the Jedi Temple. We will catch them off balance. Do what must be done, Lord Vader. Do not hesitate. Show no mercy. Only then will you be strong enough with the dark side to save Padme.

This is an incredible scene, from the most watched story in our culture. Anakin flies to the place where Mace Windu is going to arrest Palpatine, and they're fighting. He faces down Palpatine's blue lightning, the trademark of the Sith, then says he's going to kill him. But Anakin says it's against the Jedi code. Where have we heard that before? How does Mace respond? He's too dangerous to be left alive. And who said that before earlier in the movie?

You get how the scene has completely replayed itself? In Anakin's mind, **value has disappeared.** In other words, three important things are happening:

- A power play.
- Anakin's mad desire to save Padme.
- A collapse of value.

Anakin can't find a value to stand on because now the Jedi Mace is telling him the exact same thing that Palpatine said at the beginning of the movie. He's saying not to arrest him because he's too dangerous to be kept alive. **He's not able to navigate value. He's not able to see that value *evolves*.** For him, value can only be eternal and immutable that operates a particular way, which never changes and never shifts.

But actually, value that is only unchanging and eternal is undermined— and rightly so—by postmodernity. **In fact, true value is both eternal *and* it evolves.**

Eternal value is real, and it also evolves.

But it can't evolve here, it can't shift here. So we literally hear Mace Windu repeat the exact same sentence we heard from Palpatine, a shocking reversal. That comes together with Anakin's desperate need for Palpatine's help.

After Palpatine kills Mace, what does Anakin say? "What have I done?" A sense of total shame. He's now alienated from the Field of Value. You notice what happens then? He collapses, he shrinks. He literally becomes, in an instant, a different person. He just collapses.

- The person who was crying in the earlier scene is gone.
- The person who knows his child is a blessing is gone.
- The person who said to Palpatine, while saving Obi-Wan, that his fate will be the same as ours, is gone.
- The beautiful young Anakin is gone—because he's shamed.

Shame blocks Eros. Shame is the root of all evil. Of course, we must engage with and sometimes listen to shame, but here we're talking about unseen shame, unprocessed shame, unchecked shame, and weaponized shame.

Anakin can't find his way beyond shame, which is always rooted in an alienation from value. **Because value and story are the same, when we're alienated from value, we're alienated from our own story.**

• • •

To wrap things up, let's just see one last scene when Darth Vader arises. It's the ultimate shame. Anakin, who's now Darth Vader, because he has a new name, has battled Obi-Wan, who cut Vader in half. Obi-Wan didn't want to kill him, so he left him there thinking he would die. Palpatine then rescues him and rebuilds him as a technologically augmented human being. He's got the ultimate Google Glasses on. He's become this cyborg.

But inside of that cyborg is actually Anakin.

Before this, he has an encounter with Padme, who tries to stop him, and then he throws Padme to the ground. But he doesn't kill her—she's actually fine. Then she gives birth to two babies: Luke and Leia. But in his state he doesn't remember what happened, as he awakens in the new black suit, as Darth Vader. He also doesn't know that Padme has given birth to two children.

11—ANAKIN BECOMES DARTH VADER

At the medical center, Obi-Wan is with Padme after she gives birth. He leans over and softly speaks to her, "Padme, they need you... hang on." Before she dies, her last words refer to Anakin:

Padme: Obi-Wan... there... is good in him. I know there is... still...

At the Imperial Rehab Center, Darth Sidious hovers around the periphery of a group of medical droids who are working on Anakin.

Darth Sidious: Lord Vader, can you hear me?

Darth Vader: Yes, my master. Where is Padme? Is she safe, is she alright?

Darth Sidious: I'm afraid she died... it seems in your anger, you killed her.

A low groan emanates from Vader's mask. Due to his anger, objects in the room suddenly begin to implode, including some of the droids.

Darth Vader: I couldn't have! She was alive! I felt her! She was alive! It's impossible! No!!

That's the final double bind that destroys him—he's accused of killing the Mother, again. He says, in my feeling, I know she's alive. **But now he can't trust his feeling; he can't trust his body.** He's falsely accused of killing the Mother, and now he's Darth Vader.

It's the ultimate shame, the ultimate alienation from value.

7.7

SOLOMON'S SONG OF SONGS: REALITY IS A STORY OF SEDUCTION

I want to leave you with one final seduction text. It's a text of Solomon, from the *Song of Songs*, and it's possibly the most important text ever written.

There's a word in English we call "will"—as in free will, my will, the will of God. **Will is very important**—will is where I come from. It's my will to live. Schopenhauer said correctly: will is everything.

- Will is the mood of my life.
- Will is the power that courses through me.
- Will is the political will of a community.
- It's the will of a Unique Self Symphony.

This word can seem like a strange, archaic thing. But this word is everything. It comes through the Latin and the English, but one of its original sources is from the great mystic and interior scientist Solomon.

In the *Song of Songs*, the lover says to the Beloved, *mashkheni aharaka be-na rutzah*. The word for will in Hebrew is *ratzon*, and that word comes from a three-part phrase in the set of love notes between a lover and a Beloved, which is the *Song of Solomon*, from the hidden lineage—like the da Vinci codes, or the hidden lineage where the Magdalene mysteries came from, where the troubadours came from, where all the esoteric societies came from.

As mentioned, it's written that if none of the wisdom in the world existed, and if all of the texts, and all of the knowledge, and all of the traditions all disappeared, and we just had the wisdom of the *Song of Solomon*, we could wisely govern ourselves and all of Reality. All of the books are holy, says one master, but the only book that's the holy of holies, that's on the inside of the inside, that opens into the Sanctum Sanctorum, is the *Song of Solomon*.

It's not theology. It's not rigorous logic. It's not a Great Library. **It's a series of love notes between a lover and a Beloved. That's what the *Song of Solomon* is, and at the core of the Song is seduction—they're trying to seduce each other, they're trying to find each other.**

But it's not a simple text. She's completely there and then he's not around. Then he knocks on the door—*qol dudi dofeq*: the voice of my Beloved is knocking. And she says, *pashateti kutaneti khakhel elbashenah*: I've taken off my clothes, I'm in bed, how can I get up and answer the door? The whole text is them searching and searching—and they can't quite find each other.

Until finally the lover says to the Beloved, *mashkheni aharaka*: draw me after you, *na-rutzah*: and I will run towards you. So that word *rutzah*, "run," is also *ratzon*, "will"—same word.

This is the other seduction story, the holy seduction. Today we saw the unholy, shadow seduction story because we all need to know the shadow energy. It's not all sweetness and light—there's shadow energy. There's holy seduction and there's unholy seduction, manipulation. Seduction is subtle—like shame, it's insidious and multi-layered.

But underneath there's a deeper love story, and that deeper love story is about a higher and deeper seduction. Something gorgeous happens. You see, the text says, **draw me after you, *na-rutzah*: I'll run towards you.** The word "run" is the word "will." So I'll run towards you, meaning I'll be in my will. But isn't it like that moment in sexing, for example, because the sexual models the erotic? Draw me after you—what is this describing? You're kind of at the beginning process of sexing. You're in, you're in, you're in, maybe you're in, and then you cross a line. Draw me after you, *na-rutzah*: I'm running. That moment, find that moment.

So isn't that moment one in which I've given up my will? No, in holy seduction, that's actually the moment where I've *found* my will. Or you could say: **I've given up my lower will—*Shekhinati ta'ah*, the lower goddess—but I've accessed my true nature. I'm a lover. I'm in full play. This is who I actually am, and I look in your face and I scream the name of God.**

This is the truth of Reality.

At the very core of Reality, argues this sacred text, *mashkheni aharaka*: draw me after you. But oh, was there consent? We've lost the story of seduction. Of course we need consent. That's an absolute given. That's not what the story is about. In today's culture, we automatically go to consent—which is so self-evidently glaringly obvious—because we've totally lost what seduction is. The lover says to the Beloved, not "I consent," but "draw me after you." *Mashkheni*: draw me, seduce me. *Na-rutzah*: I'll run towards you, emotionally, aesthetically, artistically, politically, economically.

The sexual models the erotic.

Reality is a love story, and Reality is a story of seduction.

In seduction, I use my mind and I use my heart and my body. That's all true. We've spent much of the last ten years engaging deeply with the interior sciences, trying to re-vision and integrate all valuable wisdom streams.

But when all's said and done, what's driving the whole thing is the love story, and at the core of the love story is seduction. Who would want to live in a world where we can't be seduced? In other words, the nature of a materialist, reductive world is that there is no seduction. And in this view, because there's nothing to seduce you, seduction can only be a boundary violation.

REALITY IS AROUSAL

When I read a text, I want the words to seduce me, draw me in, get underneath my mind, find my heart and open a space that I've never seen—and love me open to Reality.

So, as we said earlier, we can replace *Know Thyself* with *Seduce Thyself*, because **Reality is arousal**. This has nothing to do with sexuality—it applies whether you're celibate, asexual, promiscuous, polyamorous, monogamous. We use sexuality as an image now, a critical and beautiful image. But the point, again, is that the sexual models the erotic. There's at least twelve billion years of Eros before sex, and there will be at least twelve billion years of Eros to come...

In Unique Self Symphony, what we say is: *we're going to take responsibility to seduce each other*. That's what we've got to do—and we also have to seduce culture. We can't just ram it down culture's throat; we can't just declare this to be the case.

We can't seduce culture unless we seduce ourselves; we can't arouse culture unless we can arouse ourselves.

You might be ask, why does he have to choose such a provocative way of saying it? *Because it's the truth.* There's no other way to say it, and it's why all the other attempts haven't worked. Da Vinci was all about seduction, day and night, and Ficino too—all of them. It's got to be everywhere alive. You can't build a company from seventy to 750 people without seducing them. But it's always holy seduction. We're breaking only the boundary of your contraction—all appropriate boundaries remain intact.

We can't create a relationship unless we're seducing each other all the time. The moment I give up my gorgeous, sacred, noble responsibility to seduce my Beloved, it's over.

Ultimately, you could say that there's only one sacred text: Outrageous Love notes between the lover and the Beloved. There's no other type of sacred text. But most scholars discover all this historical evidence and they say, this is just a "tavern" song. Of course it's a tavern song, you idiots! That's the whole point.

It's a song sung between lover and Beloved.

That's exactly what Reality is.

It's a sacred text of holy seduction.

7.8

CLOSING: I'M NOT WILLING TO BE WRITTEN IN THE BOOK OF LIFE WITHOUT YOU

So I just want to tell you one final story, about a master who's with the holy band, and they're on this very holy day of the year, on which, as Leonard Cohen writes, "The Book of Life is open," and we find out who shall live and who shall die.

So the master says to his friends, to the holy company, "Who shall live and who shall die?"

Think about your own life, and the lives of everyone you know. Will you be alive this time next year? I don't know. Will I be? I hope so. I hope we all will be—mad blessings for life.

But it's not simple. Who shall live and who shall die? The master says to the students, "I can't guarantee you anything. Life is hard, he says, but there's one thing we can do to come together that actually blows it open, so everyone is held and protected."

It's gorgeous, and we step into life together.

What could we possibly do?

He says, "If I can just give up my drive for a moment, and look at the person next to me in the hall, and say, *I'm not willing to be written into the Book of Life without you.*" At that moment, the angel of death gets confused because the Angel of Death is plucking egos—and egos don't say shit like that.

The Angel of Death goes *whoa*, and it changes everything.

CONTEMPLATION EXERCISE: THE BOOK OF LIFE & THE EVOLUTION OF LOVE

We're in Unique Self Symphony, and we're here to heal the source code of culture. That's our game. That's the only question we're asking here.

You can do this with someone else, out loud, or in your mind with an imaginal partner. Think of someone you know. We're on the inside on the inside of the inside.

The words are: "I'm not willing to be written in the Book of Life without you." You can also write this out in your journal. Reflect deeply on this as you repeat the words again and again.

Next, ask yourself the following questions and write out what comes up.

Am I ready to play a larger game?

Am I ready to participate in the evolution of love?

QUESTIONS AND ANSWERS: ON STORY, VALUE, DESIRE, AND SUFFERING

QUESTION 1: IS PLOT A PROPERTY OF STORY?

Jane: How about plot being a property of story?

Marc: Fantastic. You're exactly right. Every story has a plotline. Therefore, if the universe, if Reality, is not merely a fact but a story, and not merely an ordinary story but an Outrageous, Evolutionary Love Story, what does that mean? It's simple. **It means that Eros, or love, is the plotline of the story.**

This is how we break the postmodern predicament. This is how we restore value. This is what Putin or Xi never heard about—nor Obama for that matter. This doesn't yet exist in the Academy.

I spent ten long sessions over the past year unpacking this with Ken Wilber. He said to me, "This is the piece we didn't get in Integral Theory. We didn't get value." Ken, Zak, and I are now working deeply on this, and it's everything.[9] It completely changes the game. **Reality has a plotline.**

---

[9] See David J. Temple, *First Principles and First Values*, 2024.

Reality is moving towards more and more Eros, all the way up and all the way down.

What does Eros mean? Eros is the experience of radical aliveness, seeking and desiring ever more contact and ever greater wholeness. Is that a plotline? It sure is. We're in the source code now.

Eros has another property called intimacy (shared identity in the context of relative otherness, times mutualities of recognition, pathos, value, and purpose). So we could say that the second plotline of Reality is the evolution of intimacy. Knowing this deep down changes everything.

Is this just simplicity to complexity? No. It's the innate desire to be intimate that I share with all of Reality—not some weird pathology based on working out my early childhood issues, although those may shape the story of my intimacy in some way. The fundamental desire for intimacy is the Cosmos, awake and alive in me. Reality is not mere simplicity to complexity—yawn.

That will not prevent the collapse of value, nor will it stop all the consequences of that collapse. No. **Reality is the progressive deepening of intimacies.** I hope by now that this vital sentence resonates in an entirely different and deeper way. This is not information presented as bits and bytes, but a progressively embodied gnosis. We have to feel the progressive deepening of intimacies that make up Reality at all levels.

So we understand that it's more and more Eros, and it's more and more intimacy. **What else is a plotline? More and more uniqueness.** In other words, reaching for my Unique Self is an expression of the inherent structure of Reality in me. And if I don't live my Unique Self, then Reality is missing its own reaching, and I feel alienated from Reality itself.

Recall the text we cited on the first day from Rav Kook: "The shameless behavior of the New World at the edge of Apocalypse comes because the world is not ready to claim an explanation of how all the particular details weave together into The All." The shameless behavior, the social breakdown at the edge of the apocalypse, he wrote 100 years ago, comes from **the fact that we feel that our lives do not matter in an ultimate sense**. It's an exquisite expression of the search for meaning—every detail of my life must be connected to cosmic magnificence.

So what are we doing right now? **We're connecting the details to cosmic magnificence.** We're saying that my story is not just a story but chapter and verse in the Universe: A Love Story.

So far, we've got three plotlines:

- Eros and desire.
- Progressively deeper intimacy—from egocentric, ethnocentric, and worldcentric to cosmocentric structures of consciousness/ intimacy.
- Uniqueness.

A fourth one is that Cosmos is striving towards more and more creativity. We are participating in the ongoing creativity of Cosmos itself, unfolding in us, as us, and through us. Two more plotlines we can include in this list are Story and Value, which we've already been exploring.

Those are some of the fundamental plotlines of Cosmos.

QUESTION 2: WHAT IS VALUE?

Marc: Someone just asked, "What exactly *is* value?" Great question—let's clarify this. There are certain words where there's nothing underneath them, words you cannot reduce to other words—we call those First Principle and First Value words. What's underneath the word "desire"? Try and reduce the word desire to something else. It's very difficult to do. It's the same thing with the word "value."

But let's make an attempt here. Value means I desire a certain direction, and I experience that direction I desire as being meaningful, worth something. So you can say value is Eros, as well as meaning, information, uniqueness, story—this entire cluster of words point to it.

We can also say value means *yes, it matters*. It's aligned with the nature of the Real. It's not a fiction—it fucking matters. Notice here that there's no declaration of a list of values. Those specific values are important, but it's essential to start from First Principles. I hope that helps.

QUESTION 3: WHAT DO YOU MEAN BY "DESIRE IS MATTER"

Question: I want to know whether I understand it right when you say, "It matters." What kind of hit me was a phrase: "desire is matter."

Marc: You're absolutely right. You just put that so beautifully. Desire is at the heart of matter. Matter itself *is* desire, which seeks to create new value, which seeks to create a new whole. That's actually what it is. You hit it just gorgeously. Matter is desire, and desire is what matters.

Language is so gorgeous. What "matters" means what's meaningful, but it also means physical matter. **Physical matter is the desire of separate parts to form a larger wholes.** That's the story they should be in, and that's what they're allowed to do—*and* it fucking matters. So there's no split between those two. Look at how gorgeous language is. That's what the Hebrew word *davar* is doing, referring both to "thing" and "word" or Logos.

Do you see how this is in the structure of everything?

As you can see, this means we're doing spirituality in a completely different way because we have to do something completely different in order to re-weave a fractured Cosmos.

QUESTION 4: IS HOMO AMOR THE END OF THE STORY?

Question: As you've said, the story evolves, and values do as well, but is there some way you think *Homo amor* is the end result of the story?

Marc: Great question, thank you. But no, I don't. **Homo amor is what we need right now for the story to continue. There is no more story if we don't have Homo amor.** So, in other words, *Homo amor* is the next chapter in the ongoing story. I ultimately think this story is going to be galactic, intergalactic, and interdimensional. It'll be extraterrestrial and extradimensional. We actually live in a wild Cosmos, far more wild than we might think. We're currently in a very limited dimension of the Cosmos.

About a year and a half ago, I spent several weeks trying to plow through about forty books to get a sense of where the literature is now on extraterrestrial, extradimensional, and interdimensional questions—that's all changed now. What used to be completely unacceptable to talk about is now in all the major news outlets, but still not being widely noticed. What was blacked out essentially for over thirty-five years is now in the mainstream. It's talked about in the State Department, *New York Times*, *Wall Street Journal*, everywhere—there's an increasing recognition that there's a larger galactic story.

Homo amor is critical for participating in that story. We're going to be part of that story, and in fact, *Homo amor* is the way in. So, thank you. Beautiful inquiry.

QUESTION 5: THE RELATIONSHIP BETWEEN INTIMACY AND IMAGINATION

Simona: My question is about the relationship between intimacy and imagination, since we're saying that each crisis is a crisis of intimacy, but we were also saying that at its root, it's a crisis of imagination.

Marc: Yes, that's beautiful. We've talked before about the crisis of imagination. What Harari is saying, of course, is that value itself is a *figment* of the imagination, essentially following Feuerbach, who says God is a figment of our imagination. **The truth is that yes, God is a figment of our imagination—figment here meaning an expression. But just as important and true: *Our imagination is a figment of God.*** That's what Harari forgot.

What is imagination? It's how we're imagining Reality. So, when the spiritual traditions say, "Thou shalt not make any graven image"—the injunction against idolatry—it means that you've stopped imagining, or you've frozen your imagination in a certain set of images.

So, yes, we absolutely have to keep our imagination going.

Remember, Adam means human, humus, Earth—*adameh* in Hebrew. But the second root meaning of the word Adam is *d'mayon*, imagination. Another way to say it is that the human being is not just *Homo sapiens*, but *Homo amor*—and *Homo amor* is also *Homo imaginus*.

QUESTION 6: WHY SHOULDN'T I TRUST THAT THINGS ARE HAPPENING AND UNFOLDING NATURALLY BY THEMSELVES?

Lady G: I feel that if evolution is in us and moving through us, why should we have to do all this talking about it? My thought is: "Let things happen." I remember a sentence I once read: "The grass does not grow faster by pulling on it." That quotation spoke to me when I read it, and now I'm thinking: *What am I doing here if evolution is always already in me?*

Marc: Beautiful. This is a super important question—perhaps one of the most important. Thank you for raising it here.

Let's say it this way. We live in inescapable frameworks. We live in stories. **The primary story in culture now is that stories don't really matter, and that values are all fictions and social constructs.** This story is the basis of enormous suffering in the world—babies are dying, men and women are being killed, people are starving. At this moment, because of the stories we're telling ourselves, two billion people in the world do not have access to drinking water.

In other words, the story we tell about Reality matters, and it's important to realize that story is real, that value is real, and that we create Reality through our stories about value. So, for example, when da Vinci and Ficino in the Renaissance encountered suffering, they couldn't go into every village and heal every person. So they realized what they needed to do was tell a new story about Reality, one that would actually transform the whole thing—this was called modernity.

All the benefits and dignities (and disasters) of modernity came from a new story.

So, in other words, the way we change Reality and address suffering is by changing the superstructure of Reality itself.

Back to your question—let's recall that distinction between being naturally and inherently good. We are not *naturally* good, which is what you were pointing towards. It's like, "Oh, we're naturally good, so we can just sit back, do nothing, and let goodness flow." **We're not *naturally* good, but we are *inherently* good. This means we're intrinsically good—but goodness still requires development, cultivation, and the ongoing, evolving realization of that potential.**

Reality requires us to tell the story of that goodness. To reclaim story as a value. To reclaim value as valuable.

In other words, the nature of Reality is not that we stay in Eden. The description you just gave, which was very beautiful, is a description of the Garden of Eden. And if I were to locate that beautiful description, it would be in the pre-tragic. In other words, "Stuff just happens." We're in Eden, and there it is.

But actually, no. We get exiled from Eden. Cain kills Abel, there's fratricide, and there's enormous suffering. We have to find our way back to Eden. In much of the New Age world, they say, let's just go back to the pre-tragic. But the pre-tragic won't take us home. Nor do we want to get stuck in the tragic, like much of the nihilistic postmodern world.

We must fully accept and face the tragic in order to move to the post-tragic, to authentically find our way back to Eden. That's what we're doing.

Lady G: But then don't we actually need the suffering to get back to Eden?

Marc: Well, again, with total respect and honor, we shouldn't say, "Don't we need the suffering?" when we're talking about two billion people who need water. In other words, there's an enormous amount of suffering in the world, which is tragic beyond imagination. So we can't say that. We're not talking about the existential angst of where to live, or whom to love. We're talking about massive, brutal suffering that currently makes up an enormous amount of Reality.

And we're also talking about a level of suffering that will eliminate the future. That's what we're talking about. *We're talking about there being no future at all.* We're talking about catastrophic and existential risk.

In order to address this, we have to tell a new Story of Value. Thank you for being such beautiful voice in the room, asking such an important question. It's very easy to miss this, to look away. We all have to grapple with this.

And thank you to all the important voices in the room because these deep questions are both in the room and in society, and they're in culture. It's very critical that we presence all these voices.

So, thank you, everyone.

INDEX

INDEX

www.ingramcontent.com/pod-product-compliance
Lightning Source LLC
La Vergne TN
LVHW020420090426
835513LV00036BA/1371